Wrestling with Starbucks

Wrestling with Starbucks

Conscience, Capital, Cappuccino

KIM FELLNER

RUTGERS UNIVERSITY PRESS
New Brunswick, New Jersey, and London

Library of Congress Cataloging-in-Publication Data

Fellner, Kim, 1948–
   Wrestling with Starbucks : conscience, capital, cappuccino/Kim Fellner.
     p. cm.
   Includes bibliographical references and index.
   ISBN 978–0–8135–4320–8 (hardcover : alk. paper)
   1. Starbucks Coffee Company. 2. Coffee industry—United States.
   3. Coffee—United States—Marketing. 4. Corporate culture—United
   States. I. Title.
   HD9199.U54S734 2008
   338.7'616479573—dc22

                                        2007039075

A British Cataloging-in-Publication record for this book is available from
the British Library.

This publication is a special project of the National Housing Institute.

Copyright © 2008 by Kim Fellner

Visit our Web site: http://rutgerspress.rutgers.edu
Manufactured in the United States of America

For my parents,
Rudolph and Anita Fellner
K.F.L.Y.

Contents

Wrestling with Starbucks

Introduction
The Global Economy Comes Home

It was November 30, 1999. I was standing amid a horde of demonstrators at what was about to be dubbed "the Battle of Seattle," the protest against the World Trade Organization (WTO) that hurled global justice into the headlines and gave new meaning to our *macchiatos*. Suddenly there was a crash not twenty feet from where I stood, and the Starbucks window collapsed in a hail of glass. "Hey," I said to my husband, Alec, "That's our coffee store!"

Right there, on a cool November day, near the intersection of Fifth and Pine in downtown Seattle, our parallel universes—as consumers, global justice activists, and union members—collided. The global economy had come home to roost. And apparently, to roast.

Howard Schultz, the dynamic and driven founder of Starbucks as we know it, later recalled that the impending protests were not even a blip on his radar screen, although they were soon to rumble his world. "I don't recall any structured meeting whatsoever about the WTO here at Starbucks," he told me. "I don't remember any preparation, sensitivity, or concern. Maybe that speaks to us being naïve about our own place in the world. So I was so surprised and horrified to, in a matter of minutes, be in the eye of the hurricane. I was watching TV, and it kept rewinding on someone throwing something through a Starbucks window, people running into the store. Starbucks became sort of the de facto poster child for WTO violence and protesters in Seattle. It became a national story."

Why, we had both wondered from our separate vantage points, had it happened? At first I was merely bemused. But as I watched our politically astute friends and colleagues—many of them devoted anti-corporate activists—relate the latest episodes of *The Sopranos*, glee-fully shop for real estate, and sip their lattes, I began to fret. Political ideology notwithstanding, we were avid participants in popular culture and global capital. How could we so glibly demonize what we so cheerfully consumed? And how had a coffee company with a liberal reputation come to symbolize the ills of globalization?

At the time of the Seattle protests, Starbucks was barely a fifth of the size it had reached by 2006, but it was already a success story. For reasons known only to the gods of merchandizing and the sharp real estate strategists at Starbucks headquarters, Schultz's dream of coast-to-coast and continent-to-continent coffee havens had caught on; and Starbucks was well known enough to warrant some sharp jabs from the world of comedy. Mike Myers's *Austin Powers: The Spy Who Shagged Me*, which opened in June 1999, includes a scene in which the Seattle Space Needle is set against an ominous sky. The huge lettering around the observation deck is unmistakable: it reads "Starbucks," and inside the Needle is the lair of Dr. Evil, with two baristas among his assorted personnel. Dr. Evil has recently returned from space to find that his acolytes have been able to finance his evil empire by investing in a little-known startup named . . . you guessed it. The product placement was stellar, but some of my fellow protesters seemed to seriously believe that Starbucks, like Dr. Evil, was headed toward world domination.

And no wonder. It's big. It's everywhere. And unlike an Enron or a Halliburton, you can walk right in. Starbucks, which began as a hometown coffee roaster in 1971 and has grown into the world's trendiest coffee brand, bragged that six of its stores were landing somewhere on the planet every day. There were two Starbucks staring at each other across a shopping mall outside Seattle and two winking at each other across Connecticut Avenue in Washington, D.C. By the end of 2006, there were more than one hundred Starbucks stores in a two-mile radius of Times Square, more than 160 in central London, and twenty-two outposts in Paris, plus one at the Mecca Mall in Amman, Jordan. There were also 224 stores in China, thirty-nine of which had opened within the previous year. As fiscal 2006 ended, the company proudly claimed more than 12,000 company-operated and licensed Starbucks stores, 7,102 in the United States and 5,338 in thirty-seven other countries—on the way to a final goal of 40,000 stores throughout the galaxy. That also meant a lot of workers (close to 150,000 in 2006), both here and abroad, and an awful lot of coffee (294 million pounds) from a wide range of suppliers in twenty-four countries.

Contrary to what we all think, coffee consumption in the United States actually *decreased* by half between 1960 and 2000. But roughly a third of that coffee is now gourmet arabica rather than the more prosaic robusta that we used to drink, good-to-the-last-drop from Maxwell House or "mountain-grown" from Folgers. Furthermore, while Starbucks purchases roughly 50 percent of the arabica coffee consumed in the United States, it actually accounts for less than 4 percent of coffee beans purchased on the world market and affects far fewer coffee growers and harvesters than do the mega-corporations that purchase and market the cheaper stuff. Nestlé, Kraft Food, Procter & Gamble, and Sara Lee are the undisputed Goliaths of the coffee world, purchasing a combined total estimated at more than 60 percent.

But Starbucks, with its coffee-centric culture and relentless visibility, has become a public icon; and its success, visibility, and self-ascribed probity invite scrutiny. Throughout the 1990s and into the new millennium, there has been a steady drumbeat of reprobation from progressives and more than a few cranks. Few critics argue that coffee is inherently evil, like bombs or Hummers. Rather, Starbucks has been accused of underpaying farmers for their coffee, buying from suppliers who mistreat their agricultural workers, purchasing from farms that degrade the environment, resisting unionization, causing neighborhoods to gentrify and small cafés to wither, and representing the invasive branding that's killing small businesses and homogenizing our communities and the world. Many of the global justice activists in Seattle felt, and continue to feel, that Starbucks is emblematic of corporations, consumerism, and conformity run amok.

Yet as I traveled around the country, I couldn't help but notice that both the employees and habitués of Starbucks seemed far more diverse by race and class than were the attendees at progressive conferences I'd attended. The company's employee benefit plans were not only superior to those of industry competitors such as McDonald's, but they often exceeded those of many good-guy nonprofits. Furthermore, unless I was badly mistaken, there seemed to be more, not fewer, independent coffeehouses in a greater range of locales than ever before. So what was the real story? Was there some substance to Starbucks' touted mission statement and liberal reputation? Or was it, as many of my colleagues averred, just a cynical ploy to complement its branding and market share?

The first thing I found out is that everyone has an opinion. Say "Starbucks," and people start talking. The coffee is strong, they'll tell you, unlike the weak swill of yesteryear. The coffee tastes burnt and bitter, aptly nicknamed "Charbucks." The chairs are comfortable and the service reliable. The stores are cookie-cutter and the service predictable. The company is good on environment. It's bad on fair trade. It's a haven of civilization. It's a soulless corporate fake. Almost before I could ask the questions, friends and strangers alike would tell me what they thought, often with great relish. Their comments made one thing evident: Starbucks has insinuated itself into our shared culture as well as into our wallets and neighborhoods. It's part of how many of us define our world and ourselves, not to mention our coffee.

"I've become a Starbuckian," admitted a progressive colleague. "I'm not an addict or anything, but I do stop by a few times a week." Others spoke darkly of friends who had succumbed to dependency, consuming three or four cups per day to the tune of ten dollars or more. And at the Lebanese Taverna restaurant in northwest Washington, D.C., I found myself eavesdropping on a conversation at the next table. "Starbucks is a good employer," an earnest young man was telling a couple who looked like his in-laws. "They give health care, even to part-timers. My professor says he'd work there if he lost his job." This wasn't an isolated incident; I often overheard a Starbucks snippet on my daily rounds. Everyone had a story.

I myself confess to being an ardent coffee drinker, whose passion, born of European roots and beatnik aspirations, long predated the Starbucks wave. Growing up in an immigrant household in New York, we kids were served coffee for breakfast with what was deemed an age-appropriate ratio of milk to caffeine: two tablespoons of coffee in our milk at age five, two tablespoons of milk in our coffee at twelve. Instant Nescafé was the daily staple; but my father, raised in the Viennese coffeehouse tradition, would occasionally brew himself a stovetop espresso in an angular metal pot acquired at the Puerto Rican bodega, using special coffee from the red, white, and green tin with the exotic name, *Medaglia d'Oro.*

Coffee signified a break in a busy day, a moment to relax, and, most important, a time to talk: the coffee was poured, and the ideas poured out. Around the family table, coffee cup in hand, I learned the art of conversation, shared my secrets, planned my future. Years later, Howard Schultz would market not just coffee but "the romance of the coffee experience, the feeling of warmth and community people get in Starbucks stores."

And to a modest extent, he'd sold me. I first encountered Starbucks in the 1980s, shortly after my sister moved to Seattle and discovered the flagship Starbucks Coffee Company store at the Pike Place Market. She was an instant fan of its dark-roasted beans and its hometown reputation for good citizenship. It offered full-time health care for part-time employees, provided domestic partner benefits, and talked the language of community and environmental responsibility. When the stock went public, she became a shareholder. She had no regrets. Every dollar invested in 1992 was worth more than forty-six dollars in 2006, with every 1,000 dollar investment returning a whopping 46,700 dollars.

When it came to coffee, though, I preferred Peet's, the Bay Area godfather of new American coffee roasters, where the first owners of Starbucks had learned their craft. On return trips from Oakland, I still tucked extra bags of their signature Major Dickason's blend into my luggage. Nonetheless, as Starbucks spread across the country, it started to gain my favor. It frequently provided the best available source of coffee beans, a comfortable place to meet a friend, a welcome respite at the airport, and a convenient place to pee in strange towns. Coming out of my motel in Carson City, Nevada, I was more than happy to see the Starbucks mermaid beckoning across the highway and join what must have been half the local sheriff's department for a quick jolt before heading into the high desert.

What brought Alec and me to Seattle in November 1999, though, had little to do with coffee and plenty to do with global capital. Between us, we've spent more than fifty years working with unions and progressive nonprofits. For nearly two decades I worked with labor unions that represent janitors and nurses' aides, actors, and freelance writers; and Alec and I met as active members of the National Writers Union (currently part of the United Auto Workers). By 1999, I was heading the National Organizers Alliance, an amalgam of progressive organizers, and starting to notice that a new breed of activists was joining us in the name of global justice.

These colleagues, usually young, ranged from black-clad anarchists, to D.C. policy wonks, to artists and scientists and everything in between. As plans for the Seattle protests began to surface, I attended some local meetings and tracked preparations on the Internet. Three thousand miles was a bit far to go for a street demonstration when we have so many opportunities to protest at home in D.C., but I was smitten by the whiff of sixties-like rebellion combined with an edgy new generational style beckoning from the websites.

I had also come to believe that the World Trade Organization was up to no good. Nominally, it sought to standardize and rationalize international trade according to a regime of fairness and equity, but those equities seemed only to extend to corporations and investors. According to unions, environmental organizations, many academics, and millions of citizens in the developing world, the multilateral development banks and international trade treaties were harming workers and the planet's sustainability with policies to privatize public services and maximize corporate profits.

Examples were legion. Small farms with diverse rice crops in the Philippines were being transformed into corporate industrial plantations, destroying both the farmers and biodiversity. South Africa, slowly recovering from its legacy of apartheid, was being forced to eliminate crucial public health services to receive equally critical international loans. Despite violent protests, Cochabamba, Bolivia, was privatizing its public water supply, leaving many of its poorest inhabitants unable to afford clean water. Meanwhile, transnational corporations were trolling for cheaper labor and fewer regulations in struggling countries across the globe, even as U.S. workers battled to maintain middle-class lives, health benefits, and job protections.

The odd thing was that, a year earlier, few Americans could have told you what the WTO was. Debate about the role of capital was the stuff of academic discourse, and the impact of the global economy was the concern of Washington policy hounds. As Mike Moore, newly appointed head of the WTO (and no relation to the filmmaker of the same name), told the Council on Foreign Relations in the days leading up to the Battle of Seattle, the previous round of trade talks, which had taken place in Uruguay, "was launched in the silence of public apathy."

But thanks to the threatened demonstrations, there were suddenly major media stories about the nature of global economics and the meaning of structural adjustment. Newspapers across the country, from Buffalo to Bismarck, used local news hooks such as industry and agriculture as springboards to discussions about globalization's losers and winners. Writing in the November 28 edition of the *Rocky Mountain News*, Holger Jensen reflected the tenor of many such articles, stories that were, as never before, describing the pros and cons of the new economy and even raising questions about free market capitalism. The wildly diverse protesters, he noted, shared "a dislike for globalization, that free trade bogeyman whose ethic is survival of the fittest. And the WTO itself is riddled with ambivalence about how far it should integrate the world's economy and whether that is good or bad." Meanwhile, he added, "Rich countries fear job losses to low-wage countries as import duties are slashed on foreign-made goods. Poor countries fear the technological edge of the rich will prevent them from ever catching up. Environmentalists say the rush for profits is degrading the planet. Human rights activists decry child labor and sweatshops in developing nations. And the Third World bemoans its debt."

The reporter got it right. This confluence of many discontents ultimately gave the Battle of Seattle both its distinctive flavor and its power. But the convergence that snared and captivated me was the link between the organizational offspring of the civil rights and Vietnam antiwar movements, where I had developed my political values, and the labor movement, where I had spent so much of my working life. I loved them both, but they often hated each other.

The hostility between the AFL-CIO and the rest of the progressive sector had been forged, like Lemony Snicket's sagas, by a series of unfortunate events occurring at precisely the right intervals to alienate successive generations of young activists. In the 1950s, Senator Joe McCarthy advanced a crusade to purge anyone considered a Communist or a Communist sympathizer from public life. Most labor unions succumbed to the pressure and purged left-wing activists and intellectuals from their ranks. This weeding out process had a major impact on unions, where many of the best organizers and thinkers of the 1930s had been leftists. Those who remained were more bureaucratic and less radical about both foreign and social policy. As a result, the alliance between the intellectual and labor communities, which characterized the New Deal and continues to nurture progressive politics in other countries, was severed. In the cold war era, the AFL-CIO international affairs department, and its American Institute for Free Labor Development (AIFLD), often served as cover for CIA operations in developing countries, where they helped to destroy progressive unions, a policy that would come back to haunt the federation years later, when it needed strong labor allies abroad.

In the 1960s, the federation and many of its affiliate unions supported the Vietnam War, alienating a whole new generation of activists. The face of labor was predominantly male and white, and many unions deterred the advancement of women and people of color. Ergo, when I entered the labor movement in 1973, I knew no one who worked for unions and few people who thought well of them.

But eventually some unions had been goaded into change. A few members of my generation drifted into the ranks of organizers, lured by labor's ideals of economic fairness and dignity on the job. New legislation permitted public workers to organize, bringing more women and people of color into the membership. Ronald Reagan's attack on unions shook some unions out of complacency, and globalization began to change the realities of working America. Ever so slowly, new bonds were forged between unions and progressives. But leeriness remained, particularly between labor and environmentalists, who generally regarded each other with suspicion, if not antipathy, primarily because of perceived conflicts between job retention and environmental protection. Even relatively progressive unions such as the United Automobile Workers were troglodytes about emission standards, and the United Mine Workers continues to insist that coal can be clean.

But thanks to the work of many organizers across the labor and environmental spectrum, a shared antagonism to the WTO agenda had trumped the organizational and cultural divisions; and 50,000 demonstrators showed up in Seattle. "It was more cohesive than I had worried about," recalled Medea Benjamin of Global Exchange, one of the organizations that helped coordinate the young activists. "There were so many issues about the unions and about what they would and wouldn't do. Everybody's culture—direct action, labor, environmental, religious—was so different. But still," she smiled, "it's like sausage: you don't want to see how it's made, but when you taste it, it's great!" The size and inventiveness of the protests took both police and participants by surprise. Demonstrators basically drowned Seattle's WTO meetings in a torrent of "Teamsters and Turtles" and a storm of broken windows.

The convergence of discontents at the Seattle demonstrations had another, even less predictable byproduct: it highlighted and then magnified tensions surrounding the issues of conscience, capital, and cappuccino that lurk at the heart of our Starbucks culture. First, the protests motivated a strong internationalist response to the consequences of global finance. Activist organizations from Europe, Asia, and Africa traveled to Seattle, taking part in the action and spicing up press reports. Among the press's favorite characters was José Bové, a French sheep farmer who became a hero by ramming his tractor into a McDonald's to protest the ills of "McGlobalization." As reported by Florence Williams in the *Utne Reader*, "He took apart the McDonald's to protest American imperialism, its trade policies, and the general, noxious spread of *malbouffe*. Malbouffe, Bové has said, 'implies eating any old thing, prepared in any old way . . . both the standardization of food like McDonald's—the same taste from one end of the world to the other—and the choice of food associated with the use of hormones and . . . other things that can endanger health.' " As Starbucks expanded, it was subjected to a similar critique, both at home and abroad, and labeled as a homogenizer of culture and a symbol of corporate imperialism.

Other international participants, especially those from Africa, were integral to the faith-based Jubilee 2000 campaign that came to Seattle to demand that the World Bank and the International Monetary Fund cancel the debts of the poorest developing countries. Their presence linked global financial and trade policies that favored corporations to the persistence of poverty in these nations. This link later provided a subtext to confrontations over Starbucks' compensation to coffee farmers in some of these same struggling countries; and many of the conflicts were championed by the same nongovernmental organizations that had played a role in creating the Seattle protests.

Finally, the Battle of Seattle heralded the emergence and branding of a new iteration of counterculture, alive with giant puppets and music. It possessed a green-minded, anticorporate ethos that included a consensus model of decision making, an imaginative exploitation of new technology, and a subversive sense of humor. Starbucks became a fixture of Internet activity as the new activists employed "culture jamming" to mock corporate logos and defile transnational reputations while branding their own black T-shirt style. That culture helped revive anarchism as a strain of campus activism, especially on the west coast. In the process, it breathed new life into the Industrial Workers of the World (also known as the IWW or Wobblies), an anarchist and anachronistic labor formation dating from the early 1900s. A few years later, Starbucks found the IWW knocking at the door with a campaign to unionize baristas in New York City.

And what about the coffee giant that became a target of the Seattle protests? If Howard Schultz was unmindful of the demonstrations before they occurred, the evening news jolted him into a new awareness. "I and the company were surprised that we were in the midst of all this," he related, noting that the perpetrator of one of the broken windows was merely a sixteen-year-old girl from Bainbridge Island who been caught up in the moment. Nevertheless, the protest led the company to reassess its position in a global context. "I think we realized that in many places there was, and continues to be, significant misunderstanding and misrepresentation of Starbucks," said Schultz, who was "personally very upset" by the attacks. "The fact that we're a physical retailer, unlike a product that sits on the shelf, means it's easier to throw something through a window than it is to squish a can of Coke. It's easier for us to become a physical manifestation of the anti-globalization issues. So we had our work cut out for us to be much more aware and then to do a much better job at telling our story."

Schultz believed that the casting of Starbucks as a villain led the company into a "new-found sensitivity and perhaps new-found openness. . . . The responsibility is on us, to consistently demonstrate that we want to be the kind of business, company, organization, brand, whatever name you want to put on it, that does the right thing." Meanwhile, the company continued to grow and grow, moving into new countries, capturing new corners of the market and of every urban center.

How big is too big? And does bigness preclude goodness? There are no easy answers. Starbucks is an expansionist international corporation, albeit a relatively small one. It is the big enchilada in the trade of high-end coffee beans, a publicly held NASDAQ corporation, an aggressive competitor for market share around the world, a global employer, a cutthroat combatant for real estate, an emerging music producer, and a creator and purveyor of popular culture. Starbucks also treats its workers better than the norm but has little use for unions. It spends substantial funds on environmental sustainability but never enough to satisfy its critics. Yet in the context of the corporate universe, Starbucks is above average as both an employer and an environmental citizen—sometimes a better employer than global justice organizations, at times a better environmental citizen than labor unions. These contradicting and colliding roles—global economic imperialist and social humanist—are not so different from the ones many of us face as individuals. We are both employees and consumers, patriots and internationalists, seekers of small-town intimacy and authenticity who want big-box savings and big-city liberation, cynical disparagers of conformity and commercialism who can still be seduced by a pair of pink sneakers or a kayak and can appreciate the art in an ad from Target or Apple.

As I mulled over the inconsistencies between our political analysis and our practice, I began to feel that our lens was often too tightly focused to reveal context or interconnection. We tend to see the plight of U.S. workers as separate from environmental consequences; we see Starbucks as an exploiter of culture but not necessarily of labor; we don't connect production in the developing world with how and what we consume. To me, the collision at the intersections promised a complex and nuanced story, both alluring and elusive, about how we work, buy, interact, define, and practice our values in an era of hyperglobalization.

I began to explore these issues with what I soon discovered was a controversial notion: that the Starbucks Coffee Company, the labor movement, and the global justice movement *all* want to make the world a better place. In other words, I began by taking all of them at their word. In 2004, I was asked to write a story for *ColorLines*, a smart magazine that pushes the margins of conversation to promote racial justice. "How about something on the World Bank bonds boycott?" guest editor Francis Calpotura suggested. "I'd rather write about Starbucks," I said but warned him that the story might question some widespread left-wing assumptions about Starbucks as villain. He laughed, an instant co-conspirator. "We'll all be in trouble. But then that's what we're good at."

Having sold the idea, I now had to produce the story. I knew where to find the labor and global justice people (many were in my address book), but I knew little more about Starbucks than what I could glean from National Public Radio or the business pages of the *New York Times*. Not well suited to stealth, I approached Starbucks and told the truth: that I was a long-time union activist who had participated in the 1999 Seattle demonstrations against the WTO. And I had questions.

The welcome I received was my first surprise. Starbucks was reputed to have little tolerance for known critics. When anticonsumerism activist Reverend Billy (performance artist Bill Talen) staged a happening in a New York store, the police were quickly summoned and the reverend and some of his flock taken away. "They are not responsible people," my senior Starbucks minder Audrey Lincoff, then director of media relations, primly told me. "They destroy our property and intimidate our staff."

But Audrey and her team treated me well. Although they had never heard of me or *ColorLines*, they set up interviews with a half-dozen vice presidents and staffers. When the article came out, I got angry letters from critics on the left. Starbucks, on the other hand, while strongly disagreeing with some of my ideas about the company, wrote that I had quoted everyone accurately and I was welcome to return. So I did.

Starbucks has a carefully calibrated media policy combining openness and guardedness: it tries to appear open while retaining firm control over the information that it parcels out. But the public relations folks were helpful when they could be and always politely regretful when they had to refuse a request. Over the course of three years, I talked to people from shop floor to boardroom—sometimes sanctioned, sometimes not; sometimes informal, sometimes official. My Starbucks adventures included three interviews with Howard Schultz, three annual meetings, two visits to the Kent roasting plant, and a lot of coffee.

Unlike the guy whose goal is to visit every Starbucks on the planet, I visited Starbucks stores only as they crossed my path. I explored the various coffee outlets in my neighborhood, mulling over the differences among Starbucks, the independent Murky Coffee, and the new Dunkin' Donuts. I stopped at the Starbucks in the Pennsylvania Turnpike rest areas and visited the Starbucks in Pittsburgh's Squirrel Hill where my parents purchase their coffee beans. In that same neighborhood, I talked about the economies of straws and cups with independent coffee bar owner Kate Knorr, who turned her love for coffee and a modest inheritance into a tentatively successful small business. On business trips and vacations, I visited Starbucks and other coffeehouses. In Tokyo, Paris, London, and Berlin, I got a feel for what was lost, and gained, in translation. And I took shoestring trips to Costa Rica and Guatemala to track the beans to their source and to meet the coffee farmers whose survival lies at the heart of the fair trade debate.

As I talked with friends, I was surprised to discover how many of them had relatives or acquaintances who had worked for Starbucks. This squarely places both labor and consumption within my generally middle-class circle, a significant difference from the labor and consumption demographics of McDonald's and Wal-Mart. I worked for a day at my local Starbucks to learn what the job actually entailed. In Auburn, Washington, on the outskirts of Seattle, I sat with Jeff Alexander of the International Union of Operating Engineers. The local had organized maintenance engineers at the nearby Starbucks roasting plant, only to see most of the union workers mysteriously let go. Across the country in New York City, I watched as members of the IWW organized some Starbucks baristas at a handful of urban locales.

To help me sort through the complexities of labor in the Starbucks economy, I talked with my old colleague Andy Stern, now president of the 1.8 million-member Service Employees International Union. In 1999, Stern had decided to skip Seattle. After all, SEIU primarily represents workers in the service sector who have less to fear from outsourcing; the bedpan at the local hospital can't be emptied in India, although the aide who empties it might well have been lured from a developing nation by the promise of higher wages. "We missed globalization for a long time, and more importantly, we probably missed how significant it was to our members," he reflected. "It just goes to show how, at times, we look at the world through a limited prism of work and not through people's other lives in communities, and therefore, we've been living in sort of a cocoon."

Six years later, in 2005, Stern led seven unions out of the AFL-CIO to form the Change to Win coalition. At the heart of the split was a fundamental dispute about the nature of work in the twenty-first century and the emergence of a domestic economy with its growth in the service sector. Job creation would be less about cars and more about coffee: fewer factories, more Starbucks. At the same time, the global economy had definitely come home. An increasing percentage of Stern's schedule was spent traveling abroad and thinking about the impact of global finance on a world of low-wage workers.

I also met with Global Exchange founder Medea Benjamin, who had helped organize the Seattle protests. Medea is thin and wired, not fragile but fierce, all bones and sharp angles, with determined eyes. She grew up as Susie Benjamin on Long Island, the daughter of a successful developer who has supported and championed her activism. "I was a rebel from early on," she laughs. "In high school, I was appalled by the war in Vietnam and racism." But it was a trip to Mexico that really hit home. "The intense poverty really struck me, hit me between the eyes," she told me. "I didn't realize how privileged I was to have a roof over my head and food." She eventually moved to the Bay Area, and in 1988 she and three colleagues founded Global Exchange. During the next decade, the group combined entrepreneurial savvy, innovative tactics, and a bold fighting spirit to link the desperate plight of Third World workers with the profits of First World corporations. At the time of the Seattle protests, Global Exchange was demanding that Starbucks buy fair trade certified coffee, and Benjamin continues to consider the company's declarations of virtue as a cynical vice.

All the while, my questions continued to pile up. How do we decide whether a company is good or bad? Is becoming a manager or an owner the only road left to success? What does that mean for those who remain on the shop floor? How had the idea of a shared global culture changed from a leftist vision for world peace into a business strategy for world domination? And why Starbucks?

To root out answers, I concentrated not on the extreme edges of possibility but in the shifting middle ground where most of us struggle to balance our values and our actions. I wanted to revisit the slogans made famous by my generation. Do we really think globally and act locally, or is it the other way around? What does it signify for the personal to be political, the political to be personal? Can we reconcile our hunger for justice with our thirst for a decent cappuccino?

This book is where my travels brought me. First, I walked through the doors of the Starbucks Coffee Company and explored the issues of conscience, capital, and cappuccino from the inside out. Then I examined the collisions at the intersection where our values meet the global economy. Finally, I searched out a meeting place where, perhaps, we could sit in comfortable chairs and discuss our differences over a cup of coffee.

1 | The Empire Strikes Gold

If you'd accidentally walked into Seattle's McCaw Hall on March 30, 2004, you might have mistaken the spectacle for a Vegas-style stage show. There were musical acts, jugglers, video comedies, and a procession of percussionists. Someone read David Letterman's Top-Ten List, "Things You Don't Want to Hear in Starbucks." Three thousand audience members whooped and cheered.

Performance it may have been, but the purpose was not entertainment: this was Starbucks' annual meeting. The attendees were stockholders—some of them large, most of them small—enjoying their yearly chance to sample free Starbucks treats and learn how the company was doing. Among them were baristas checking up on their Bean Stock, a stock option available to any employee who works at least 240 hours per quarter. "I've never had a chance to meet Howard Schultz in person," confided one young employee, "so I decided to come and see for myself."

And then there was the suspense: trying to guess the identity of this year's guest performer. Good music has always been part of the Starbucks store environment; but this year's guest artist, who turned out to be Emmylou Harris, was also part of the business plan. After she wowed the crowd with "Red Dirt Girl" and John Lennon's "Imagine," the company announced that she would feature on the upcoming Starbucks/Hear Music Artist's Choice CD, one of a series of compilations starring great musicians and sold only at Starbucks. The company was also kicking off another music venture: in-store kiosks allowing customers access to a library of 250,000 songs to download onto custom-made CDs.

But the real star of the morning (aside from rising stock prices) was founder and chairman, Howard Schultz, who conducted the drummers on stage with the same flair he uses to conduct the company. In a style seamlessly combining the conversational and the charismatic, he spread news of growth and profit. And if the annual meeting—and the company's aspirations—had as much to do with show business as Wall Street, the numbers hardly needed hyping. Starbucks' fortunes were rising; and 2003 had been a very good year indeed, with net sales of 4.1 billion dollars (almost twice what it had earned in 2000) yielding a net income of 265 million dollars. Schultz later told the press, "Both domestically and internationally, we probably underestimated the size of the global opportunity that we have."

The company has aggressively chased that opportunity in every possible way.

In 1999, when I first began to pay attention to Starbucks, the company had 2,498 stores and a net profit of less than 102 million dollars—but its detractors were already viewing it as a predator. As the 2006 fiscal year drew to a close, the company boasted 12,440 stores and a profit of 564 million dollars after an accounting adjustment. In real dollars, the earnings were even higher: 581 million dollars. You don't need special training to understand that math: for seven years Starbucks was all feast, with hardly a day of famine.

Its success could be attributed to years of smart ideas, adept management, the cultivation of mystique, and a lot of moxie. Starbucks innovates. Starbucks takes chances. This is the company that made drinking coffee an "experience," brought you the Frappuccino, and in 2000 opened a store in Beijing's Forbidden City. Not even six hundred years of Chinese insularity could stop the company's relentless drive to open stores, expand sales, add products, and make money. And although the Forbidden City store finally succumbed to public outcry over degradation of the country's cultural heritage, the controversy didn't slow the chain's expansion into the rest of China, where it now boasts more than two hundred outlets. Nor had missteps (such as a prolonged refusal to offer nonfat milk) or setbacks (such as a huge 1994 spike in world coffee prices) stopped the pace of innovation, risk taking, and profits. So even if stockholders had reservations about the music kiosks, those who had taken the time to attend this carefully scripted annual meeting were not about to argue.

Chairman Howard Schultz and then-CEO Orin Smith plied the crowd with numbers, answered questions, and urged stockholders to stay with the company's extraordinary expansion toward sector domination. Wal-Mart, for all its fearsome aggression, has only about one-quarter of the general merchandise and groceries sector. But as of 2005, Starbucks owned more than a third of the nation's total coffeehouses and a whopping 73 percent of the market value.

Nothing, it seemed, was like Starbucks. Though, of course, for years even Starbucks wasn't really like Starbucks. Yes, there was a store called Starbucks across the street from Seattle's Pike Place Market, opened by three sixties-style coffee mavens and named after the first mate in *Moby Dick*. But that Starbucks was just a cool local business that sold high-end coffee beans. To become a phenomenon, Starbucks had to meet Howard Schultz.

The Starbucks mermaid peers coyly from a little clock tower atop a refurbished Sears warehouse near the port of Seattle. Security at the eighth floor check-in desk is efficiently pleasant: a staff member inquires about your business and issues a name tag. Then you help yourself to coffee (of course) and read newspapers in a comfortable chair until your host arrives to lead you through the door into the corporate heart of the Starbucks Coffee Company.

The building is stylishly industrial, the vibe professional yet informal, upbeat without jangling the nerves or the eyes. On my first visit in 2003, I was struck by how the design favored public and communal areas. Most of the vice presidents have small offices, many without windows. But there's a fine array of coffee-making accoutrements in the employee kitchen, complete with a real whipped cream dispenser. I liked the open spaces, the inviting armchairs, the comfortable places for employees to eat and talk, and the slightly whimsical coffee-related art that lines the public halls.

Howard Schultz is nothing if not disarming. He introduces himself as "Howard" and works in a pleasantly understated office. He's tall and fit, nice-looking without being abrasively handsome, and often dresses as if for an informal—not casual—office party. His visitors may sense the under-hum of impatience that sometimes accompanies busy, driven people; but Howard's body language remains open, he listens intently, and he thinks before answering. And when he says he cares about values more than profits, I'm inclined to believe him.

"In the early stages," he told me, "we were literally fighting for survival, trying to build a company that would just pay our salaries. We weren't trying to build a global enterprise. What was institutionalized in the early stages of the company is that we were going to try and build a different kind of company, specifically a company that our parents, collectively, didn't get a chance to work for, a company that had conscience, that tried to be responsible, a company that we would go home and be proud of, a company that did the right thing."

In 1990, the first year that Schultz's Starbucks turned a profit, staff members collaboratively drafted its mission statement and five guiding principles. A diversity principle was added in 1996; and since then, the statement, which appears on the back of the official Starbucks business card, has remained intact.

Schultz and others point out that profitability, "essential to future success," comes last among the principles, below respect, dignity, diversity, community, and good coffee. And they assert that the key to profitability lies in following the other principles. For both individuals and companies, however, balancing profits and other values is no easy matter. And for Starbucks, that struggle originates with Schultz.

The story of Howard Schultz's origins is oft-told and well-honed. He grew up in the projects in Brooklyn's Canarsie neighborhood. But although his childhood was working class rather than poor, the housing blocks not menacing but modest, he was stung with a sense of privation. Economic scarcity, family humiliation, and his need to escape underpin almost any personal interview. "I grew up in a working-class family, where there was so much pressure and uneasiness around the fact that there just wasn't enough money," he told me, "and that shaped how my parents conducted themselves. As I got a little older, I began to realize that my father's self-esteem was linked to how he was treated in the workplace. As a blue collar, a war veteran, a high school dropout, I think he was not very confident in his ability."

Fred Schultz, Howard's dad, held a variety of jobs, which included laboring in a factory and driving a diaper truck. The work was unsatisfying and poorly compensated. "He was a bitter man, shaped by the experiences he had as a working adult," Howard recalls. "And I witnessed that. I think there's a point in your life

starbucks mission statement

Establish Starbucks as the premier purveyor of the finest coffee in the world while maintaining our uncompromising principles while we grow.

The following six guiding principles will help us measure the appropriateness of our decisions:

———

Provide a great work environment and treat each other with respect and dignity.

———

Embrace diversity as an essential component in the way we do business.

———

Apply the highest standards of excellence to the purchasing, roasting and fresh delivery of our coffee.

———

Develop enthusiastically satisfied customers all of the time.

———

Contribute positively to our communities and our environment.

———

Recognize that profitability is essential to our future success.

where you accept your parents for who they are. But you also start asking questions and judging them as people as opposed to just as parents. And the people I saw were kind of beaten down, where the American dream was truly fractured and there was hopelessness and despair."

Fred Schultz had no health care to cover the medical costs of a broken ankle and no pension when he died. From that experience, Howard Schultz learned a double lesson: make good money, and provide good health care. Succeed, but not at the expense of decency and the dignity of others. Years later, the dual track of profit and principle became the hallmark of Starbucks culture.

Schultz went to Northern Michigan University on a football scholarship. He was happy to be far away from Brooklyn: Northern

Michigan was more than two hundred miles away from Milwaukee, the nearest big city. He enjoyed college life, worked at a conventional mix of part-time jobs to help pay for his schooling, and in 1975 graduated with a bachelor of science degree in communications. From there, he went into sales, first at Xerox, then as a rep for a Swedish housewares company, Hammarplast, where he rose to become vice president for U.S. sales. He was making good money and had taken an important step up from his roots, but so far he'd done nothing newsworthy. Then in 1981 he stumbled onto Starbucks.

Schultz's interest was piqued when he noticed that a tiny four-store retailer in Seattle was selling more of a certain kind of drip coffeemaker than Macy's was. He hopped a plane and flew to Seattle, where he checked out the company's flagship store at Pike Place Market. He loved what he saw, became obsessed, and hounded the Starbucks owners to let him in on the venture. The owners, Jerry Baldwin and Gordon Bowker (a third, Zev Siegl, had bowed out in 1980), eventually invited him to join as head of Starbucks marketing. And despite the owners' reluctance, from the get-go Schultz dreamed of making the company bigger, and bigger still.

According to official legend, the magic happened on a 1983 trip to Italy, when Schultz fell in love with the coffeehouse concept. He was astounded at the breadth of coffeehouse culture; the country had 200,000 coffeehouses, 1,500 in Milan alone. In his business autobiography, *Pour Your Heart into It*, Schultz describes how he wandered the neighborhood coffee bars, observing their regular customers and skilled baristas, and had an epiphany: "Starbucks had missed the point—completely missed it. . . . The connection to the people who loved coffee did not have to take place only in their homes. . . . What we had to do was unlock the romance and mystery of coffee, first-hand, in coffee bars. The Italians understood the personal relationship that people could have to coffee, its social aspect. I couldn't believe that Starbucks was in the coffee business, yet was overlooking so central an element of it."

As any beatnik, hippie, or big-city Italian American could tell you, Schultz didn't have to go all the way to Milan to find a good coffeehouse. In San Francisco's North Beach, as in many Little Italies around the United States, more or less authentic Italian coffeehouses were catering to their communities. In 1956, Italian immigrant Giovanni Giotta, trying to create a little slice of home, opened the Caffe Trieste on Vallejo Street; and soon the postwar counterculture discovered the Trieste and its neighborhood imitators. On April 2, 1958, in the wake of a series of public poetry readings in North Beach, *San Francisco Chronicle* columnist Herb Caen coined the term *beatnik*. The word was first loathed and then embraced by the beats, who continued to hold forth at the Trieste and created a community that began in North Beach and spread nationwide. The Trieste, by the way, is still open on Vallejo Street and has recently been franchising itself around San Francisco and nearby Sausalito. For a fee, you, too, can open a Trieste. *Ça va les beats.*

You could, in fact, argue that it wasn't Schultz but author Jack Kerouac who popularized these places in the U.S psyche. As William Burroughs wrote in 1985, "Kerouac opened a million coffee bars and sold a million pairs of Levis to both sexes." Yet Schultz seems to have been unaware of the beat culture and the hundreds of coffeehouses that dotted the American landscape from the 1950s on. And apparently he did not frequent Berkeley, California.

By the early 1970s, the components of modern Starbucks—high-end coffee bean stores and stay-as-long-as-you-want espresso cafés—were already in place throughout the Bay Area. Around Berkeley there were places like the Caffe Mediterraneum (or, as it was universally known, "the Med"), which opened in the 1950s, and its progeny—the Intermezzo, the Roma, and the chess player's hangout, Hardcastle's. Others came and went, all offering espresso, cappuccino, macchiato, caffe latte, and granita, an icy precursor of Starbucks' Frappuccino. Music played, people studied, and coffee drinks to go were everywhere. In addition, a grim-faced Netherlander named Alfred Peet had already opened his North Berkeley store specializing in unusually fine imported coffee beans, which he roasted on the premises. In short, the Starbucks model preceded Starbucks; it just stayed in Berkeley and other college towns around the country. It rarely ventured into the suburbs and ventured even less often into the popular mind. So Schultz had to make the *hajj* to Milan to see what he hadn't noticed around the corner.

Which brings us to the multibillion-dollar question: why did Schultz suddenly see it, and why did we buy it? Americans had had ample opportunity to open a nation of coffee bars before Schultz came along, but they hadn't done it. So why has Starbucks become so integral to our cultural psyche? This question has generated reams of commentary, alternately erudite and banal, caustic and fawning, about the intentions of Starbucks and our receptivity as consumers.

But once you pare away the layers of pop psychology and cultural analysis, you can begin to get a clearer picture.

Schultz's epiphany was a real one. He was captivated by Italy's coffee bars and by their function as centers of comfort and community; and he thought that Americans, portrayed as increasingly isolated in their homes and cars, alienated at their jobs, and adrift in existential angst, would feel the same way. In 1989, Ray Oldenburg, a sociologist, published *The Great Good Place*, touting the value of community meeting places such as bars and cafés as critical to a society's health. Oldenburg lamented the school of urban planning that substitutes malls for Main Streets and an ascendant culture that is increasingly turned inward, cocooned in larger homes, while public spaces and the relationships they have traditionally nurtured evaporate from our lives. Unlike much of the world, we lack the comfortable havens that build community and foster conversation, where, as Oldenburg told me, "you come in alone, and sit down with friends."

Schultz appropriated the concept of a "third place" between home and work as the perfect definition of Starbucks' role. "We're in the business of human connection and humanity," he often asserts, "creating communities in a third place between home and work." Oldenburg himself is somewhat bemused. He's never met Howard Schultz. "I think he avoided me in the early years because I would have scoffed at him," Oldenburg hazards. And although he thinks the company may be trying for third-place status—"I know there's one near me where the book club meets"—his few forays into the chain have been less than encouraging. "The seats were uncomfortable, the staff was impatient if you stumbled over your drink order, and they were rude—not at all like a third place. I have my own places. This afternoon was Thirsty Thursday down at Cooter Brown's in Pensacola, and a bunch of us sit around and have a beer."

Still, Schultz succeeded in making the third-place label part of the accepted media explanation for the company's success. Writing in *MSN Money*, Jon Markman says that he drinks two cups of coffee at home; but even so, something pulls him to Starbucks: "I want a third cup in large part because, like many others, I am a sucker for the ritualistic experience of what founder Howard Schultz has termed the 'third place' of American life. It's a place without the stresses of the home or the office, a neutral ground where there are always 'friends' behind the counter. In our largely impersonal, digital and ethereal world, returning to the homey confines of one's own Starbucks, staffed with people who care enough to remember something about us, provides a primal human connection."

What Schultz captured from the streets of Milan was not just the community-building potential of the coffeehouse but its essential commonality: the idea that its appeal could be expanded across class and neighborhood rather than remain exclusive to the college town or urban Italian enclave. The walk-up bar, the arrayed bottles, the Italian names on signboards, the displayed bulk or packaged coffee—all these had been in evidence around the United States. What Schultz and company did was to make them available nearly *everywhere*. The result may not have been the same as the indigenous neighborhood hangouts that constitute authentic third places, but Schultz realized that many of our communities lacked *any* place where people could take a break to meet, talk, read, or work in comfort.

He also combined the community and democracy of the European coffeehouse with the consistency and branding acumen of American capitalism. At its heart, Starbucks is a chain store that sells coffee, milkshakes, and sweets; but add the name, the packaging, and the aura, and *voila*—or should I say *ecco?*—a Starbucks is born.

The word *brand* derives from the old English word for "burn," as in burning a ranch's name onto cattle. Since the advent of mass production and mass media, however, branding is about burning a product into our brains by making it difficult to avoid and ascribing it with characteristics that transcend its physical reality. Coffee branding as we more or less know it probably began late in the nineteenth century, when branded coffee began to replace bulk coffees in the nation's grocery stores. By 1915, 86 percent of coffee was prepackaged rather than scooped out of a bin, and both manufacturers and retailers jumped into mass advertising on a national scale. By the 1970s, we all knew that Chock Full o' Nuts was "the heavenly coffee," that Yuban coffee was "deep, dark, delicious," and that good coffee came from Colombia, where Juan Valdez picked the beans by hand and carted them down the mountain on his mule.

But even as these ads were insinuating themselves from the TV screen into our memories, the nature of the message was evolving from branding products to turning the corporate name itself into a brand imbued with psychic qualities. As journalist Naomi Klein describes in her provocative book *No Logo*, companies began to market their aura as well as their products. Over the course of several decades, ad agencies moved "away from individual products and their attributes and toward a psychological/anthropological examination of what brands mean to the culture and to people's lives." Today, branding is both a sophisticated process and an established ideology, enabling Starbucks to endow its offerings with a cultural significance that transcends their reality as food products or CDs.

Although the original Starbucks possessed a distinctive coffee and artisanal cachet, late-comer Howard Schultz was responsible for introducing the concept of deliberately marketing the intangibles. The people associated with Starbucks in 1982 remember how different he was, a New Yorker who talked, walked, and thought fast and was endlessly ambitious for himself and the company. From his first days as head of Starbucks sales and marketing, he cajoled the owners to expand and then lobbied to sell coffee drinks in addition to fine beans. When he bought the company in 1987, there was no stopping him.

Schultz intuitively knew how to make Starbucks into the kind of epidemic Malcolm Gladwell later described in *The Tipping Point*. Gladwell suggests that some behaviors or fads are, like diseases, contagious: that incremental causes or changes can add up to big effects and that there is a moment at which the balance shifts and you have an epidemic. "The tipping point," says Gladwell, "is the moment of critical mass, the threshold, the boiling point." And that epidemic moment occurs because of three transforming factors he identifies as "the Law of the Few, the Stickiness Factor, and the Power of Context." The theory seems made for Starbucks, or vice versa.

The Law of the Few posits that an epidemic can be helped to the tipping point by a relatively small number of individuals, who become the connectors, mavens, and salespeople who link people with the idea or product. Starbucks initially starred Schultz himself in all three roles—networker, facilitator, and salesman-in-chief—to carry the message about Starbucks coffee and cool. But he quickly drew in and animated others who had those skills, such as veteran Seattle coffee bar owner David Olsen. Not only did Starbucks coffee taste better than its competitors, but its stores also had better taste and a clean, distinctive design. The original Starbucks provided a base of connectors and mavens who appreciated the roast, bought the rest of the concept, and became salespersons who spread the word.

Furthermore, the message and the production were "sticky" in that the stores stood out from the crowd, were memorable, and motivated people to return—so much so that, for years, Starbucks did little conventional advertising. Some of that stickiness was embedded in the unconventional expansion pattern, clustering stores in close proximity to each other based on traffic and perceived micro-neighborhoods. This may have created the aggravating sense of everywhereness that fuels late-night comics and infuriates critics, but it also worked to sell a lot of coffee. "They did scale very well," said Rob Walker, who writes the "Consumed" column for the *New York Times Magazine*. "I think their coffee's fine, but I'm frankly mystified about why people rave about their physical spaces. I think they're nothing special. But I'd be interested in talking to their real estate guy. I think the appeal is mostly familiarity, scale, convenience. And reliability, you know what you'll get."

But as we both agreed, there was a little more to it than that. Drinking Starbucks not only appeals to the senses, but it automatically conveys a rise in social status—and here you have the power of context. Guided by Schultz's vision, his coffee stores became an "affordable luxury," imbued with the romance of coffee and a touch of the Italian coffeehouse combined with a claim to social responsibility and a human connection that transcended the physical exchange of goods for cash. For a time, at least, brandishing a Starbucks cup signaled your education, sophistication, and exclusivity, or at least your aspirations to those qualities. You, too, could order something called a latte, even if you couldn't find Italy on a map; and you could see Jude Law or Meryl Streep clutching the self-same cup. "It's the boho factor," veteran Starbucks roaster Tom Walters thought. "We may not live in the same neighborhood, we don't wear the same clothes, we can't afford the same car, but we can drink the same coffee." In fact, Starbucks serves more than 50 million consumers a week. As of 2005, regular Starbucks customers averaged eighteen visits a month, which, according to an article in the *Guardian*, translates into "the world's most frequently visited retailer."

For added status, the frequent customer can purchase a stored value card, a little Starbucks prepaid debit card for your drinks. The cards were introduced in 2001, and their popularity and profitability induced envy in other retailers. There was one with a special limited-edition design in my mom's shareholder packet, which I used to keep track of my coffee-drinking expenses during this project. I was forced to admit to a little twinge of satisfaction as I handed it over at the register, with the same mixture of disgust and guilty pleasure I felt about being a premiere flyer on United Airlines, although the latter, at least, had some tangible benefit. The card was also popular among the younger set; my sister often purchased five-dollar cards as the little rewards handed out to kids as part of the Passover Seder. As of mid-2007, there were 120 million cards in circulation, and the dollar amount had surpassed 2.5 billion. Definitely sticky.

Schultz proved inspired in his hunch, unshakeable in his determination, canny in his execution, and just plain lucky. According to one financial expert who has followed Starbucks for decades, Schultz often neglects to mention the luck factor as an important component of his success. "Howard deserves a lot of credit for his persistence and his focus on creating and protecting the brand," noted the Seattle insider. "But he happened into a business that has a lot of give in it. His profit margins are so huge that he was able to take chances—and often fail—where other businesses could not. If he were in some low-margin business, he wouldn't be a genius."

Still, the time was right. And as it turned out, Schultz was right: we did want an alternative to the pub, a youth- and woman-friendly place to meet, drink coffee, hang out, and linger over our laptops. As a consequence, Starbucks has achieved what few other companies in the *Fortune 500* have done: it has gone from eleven regional stores to household word, from obscurity to ubiquity.

But when Schultz returned from Italy back in 1983, Jerry Baldwin and Gordon Bowker didn't fall for his epiphany. Their passion was finely roasted coffee beans; and the opportunity to purchase Peet's, the legendary East Bay coffee roaster, seemed far more enticing than a harebrained venture to bring coffeehouse culture to the masses. So the owners of Starbucks bought Peet's, and Howard Schultz left Starbucks to open a coffee bar named Il Giornale.

Ultimately, running both Starbucks and Peet's proved too much for Baldwin and Bowker, and running Il Giornale was not quite enough for Schultz. In 1987, the original Starbucks owners decided to focus on Peet's and sold Starbucks to Schultz. The beginning of Starbucks as we know it had arrived. Gordon Bowker does not admit to any regrets. "I don't think about it," he says. "It's not what I wanted to do."

Schultz has no regrets either. During the next five years, Starbucks grew from 11 to 165 stores, and the pace of expansion never slowed. On June 26, 1992, which Schultz once called "the happiest day of my business career," the company went public, determined to make gourmet coffee synonymous with Starbucks from coast to coast. How well he succeeded you already know.

2 | Running the 10-K

To present a company's best face, annual meetings tend to include plenty of spectacle and flash, a way to show stockholders, the press, and the public that the company is simultaneously comfortable and innovative. These meetings also spawn a forest of paperwork. To follow Schultz's parallel visions of profit and principle, I began with two Starbucks reports: the annual 10-K that every public company must file with the U.S. Securities and Exchange Commission, and the annual Starbucks Corporate Responsibility Report. These reports are looking-glass images—one justifying the business in market terms, the other validating it in human terms.

The Starbucks 10-K is a catalogue of achievements, goals, and risks anchored in numbers. Gray and single-spaced, the document is a bracing antidote to the chatter and hyperbole that frequently surround the company. It's where you get a chance to rummage through a company's clean, folded linen, looking for loose buttons and stains that haven't quite disappeared in the wash; a place where you can hunt for lost socks. That is, if you know where to look.

I handed the 2005 report to analyst and activist Randy Barber of the Center for Economic Organizing. A few weeks later he offered this summary: "When you go by the numbers, this 10-K looks and quacks not like a culture, but like a corporation," albeit one that was doing very nicely indeed: it had plenty of profits and considerable growth coexisting with minimal debt.

The 10-K also reminds you that *big* is relative. Given all the hype, not to mention the company's obsessive presence in downtown America, you'd be forgiven for thinking Starbucks is bigger than it is. In fact, it's only been in the Fortune 500 since 2003, although it continues to work its way up the list. As of 2006, it sat in the lower middle, at number 338, between Dynegy, a company that produces and sells energy, and Safeco, an insurance company. The kingpin coffee purchasers—Altria (until recently the parent company of Kraft) at number 20 and Procter & Gamble at number 24—far outrank Starbucks on the charts. Nestlé, the biggest coffee ogre, is a Swiss company and therefore not part of the list, although it makes Starbucks look puny. On the other hand, in 2006 Starbucks was the third-largest food service player among the Fortune 500, smaller than McDonald's or Yum! Brands (home of Kentucky Fried Chicken, Pizza Hut, and Taco Bell) but bigger than Wendy's.

Like its founder, however, what Starbucks does have is a strong desire for upward mobility. Starting on the first page of its 2005 10-K, Starbucks pressured itself to outdo its own performance. "The Company's objective is to establish Starbucks as the most recognized and respected brand in the world," paragraph 1 announced humbly. "To achieve this goal, the Company plans to continue rapid expansion of its retail operations . . . and to selectively pursue other opportunities to leverage the Starbucks brand through the introduction of new products and the development of new channels of distribution."

But *respected* and *recognized* aren't always synonymous. To accomplish these twin objectives, Starbucks needs to make profits that meet Wall Street's projected targets and grow ever more rapidly. It has to expand its reach abroad, especially in China, and protect its brand; but it needs to do so while retaining the trust and patronage of you and me, the coffee consumers. And it needs to accomplish all these tasks while meeting its obligations as a publicly held corporation.

There is a difference between private and public ownership. The latter is both more regulated and less controllable. To be a listed corporation means that the company can be used by speculators as well as various investors, all of whom have a piece of it. Publicly held corporate management must deliver profits and meet expectations.

Starbucks stock (SBUX on the NASDAQ) has done what stocks do: it has danced. Nevertheless, for more than a decade its averaged and sustained growth was undeniable. As Brian Lund, a columnist for the snappy stock advice website *Motley Fool*, pointed out in 2000,

"One reason we don't comment on Starbucks is that nothing much happens at the company, except that it maintains its strong business momentum." That momentum has been characterized by increased market capitalization (the amount of money it would take to buy the company) from 300 million dollars in 1992, when the company first went public, to 12 billion dollars in 2003 and roughly 20 billion dollars by the end of 2005. Furthermore, the 10-K showed that this growth was achieved from profit. In 2003, the company invested a bucket of dough in a new plant and new stores yet still had cash reserves of 335 million dollars. The corporation had virtually no short-term debt until it established a revolving line of credit in 2005.

Financial types and the media tend to give Wall Street (aka "the market") both animal and human characteristics. The Street is not merely bullish or bearish in its upward and downward swings; it's like a finicky eater who regularly sends back its dinner because it's over- or underdone. It squishes the numbers around on its plate. Were the same store sales for May of this year better than for the same month last year? Did they replicate as quickly as they said they would? Most of all, did they do as well as the company or the analysts predicted? If the market gambled on a venti caramel latte and only got a grande vanilla, it sends the drink back to the kitchen with a reprimand. And down goes the stock—which apparently isn't always as bad as you might think. If analysts consider the stock overpriced or overheated (that is, more hype than value), the downward drift may bring the price more in line with what pundits consider to be appropriate. At that point, analysts consider it a better value and tell you to buy.

Analysts occasionally broke the monotony by warning of a coming downturn for Starbucks, if not a collapse. After all, how big could it get, and how much coffee could we possibly drink? In 2006 and 2007, there was more such gossip than usual. A 2006 midsummer spike in gas prices plus a slide in the housing market fueled anxiety-ridden reports of consumer cutbacks in disposable income and discretionary purchases; and Starbucks showed an increase of only 4 percent in same-store sales as opposed to market expectations that were closer to 7 percent. Starbucks blamed the blip on too many customer orders for Frappuccinos, drinks that take a relatively long time to prepare and therefore slow store lines. Bloggers greeted this rationale with hoots, analysts with skepticism. "Hot customers put Starbucks on ice," quipped the *Age* in Melbourne, Australia, as shares dropped

11 percent. No matter that the stores had registered a healthy profit of 16 percent for the previous three months: the stock price took a hit.

The stock continued to slip throughout 2007, and pundits alternately fretted and gloated over the company's 23 percent drop in market value. So far the downturns have been transitory and ultimately insignificant. But as the 10-K filing notes, "Management believes the price of Starbucks stock reflects high market expectations for its future operating results. In particular, any failure to meet the market's high expectations for Starbucks comparable store sales growth rates, earnings per share and new store openings could cause the market price of Starbucks stock to drop rapidly and sharply."

More pressure. But Starbucks had a strategy to meet its expectations: expand and brand. In 2005, Starbucks added more than 1,000 outlets in the United States and debuted in Jordan and the Bahamas. It also opened eighteen more stores in China, bringing the year's total to twenty-four. "Starbucks expects the People's Republic of China to be one of its largest markets outside of the United States," the 10-K asserted; and indeed, by the end of 2006, the number of SBUX emporia in China had swelled to more than two hundred, and citizens of Cairo and São Paulo had the opportunity to guzzle Frappuccinos in their very own towns.

Unlike a Dunkin' Donuts or a Burger King, Starbucks does not franchise its stores, preferring to retain full ownership and control of its operations and revenues. The 2005 report revealed that, out of a total of 10,241 Starbucks stores, 6,000 were company-operated, up from 5,265 the year before. More than three-quarters of those stores were in the United States, the other 1,133 spread across nine countries, including China. The company-operated stores, foreign and domestic, accounted for roughly 85 percent of SBUX net revenues.

The rest of the stores are not exactly franchised but are licensed to corporate business partners for locations, here and abroad, where the company would have difficulty securing the necessary real estate or operating the business. These represent the largest share of what the company calls its specialty sector. Think airports, turnpikes, and the kiosk at your local Safeway or Stop & Shop supermarket. They look like smaller versions of your old familiar Starbucks (though without the comfy chairs), but they are in fact a mutation that is spreading rapidly through the company's dominion. While these locations are still only a small part of net revenues (roughly 6 percent in 2005), they're on the rise. The Starbucks outlets at hospitals and campus coffee shops are food service contracts.

The remaining Starbucks revenues comes from a grab bag of other collaborative enterprises: with Pepsi-Cola for bottled Frappuccino drinks; Dreyer's for ice cream; Jim Beam for coffee liqueur; and even Suntory for the chilled canned coffee drinks I encountered during a teaching stint in Japan, where they are dispensed from vending machines as popular pick-me-ups.

Starbucks has also grown by acquisition. In 1999, Starbucks purchased Tazo Tea, developing its tendency to pick up reputable small companies whose offerings fit well with the business. Over the years, it has also bought up a number of competing coffeehouse chains and roasters. In 2003, the company bought Seattle's Best Coffee and Torrefazione Italia, simultaneously eliminating two smaller rival brands and gaining 150 locations. While Starbucks abolished Torrefazione as a coffeehouse in 2005 (the store still sells wholesale roasted coffee and Italian pottery), Seattle's Best remains a distinct brand of stores and roasts within Starbucks; and many purchasers of Seattle's Best have no idea they're buying a Starbucks product, although the workers are now Starbucks employees. When I asked why the company had retained the name, Starbucks vice president Audrey Lincoff explained, "There are a lot of customers who really like the milder Seattle's Best roast, and unlike Starbucks, they have some popular flavored coffees." Of course, the company also softens its ubiquitous image by hiding behind another label. In 2005, Starbucks purchased Ethos Water; and in 2006, it bought Dietrich, a small coffee chain based in Portland, Oregon.

Starbucks also bought its way into the music biz. As Allison Overholt noted in an article for *Fast Company*, the leap from coffee to music followed the advice of the late marketing guru Theodore Levitt of the Harvard Business School, who cautioned against myopia in defining a company's true business. In Levitt's famous words,

> The railroads did not stop growing because the need for passenger and freight transportation declined. That grew. The railroads are in trouble today not because that need was filled by others (cars, trucks, airplanes, and even telephones) but because it was *not* filled by the railroads themselves. They let others take customers away from them because they assumed themselves to be in the railroad business rather than in the transportation business. The reason they defined their industry incorrectly was that they were railroad oriented instead of transportation oriented; they were product oriented instead of customer oriented.

"It's easy to interpret the non-coffee acquisitions as possibly showing a lack of focus," says Alyce Lomax, who writes about Starbucks for *Motley Fool*, "but I think they all fit well within Starbucks' culture and positioning as a lifestyle brand. Premium tea fits well, as does a water provider that fulfills social responsibility by donating to clean water efforts in developing countries."

Schultz's early success was the leap from coffee as beverage to coffee as lifestyle, upscaled to accommodate the upscaling incomes of aging boomers. To Starbucks' initial surprise, the proposed or reflected lifestyle also proved congenial to moms with strollers, young teens looking for cool hangouts, and students in search of study hall alternatives. This discovery was immediately incorporated into a sophisticated brand plan. George Washington University, for example, has a Starbucks in the library plus two more on campus and one nearby. In addition, Starbucks became an early retail adopter of new technology, ahead of the curve in making its stores computer-friendly and Wi-Fi accessible and branding its image accordingly.

All it needed was a soundtrack. On June 5, 2007, computer and coffee culture united to open a new dimension in superstar super-promotion: every Starbucks store played Paul McCartney's new album, *Memory Almost Full*, all day, throughout the inhabited universe. "Customers from Taipei to Topeka have the opportunity to experience this extraordinary album all within a span of twenty-four hours," said Ken Lombard, the president of Starbucks Entertainment, who runs the company's Hear Music label. McCartney was the first artist signed to record an original album on the label. A week after its release, the album was number 3 on the Billboard sales charts, McCartney's first success in more than a decade, with 47 percent of those sales taking place at Starbucks stores.

According to Schultz, the beginning of Starbucks music involved serendipity more than direction. In 1994, the company had a Seattle store manager named Timothy Jones, who had long worked in the record industry and was supplying the company with in-store tapes. He suggested to Schultz that Starbucks compile its own tape or CD. In late 1994, Starbucks marketed a Kenny G holiday CD; and according to Schultz's book, it "flew off the counters." Through a chance connection, Starbucks met with Capitol Records, which had acquired the prestigious Blue Note jazz label and its entire classic catalogue. Schultz himself is a jazz aficionado and was solidly behind using Blue Note's collection of fifties and sixties jazz. The first result was

Blue Note Blend, released in tandem with the 1995 opening of Starbucks' biggest New York store at Astor Place. *Blend* eventually sold a respectable 75,000 copies. Then in 1999, the year of the Seattle protests, Starbucks acquired Hear Music, a small music retailer and record label based in San Francisco. Hear Music was known for treating its music the way Starbucks treated its coffee; it was reputed to be the first to provide listening posts (replacing the listening booths that used to grace record stores), where customers could sample CDs before purchase in an environment of style and connoisseurship. Starbucks paid 8 million dollars for the label and brought its founder, Don MacKinnon, into the company as a vice president for entertainment. With music already a part of the Starbucks in-store environment, the company began to experiment with ways to strengthen customer awareness or, as it's called, buy-in.

A few months after the company had touted the Hear Music bars at the 2004 annual meeting, I went to the Fremont section of Seattle to check one out, accompanied by Alec and my ninety-one-year-old dad. Fremont is notable for its twenty-foot statue of Lenin, shipped over from a dump in the Czech Republic and now residing in front of a Taco Del Mar and a gelato stand. At the Starbucks a few blocks away, the company was proposing its own vision of revolution: legal CDs you made yourself while sipping coffee. The process wasn't as complicated as Lenin's *The Development of Capitalism in Russia*, but it wasn't that easy either, as we soon discovered. "Listen to songs, create a custom mix, burn an album to CD at Starbucks," the company proudly advised. "Once you've found what you like, you can take home the album on CD in minutes or make your own CD mixes from the songs you choose."

The key misunderstanding for us was the "in minutes" part. With 250,000 songs to choose from, we needed (sticking with the Marx-Lenin metaphor) a five-year plan. People who knew exactly what they wanted and remembered artists, titles, or key words might have had an easier job. For me, just checking out the library took a lot of time. The mechanism was less complex than an ordinary remote control, but we novices did require barista help during the process. Still, within an hour—and after three macchiatos, which may be the point—I came away with an eclectic CD. We never played it enough to justify the ten dollar cost, maybe three times in three years, but I did have fun.

It was evident, however, that as iPods and their cousins became the norm, people with file-sharing savvy didn't really need this clunky venue to download music, and duffers probably wouldn't use it. Without mentioning the word, Starbucks acknowledged failure in 2006: "After two years of testing the machines at 15 stores in Seattle and 30 stores in Austin, Texas, the coffee retailer has pulled them out of all but five locations in each city and will not install them in future coffee stores. The machines will remain at Starbucks' three large-scale music stores, called Hear Music Coffeehouses, in Santa Monica, Calif., San Antonio, Texas, and Miami, and go into future music stores."

But as Malcolm Gladwell notes, what characterizes successful quests for stickiness is a willingness to test one's intuitions and calibrate one's approach based on the results. The implosion of the machine-made CDs didn't stop Starbucks from succeeding, sometimes wildly, in some of the other music ventures featured at that annual meeting. By the time Emmylou Harris sang for the stockholders in 2004, Starbucks was headed toward its first Grammy for Ray Charles's final album *Genius Loves Company*, featuring a dozen duet tracks with people such as Norah Jones, Elton John, Gladys Knight, and Van Morrison. The CD became a fixture on the top-ten list and by mid-November had been certified multi-platinum in the United States and overseas. Of the more than 2 million copies sold in the United States, 30 percent came from Starbucks stores. In other words, at a time of declining retail CD sales, a coffee bar sold 600,000 copies of a full-price recording by a man who had already cut 250 records. In 2005, at the Grammys in Los Angeles, *Genius Loves Company* won eight awards—certainly a first for a chain of coffee bars and pretty good for any CD or producer.

During the 2005 Starbucks annual meeting, Lombard elucidated a core strategy for growing the music business. Baby boomers were intimately bonded to music in a way that had transformed both the industry and the generation. Now, however, "adult customers feel disenfranchised." They could no longer turn on the radio and hear their music. Starbucks was going to change that. The idea resonated with me; and a few days later, when I reported this nugget to a colleague, he immediately called his broker to buy Starbucks stock.

Over the years, Starbucks has released more than 170 reissued titles by artists ranging from Tony Bennett to the Dixie Chicks. The company is seeking to develop a range of offerings that satisfies both aging hipsters and a younger generation of music trendsetters; it's constantly trying to balance the comfort of the center against the excitement of the edge. Ergo, Starbucks followed its Paul McCartney album with the announcement that a Sonic Youth compilation, appealing to a younger and hipper crowd, would be next. And unwilling to be a latecomer in the burgeoning satellite radio business, the company joined XM Satellite Radio to create what is essentially the coffee bar channel. As they say, "Now you can access the Hear Music song library in living rooms, offices, car stereos and online, coast to coast and 100% commercial-free on XM channel 75." In 2006, the Hear Music catalog became available on iTunes. Starbucks actually has selling rights to more than 200,000 cuts.

Building on its developing musical muscle, the company decided to branch into other cultural realms. In 2005, Starbucks opened an office in Los Angeles, with the goal of being closer to the entertainment industry. Although its first foray into film promotion, "Akeela and the Bee," was deemed something of a failure (the film's revenues were weak despite the Starbucks connection), Ken Lombard told me it had been a good first effort; and by 2007 the company was preparing to put its name behind another film. The company's move into books was more immediately gratifying. Its first offering, *For One More Day*, by Mitch Albom, sold more than 90,000 copies in six months, a success the company topped in 2007 with its second book, *A Long Way Gone*, by former child soldier Ishmael Beah. The Starbucks imprimatur helped launch Beah as both an author and a celebrity. Nevertheless, music, though highly visible and audible, as well as the rest of the entertainment package remain minor parts of Starbucks' total revenue, accounting for about 3 percent. But that 3 percent was worth a bucket of publicity and added to the buzz, even if some of the ventures ultimately failed.

"Hear Music may seem like the furthest from the core mission," Alyce Lomax of *Motley Fool* acknowledges, "but small amounts of media make sense for Starbucks, which can function as a tastemaker. I believe Starbucks' brand seeks to address customers who consider themselves to be of discerning, individualistic tastes, and of course music is part of the coffeehouse tradition. They may not make up the lion's share of Starbucks' sales, but they help shore up the brand, which is very important for this company."

The newsworthiness of the company's lofty cultural aspirations was given the official stamp of significance on October 22, 2006, with a front page story on "The Starbucks Aesthetic" in the "Arts and Leisure" section of the *New York Times*. Though journalist

Susan Dominus was a trifle snide, she grudgingly acknowledged the company's potential for success. The entertainment world and the media who cover it can't help notice that Starbucks has become a player. As Dominus observed, "the chain is increasingly positioning itself as a purveyor of premium-blend culture." But seeing as upscale newspapers go with upscale coffee, and the chain is one of the nation's largest sellers of the *New York Times*, only a very daring writer and a courageous editor would have devoted major space to a negative article about Starbucks. As Howard Schultz enthused to Dominus, "At our core we're a coffee company, but the opportunity we have to extend the brand is beyond coffee; it's entertainment."

And what about those vaunted beans that first made Starbucks famous? "I'd be surprised if 5 percent of Starbucks' business is beans," scoffed Gordon Bowker, one of the three original founders of Starbucks, who is still a major shareholder and board member at Peet's. As it turns out, he's right. Although the sale of whole bean coffee at Starbucks stores, supermarkets, and warehouse clubs—notably Costco—remains part of the mix, the 10-K suggests that whole bean coffee accounts for less than 5 percent of Starbucks revenues; and the word *bean* plays only a bit part in the 10-K description of company stores.

Peet's stores, by contrast, are beaniacs: "Our stores are designed to facilitate the sale of fresh whole bean coffee and to encourage customer trial of our coffee through coffee beverages," proclaims the Peet's 10-K. Forget about respect; piffle to global recognition. Rather, "each store has a dedicated staff person at the bean counter to take orders and assist customers with questions on coffee origins and on home brewing. Upon order, beans are scooped and ground to the customer's specific requirements."

These days, all the beans Starbucks buys and roasts, whether whole or ground in your morning drink, account for just 10 percent of COGS (finance-speak for "cost of goods sold"), the cost for obtaining raw materials and producing the goods we eventually buy. Beans may be the font of Starbucks' existence; but even with a 2005 purchase of 312 million pounds at a cost of roughly 400 million dollars, beans are only a small part of its expenses.

Based on what the company spends, you could, with some justification, just as soon label Starbucks a real estate, health care, or milk company. Making sure you trip over a Starbucks no matter where you roam, for example, rivals the cost of the beans in your cup.

Increasingly, there is competition in the retail sector for those desirable street corners and inviting locales that lure in customers. The ability to select the perfect spot, over and over, in a proximity that seems counterintuitive, has been a consistent company strength and increasingly the bane of other retail coffee vendors. As CIBC (formerly the Canadian Imperial Bank of Commerce) world markets analyst John Glass told *Newsweek*, "The two things that make them great are real estate, and making sure no one has a bad experience in their stores."

There are a growing number of stories about Starbucks' predatory capture of prime locations, often by negotiating exclusive deals with landlords at prices higher than any smaller business could afford. In 2006, the owner of a small espresso bar filed suit against Starbucks for stifling competition via such arrangements to satisfy its "insatiable and unchecked" ambition. It wasn't the only such story. A well-known coffee expert and sometime coffee bar owner seeking to open a café in a new development district was outraged to be refused space within a multiblock area because of a deal that Starbucks had made with the project owners. It's fine to be competitive, he thought, but wrong to create a monopoly through real estate manipulation.

Although the figures are not explicit in the 10-K, Starbucks' 2005 expenditures for U.S. employee health care rivaled its U.S. coffee costs. Schultz told me, "I've said to our team, I've said to our board, that there is nothing that I will do with regard to the growth, development and profit of the company that will ever take away the health care benefit for Starbucks employees. It's a huge thing because, between 2007 and 2009—we don't have the exact time period—our health care coverage cost will be greater in dollars than the entire budget for buying raw coffee. . . . it's unbelievable."

And then there's milk. The strange truth is that Starbucks spends almost as much on milk as on coffee. Not on the milk that fills the stainless carafes standing on the sideboard and labeled *whole, skim,* and *half-and-half,* although that adds to the total. No, it's on the milk that goes into the lattes and their progeny: from seasonal gingerbread latte, peppermint mocha, or eggnog latte to perennial favorites such as vanilla latte, mocha nut latte, and the infinitely variable syrup-flavored lattes. But even more milk goes into the equally and seasonally variable cold drinks, the Frappuccinos that have turned Starbucks from a coffee bar into a latter-day soda fountain: caffe vanilla Frappuccino, caramel Frappuccino, java chip Frappuccino, and on down the line, ending with plain old coffee Frappuccino—all, of course, trademarked.

Overall, this is at least good for the dairy industry. According to the U.S. Department of Agriculture, by 2001 Americans were consuming fewer than eight gallons per person of whole milk, compared with nearly forty-one gallons in 1945 and twenty-five gallons in 1970, although they were making up for that consumption somewhat in the form of lower fat milks. At the same time, ice cream consumption has stayed relatively level since the end of World War II, with Americans, according to the USDA, "eating a little less ice cream overall but more of the higher priced, higher milk fat premium and super-premium ice creams as well as frozen yogurt and other frozen dairy products."

That's the sort of the change that's taken place at Starbucks as customers have glommed onto the Frappuccino. Officially, it's a blend of brewed Starbucks coffee, milk, sugar, maltodextrin, and pectin. Less officially, it's instant coffee mixed with dry milk and sugar and sent to the stores in the form of a powder. The result bears about as close a relationship to a cup of Starbucks coffee as a bouillon cube does to a cow.

Then there's the milk that fills the out-of-store production, milk that never even passes through Starbucks. Tanker loads go to Dreyer's (a subsidiary of the international giant, Nestlé), which makes Starbucks ice cream, a high-calorie collection of flavors sold everywhere from Safeway to 7-Eleven. More is turned into bottled Frappuccino, sold in six-packs at well-known and lesser-known retail outfits; and for those who just can't wait for an individually blended drink, they're available in Starbucks stores as well. Another RTD (ready-to-drink) coffee-milk concoction is the Starbucks Espresso DoubleShot, a 6.5-ounce can of strong coffee doctored with cream and sugar. It may generate scorn from true coffee connoisseurs, but it cheers up the dairy farmer. And although Starbucks workers don't much like making them, Frappuccinos have been a magnet for younger customers and a godsend for the company's, and the population's, ever-fattening bottom line.

But maintaining that bottom line takes work. The vagaries of Wall Street, where a healthy profit is less important than fulfilling the expectations of market gamblers, are only a few of the hazards the company faces in meeting its ambitious goals; and the 10-K catalogue of risk factors makes very interesting reading: it mentions everything from health pandemics to drought, local competition to the deterioration of

U.S.-China relations, labor costs to customer disenchantment. Blink, and you may find your view of the company metamorphosing from ravenous monster to fragile heroine in the path of an oncoming train.

What emerges vividly from the list of hazards is a looming threat to the value and reputation of Starbucks' good name—the real core of the enterprise. In 2004, when *Time* named Howard Schultz as one of America's one hundred most influential people, the magazine didn't give him the award for inventing good coffee or café culture but for merchandising. Said *Time*, "Starbucks has become a global iconic consumer brand, as well as the place millions of people hang out, read, listen to music, take off their shoes and hop online."

That evolution can be traced in reportage about the company. During 2006, Google dumped links to roughly 5,000 articles about Starbucks into my mailbox, ranging from prosaic stock reports to the wildly metaphorical. Between January 1, 1981, and April 30, 2007, there were 2,688 references to Starbucks in the *New York Times* alone (although the first reference was actually to a country-western disco with the same name). The first real reference to Starbucks as we know it appeared in a 1989 general article about Seattle coffee culture. "No one in Seattle," wrote food critic Marian Burros, "just walks into a store and buys [an espresso] machine; a demonstration is a must. In addition, Starbucks offers seminars on the proper use of the machines. Howard Schultz, who went to work for the company in 1982 and bought it in 1987, said there were waiting lists for the seminars." That's it. Nothing suggests that Schultz or Starbucks are about to swamp the competition or change the culture. Burros thought that the coffee culture was already there, just that no one retailer owned it.

As the years passed, especially after the company went public, the *New York Times* references multiplied at about the same rate as the stores. In 1992, there were thirteen references, almost all about earnings and business, plus one on coffee culture and one on benefits for part-timers. In 1999, the year of the Seattle uprising, there were 165 references; by 2001, there were 251. In 2006, there were 354, about one per day, spread throughout all sections of the newspaper. Yet while Starbucks clearly reached a tipping point when it stopped being a chain of coffeehouses and became *the* global coffeehouse, it's hard to identify the exact moment. By following Levitt's advice to constantly expand the definition of the business and the brand, the company achieved world domination in steady, well-planned, incremental steps, leaving only the question—the subject of endless chatter—of when and how it might suddenly fall from grace.

The Sunday *New York Times* of April 22, 2007, offers a glimpse of what Starbucks has become. There are six references to the company in six different sections of the paper. Two are even about coffee. A story about Chiapas, Mexico, in the "International" section reports that Mr. Moshán Méndez's cooperative sells to Starbucks, which "pays higher prices to farmers who meet its standards." Meanwhile, a "Fashion and Style" story about fair trade coffee in Brooklyn asserts that, while large companies such as Starbucks now offer fair trade, the cool and the hip still eschew the chain for independent fair trade coffeehouses. The "Travel" section offers some tourist advice: head to the Hôtel Langlois if you "want the experience of what's left of the authentic, historic Paris, the Paris with few chain clothing stores and Starbucks." In "Sports," a woman tells a reporter that she "grabbed the bat and chased [Yankee shortstop Derek] Jeter into a Starbucks for his signature because I knew Dustin would love it," while in "Business" Starbucks employees report that tycoon Philip F. Anschutz arrives for work at 5 A.M. dressed in cycling clothes. "He often waves to them, they say." Finally, in the "Book Review" section, we learn that "Change has come to Tula Springs, La. Readers familiar with St. Jude Parish from James Wilcox's first novel, *Modern Baptists* (1983), may have trouble recognizing the place today. There's a Starbucks in the Piggly Wiggly."

Starbucks is progress. It's hegemony. It treats farmers well. It doesn't treat them well enough. Join the stars and successful people by going there. Join the cool and politically conscious by scorning it. Brand value, as the 10-K notes, is a fragile thing. "Consumer demand for the Company's products," reads the 10-K, "and its brand equity could diminish significantly if Starbucks fails to preserve the quality of its products, is perceived to act in an unethical or socially irresponsible manner or fails to deliver a consistently positive consumer experience in each of its markets."

Pressure indeed. And also vulnerability. It is this sensitivity to public image that makes Starbucks such an appealing target for attack and motivates the company to work hard at looking like the good guy, even as it takes over the world.

If the 10-K speaks primarily to worth, Starbucks' social responsibility report is its public statement of worthiness. Here, stark numbers and

single-spaced, austere documentation give way to heartwarming photographs and enthusiastic prose that overflows with cultural and
multicultural affirmation. This is the other half of the Starbucks
equation. As Schultz told me, "We have to make a profit as a business, but at the same time we have to be committed to being the kind
of company that demonstrates a social conscience and benevolence
in everything we do and, most importantly, a deeply rooted sensitivity to not just the global, but the local environment."

Local or global, those sensitivities tend to parallel the factors that
define the company's financial commitments. Coffee buying equals the
well-being of the farmers who grow it. Real estate underlies debates
about community gentrification and homogenization. Health care is a
critical battleground in the American workplace. The debate over arti-
ficial growth hormone in milk speaks to the environmental and health
hazards promulgated by corporate greed. Dig even deeper, below the
specific issues, and you arrive at the core question: does the company
achieve its wealth at the expense of the global community?

Corporate social responsibility (known as CSR) is akin to
emergency-room CPR: it's an attempt to rescue corporations from the
brink of public moral collapse, an effort to make us believe that company profits are good for us as well as them. And these days, CSR is
all the rage as corporations go after the niche market share that
accrues to a brand perceived as morally good. According to a 2006
report by the Harvard Business School, "Governments, activists, and
the media have become adept at holding companies to account for the
social consequences of their activities. Myriad organizations rank
companies on the performance of their corporate social responsibility
(CSR), and, despite sometimes questionable methodologies, these
rankings attract considerable publicity. As a result, CSR has emerged
as an inescapable priority for business leaders in every country."

Polls show that consumers at least *say* they care about CSR and
give it some weight in their buying preferences. According to a 2005
survey by Fleishman-Hillard and the National Consumers League,
fully 52 percent of interviewees said they actively sought out CSR
information at least some of the time; and an astonishing 35 percent
said that, product quality being equal, CSR was the primary factor in
creating consumer loyalty, greatly outranking availability and price.

Historically, this affirmation of goodness is redundant.
Corporations were initially quasi-public enterprises licensed by the
state to contribute to the public good. From the start, people got rich

from investing in and operating corporations, but wealth was never the sole stated objective. Yet this public service character slowly eroded; and when Milton Friedman proclaimed that a business's only duty was to make money, the U.S. government began to encourage a profits-only mentality.

Obviously, Starbucks doesn't share that view. "The only thing we have at the end of the day is not how big we are, how many people we hire. The only thing we have is what we stand for, what our purpose is," Schultz told me in our first meeting. "What we stand for today is the same as it always was, and that is to build a company that has a conscience, that achieves a balance between profitability, shareholder value, and fiscal responsibility, and is also a company that has a heart, that demonstrates benevolence and sensitivity to the constituencies that we feel are important."

CSR is also important to how the company has chosen to define and market its brand. The Starbucks advertising budget is miniscule compared to that of most corporations; but as doubters and detractors have become louder, the company has touted its socially responsible image more aggressively. In 2006 and 2007, Starbucks ran a series of elegantly conceptualized newspaper ads, many of them full-page, in the *New York Times* and the *Washington Post*, all tastefully signaling the company's good, progressive citizenship. "It's a Matter of Degrees," says an ad on the need to stop global warming, which also announced a Starbucks partnership with Global Green, U.S.A. "What Makes Coffee Good?" asks another ad, which then explains that the company's C.A.F.E. Practices are good for farmers and therefore good for business and thus result in good karma all around.

Generally, the folks in Starbucks management are smart enough to understand skepticism. As David Pace, executive vice president for partner resources, acknowledged, "Our guiding statement is probably not that different from [the statements of] people who are involved in scandals. The difference is our commitment to it." The company's corporate social responsibility report tries to beat the Starbucks drum (but not too loudly) while deflecting critiques, mostly from progressive organizations dedicated to environmental, farmer, and employee social justice issues—all without seeming defensive. Inviting readers of the 2005 report to look beyond the coffee cup, the company displays its accomplishments and goals for improving the world by posing and then answering, to its own advantage, challenges such as "Why isn't all of Starbucks coffee Fair Trade

Certified?" and "Everywhere I go, I see Starbucks. Pretty soon every place will look the same."

On the plus side, this corporation pays attention to criticism. Yet the answers tend to be conciliatory, if oblique: "Starbucks doesn't rely on a 'one size fits all' mold for our stores. . . . we are respectful of a neighborhood's desire to preserve its look and feel, its historic buildings and/or its unique architectural attributes." That's fine. But it's probably not the answer the hypothetical questioner had in mind. The real concern of real questioners is "You're too damn big, and your ubiquitous branding is squelching the unique character of our community." The news clippings and Internet postings that fill my inbox are rife with such grievances. Emily Byers, a young conservative columnist for the online edition of Louisiana State University's *Daily Reveille*, moaned about the impending arrival of a Starbucks on campus, where a local enterprise on the verge of bankruptcy would be "replaced by the McDonald's of coffee shops in all its commercialized glory. . . . I certainly prefer to purchase my café au lait at a local coffee shop, a place where people want to stick around, not bustle through like a nameless herd that hurries off like cattle on a caffeine buzz. . . . Starbucks reeks of the sort of unbridled consumerism I just can't stand."

Starbucks does a better job of addressing the real issue further down in its report: "As we have grown our network of Starbucks stores, thousands of independent coffeehouses have also sprung up. With more than 21,000 coffeehouses in the U.S., of which a third are Starbucks, consumers can choose from a wide variety." It's a point that David Heilbrunn, manager of Coffee Fest, a trade show for independents, readily acknowledges. "When we started out in 1992, 90 percent of people didn't know what a latte meant," he told me. "If it wasn't for Starbucks, we wouldn't be doing what we're doing today." Figures from Mintel, a Chicago consumer research company that follows coffee trends, affirm that the number of independent coffee emporia has grown dramatically, from roughly 7,500 in 1998 to almost 14,000 in 2005.

Elsewhere much of the social responsibility report's prose is crafted to exude sincerity and uplift. "Starbucks success in new and established markets hinges on our ability to cultivate meaningful relationships with our customers, local community leaders and neighbors—relationships that are built on trust," it sermonizes. "We know our trust is earned when we keep our promises and uphold our commitment to contribute positively to our communities and our environment, a guiding principle of the company."

The fact that this prose is easy to mock doesn't make it untrue. But it isn't necessarily the whole truth either. The fine print tells you, for example, that Starbucks "recognizes our partners' right to unionize" and does "not take action or retaliate against partners who express their views about unions or who take part in union activity." Nevertheless, all the unions that have dealt with Starbucks and some ex-employees, here and in Canada, speak convincingly about company hostility toward union organizations and retaliation against workers who dare to forego corporate benevolence for a union card. Some dregs lurk in that coffee cup.

Still, the report contains a great deal of substantial and compelling material, and it's chockfull of facts and figures. Many people tend to equate social responsibility with corporate donations, and Starbucks does have a philanthropic foundation. But like most other corporate giving programs, the Starbucks foundation tends to offer grants to the blandly benevolent; and who's going to argue against literacy programs and aid for tsunami victims? Better to linger over the maps of commodity-supplying countries, following the colored dots showing coffee, tea, and cocoa production across the continents. Better to watch the company struggle with the issue of greenhouse gas emissions as it acknowledges the dangers of global warming. Better to track the journey of a Starbucks paper cup from pulp mill to counter or to follow the chain of corporate accountability. The report touts company efforts to build community, promote environmental sustainability, create a nurturing workplace, and expand diversity. We can find out that Starbucks is looking for ways to conserve electricity and water. We can ponder the fact that 64 percent of its workforce participated in its 2005 partner survey, up from 46 percent in 2003, and that 87 percent of the partners say they are moderately or very satisfied on the job.

Roughly a quarter of the document is devoted to coffee sourcing—where Starbucks coffee comes from, under what conditions it is grown and processed, and how farmers are compensated—and rightly so, because cold-hearted profiteering on the backs of poor coffee farmers ranks with cultural homogenization as the most gripping public accusation against the company. The report cites the premium prices that Starbucks pays to farmers and explains its Coffee and Farmer Equity (or C.A.F.E.) Practices, developed to encourage and monitor economic transparency, environmental sustainability, and social equity among coffee suppliers. Farmers who meet tough criteria are rewarded with boosts in the per-pound price of their beans. The report includes predictable stories of affirmation from Third World farmers but also a picture guide to the various coffee certification systems. It compliments other organizations that certify fair trade and sustainable environmental practices, modestly listing C.A.F.E. Practices as one effort among many and listing the websites of other exemplary groups. In the process, the report manages to note that Starbucks' purchase of Fair Trade Certified beans rose from 4.8 million pounds in 2004 to 11.5 million pounds in 2005, making the company the largest purchaser of Fair Trade Certified coffee in North America.

And then the report adds an extra ingredient, the flavor that makes Starbucks a little different from the norm. Just as *Consumer Reports* rates cars and blenders using little circles—empty, half full, or completely colored in—to demonstrate quality, Starbucks self-rates its progress against its stated annual goals. Admittedly, the company's self-evaluation might be more generous than the ratings of others; but at least it knows, and you know, what the goals were and how the company thinks it's doing. This is in sharp contrast to, say, Procter & Gamble, a much larger player in the world coffee market, whose social responsibility report offers high-minded rhetoric with little backup information by which to evaluate its assertions.

"We shaped the company early on to be very different," says Schultz, "and that was a triangle that was inverted. At the top of the triangle was our people, and underneath that was our customers, and underneath that, lastly, was our shareholders. We said, then and today, that we're going to build long-term value for our shareholders; but the only way we're going to do that is if we build long-term value for our people, and as a result of that our customers will be satisfied."

The trouble with this vision is that it's not supported by the law. Shareholders, especially major shareholders, have both their money and the Securities and Exchange Commission on their side. Bo Burlingham, editor-at-large of *Inc.* magazine and the author of *Small Giants: Companies That Choose to Be Great instead of Big*, thinks it's clear that publicly held companies, regardless of what they say, are bound by law and custom to make maximum shareholder return a condition for taking investors' money. "There are choices," he told me. "You don't have to go public, you don't have to grow as big as possible. But if you decide on that route, you need to do it with your eyes open. I totally respect people like Schultz; I respect what he's tried to do in terms of conducting business in a way that he feels will enhance the society and have good positive impact. It's not that they can't choose public good, but they have to live up to their promises to their stockholders."

Customers, of course, can weigh in by either patronizing Starbucks or taking their trade elsewhere. But with labor protections being eroded and nullified at every turn and large equity funds trolling the landscape in search of companies to pillage, employees and coffee farmers have little to back them up but the company's intentions of good will. And that may not always be enough. When Starbucks' ship encounters a really bad sea, someone may be tossed overboard, and it's not likely to be the shareholders.

"The problem," says Burlingham, "is that when you go public, your responsibilities have the potential to come in conflict with your ideals. Then you have a fight on your hands. Schultz has fight on his hands."

3 Banking on the Bean

Back in the 1970s, my husband, a premature caffeinista, talked with Alfred Peet, acknowledged godfather of the high-end coffee business, about the nature of north-south trade. "Isn't it true that you can't grow coffee without cheap labor?" Alec asked.

Mr. Peet leaned on the counter and smiled. "No," he said. "You can't grow coffee without *dirt* cheap labor."

This is where the global coffee controversy begins. Forget the mumbo jumbo. Although the history of coffee is intricate and its trading arcane, you need just a few bits of information to get to the nub:

1. Coffee has been traded for more than five hundred years and has always reflected the benefits and injustices of the prevailing level of globalization.
2. Coffee grows in the less developed countries of the global south, where the trade has been dominated by colonial powers and made profitable by the exploited labor of indigenous people of color. In general, poorer countries grow it, and richer countries purchase and consume it. Today, about 80 percent of the world's coffee comes from the Americas, the remainder from Southeast Asia and Africa.
3. There are two kinds of coffee: robusta, which provides about 35 percent of the total, and arabica. Imagine a caste system for

coffee: the lower the altitude at which it grows, the lower the quality, and the lower the price. The major growers of robusta, the lowly and least finicky kind, include Vietnam, Indonesia, Brazil, and Côte d'Ivoire. The lower grades go to transnational corporations and other mass marketers and are often blended with higher-grade beans to produce the taste that Americans once recognized as coffee. Arabica, the higher-caste coffee, grows mostly on small farms in Central America and, in smaller amounts, in parts of Africa and Southeast Asia. Think Sidamo, Sulawesi, and Java. It prospers at altitudes between 1,500 and 6,000 feet. The loftiest and best arabica coffees, technically known as "strictly hard bean," go to Starbucks and other specialty coffee roasters.

4. Robusta is traded primarily on the London International Financial Futures Exchange. Arabica is traded primarily at the New York Board of Trade on the Coffee, Sugar, and Cocoa Exchange; the coffee part is commonly referred to as the "C market" or the "New York C."

5. The U.S. part of the equation is all about purchasing, roasting, and distribution. In what used to be called imperialism, we take raw materials—in this case, coffee beans—from elsewhere at the cheapest possible cost to ourselves. Then we process them, adding value along the way, and sell them for the highest possible price.

6. Except for a small amount of highly publicized coffee from Hawaii and indifferent coffee from Puerto Rico, the United States doesn't grow coffee. So unlike sugar, rice, or cotton farming, the coffee business doesn't have lots of trade legislation to protect domestic farmers or restrict imports. This militates against some of the more brutal forms of predatory trade behavior at the expense of poor nations—as when U.S. government subsidies enable cotton growers to dump expensively produced cotton on the world market at prices competitive with the cheaply produced cotton grown in West Africa. Even without blunt instruments of inequity, however, there's still plenty of room for exploitation.

7. "Fair trade" is an organized attempt to change the equation so that growers and harvesters in poor countries get a larger share of the profits earned by the corporations that roast and resell the beans in richer countries. Fair Trade Certified coffee, administered

internationally by the Fair Trade Labelling Organizations International, and in the United States by its affiliate TransFair USA, ensures that growers get paid a fair minimum price per pound for their beans. But in the past ten years, competing certification systems, with varying priorities, have emerged. Rainforest Alliance has traditionally led with environmental standards, and Starbucks believes its own C.A.F.E. Practices can achieve similar and often better results. Alfred Peet, a confirmed free-trader, would probably hate them all.

8. Although it appears to be everywhere, Starbucks is far from the biggest fish in the coffee pond. The company buys less than 4 percent of the world's coffee. The sharks are Nestlé, Kraft (formerly General Foods, then Philip Morris, then part of the Altria Group, and now once again Kraft), and Procter & Gamble. A fourth giant, Sara Lee, recently sold its coffee brands to the Italian firm Segafredo Zanetti Coffee Group. In the United States you know these brands as Nescafé, Maxwell House, Folgers, and Chock Full o' Nuts, among others. Together, they purchase more than 60 percent of coffee traded on the world markets. This doesn't mean that Starbucks, the undisputed kingpin of gourmet coffee roasters, is insignificant. Rather, the company dominates a smaller and more profitable sector of a much larger coffee universe.

To unravel the mysteries of Starbucks' role and its impact, we need to take a brief tour along the historical and economic routes that the bean travels on its way to your cup.

There's a tendency to take coffee rather lightly. It lacks the gravitas and danger of mining or oil, the macho of manufacturing, even the aura of subterfuge in the financial markets. It is, after all, just coffee—a food without nutrition and a drug of slight danger. Despite a lively mix of scientists, nutritionists, and alarmists who are convinced that caffeine addiction is a major hazard, coffee has thus far maintained its position as a relatively harmless pick-me-up and a benign indulgence.

But the strange fact is that coffee is second only to oil as the most valuable international article of trade. It's as rife with geopolitics as any other commodity and can be as exploitative as any form of plantation agriculture. In short, it's serious business and has been for a very long time. Coffee is a major earner of international currency for at least forty nations, most of them among the world's poorest.

Countries such as Nicaragua, Guatemala, Angola, and Ethiopia depend on it, as do less desperate economies such as Colombia, Costa Rica, Vietnam, and Indonesia, not to mention the world's largest coffee producer, Brazil, which provides roughly a third of the world's coffee. An estimated 25 million small farmers are entirely dependent on coffee for their survival, and the numbers of people who rely on the crop for their income range up to 125 million. According to Worldwatch Institute, "Farmers harvested nearly 7.4 million tons of coffee beans in 2002—an all-time high and almost double the harvest in 1960."

On the consumer side, coffee drinkers put away nearly half a trillion cups a year, and coffee rivals tea as the world's most popular beverage other than water. While the highest coffee consumption per capita is in northern Europe, U.S. coffee drinkers account for one-third of all the coffee consumed worldwide.

The history and politics of the coffee trade are fascinating enough to spawn many books of their own, and you'll find some of my favorites listed in the source notes. They all agree that coffee has been globalized since the early Middle Ages, spreading from its original home in Ethiopia through Yemen to the Middle East and, by the 1600s, along the trade routes to Europe, when the first coffeehouses appeared in Holland, Italy, and England. It didn't take long for them to become all the rage—or for the colonizers of Africa and the Americas to recognize a potential new source of wealth.

The arabica coffee that originated in Ethiopia and dominated the early coffee trade was highly prized and carefully tended, the root stocks purloined by entrepreneurial traders and transported to the Americas. Robusta, which was hardier and easier to grow at lower altitudes, came to prominence in the mid-1800s; it was cultivated in the colonial territories of Africa and Indonesia, and eventually in Brazil as well, to satisfy the burgeoning demand for the brew in Europe and America.

As is generally the case for plantation crops, coffee production was built on the "dirt cheap" labor of slaves and indentured farm workers, who paid dearly with their liberty and sometimes with their lives. Economic injustices were compounded by racism, with European colonial landowners subjecting African, Indian, and Asian land and labor to expropriation and exploitation. In *Uncommon Grounds*, a history of coffee, author Mark Pendergrast itemizes the woes of the world's coffee belt, quoting an 1881 work by Francis

Thurber on coffee growing under the Dutch in Java and Sumatra: " 'The price received by the natives from the government is placed at a figure low enough to leave an enormous margin of profit to the government.' The Dutch, thereby 'have maintained a most grinding despotism over their miserable subjects, levying forced loans and otherwise despoiling those who . . . have accumulated anything beyond their daily subsistence. . . . Even the little children came up, ducked their small shaven heads in comical homage to the great white sahib, and held out very small brown hands for the price those hands were supposed to have earned at the rate of a penny a-day.' "

This pattern of abuse pursued coffee into the twentieth century. In Central America, dictators consolidated both land and wealth in the hands of the elites. As Pendergrast relates, "By the 1930s, coffee accounted for over 90 percent of El Salvador's exports. Indians worked ten-hour days for twelve cents. They suffered, as a Canadian observer wrote at the time, from 'low wages, incredible filth, utter lack of consideration on the part to employers [under] conditions in fact not far removed from slavery.' In the rebellion that followed a few years later, more than 30,000 Indians were murdered by the military and the plantation owners." The case of El Salvador is hardly unique. Around the world, countries with a colonial history often have an accompanying history of peasant revolts, which, in modified form, continue after formal colonialism ends. The legacy of repression and mayhem remains throughout the coffee-growing world, a sharp counterpoint to the aura of comfort that surrounds gourmet coffee emporia.

Politics aren't the only factor plaguing the world of the coffee bean. In fact, coffee growing is one of the most volatile, uncertain businesses in the world, easily capsized by droughts and frosts, like the ones that hit Brazil at irregular intervals. There's also pestilence, in the form of coffee rust and coffee borers, which can decimate a crop or destroy a country's stock. These fluctuations in conditions create fluctuations in price, which in turn create expansion and contraction cycles of coffee growing. When coffee is scarcer and the price of coffee rises, new growers enter the market. All too often, in the five years it takes for coffee plants to become productive, coffee is once again plentiful, and the price has fallen below the point that will amortize the cost of growing. A long string of good coffee-price years can keep a farming family solvent and well fed, but many people go broke trying to make it. The tree crop cycle continues to fuel the boom-bust pricing syndrome. The alternating periods of scarcity and glut are a constant of coffee history; and no amount of trade legislation, fair trading, or above-market pricing will sufficiently make up for an extended surfeit of coffee. But that hasn't, and doesn't, stop people from trying.

By the beginning of the twentieth century, coffee was already wildly traded across continents. The United States was consuming the lion's share; and Folgers, Chase & Sanborn, and Hills Bros. were already household brands. Business was booming, and the producer countries, many emerging from colonial rule, did not want to be left behind.

In the first half of the century, Brazil, which then produced three-quarters of the world's coffee, and Colombia, an emerging coffee producer, embarked on several convoluted decades of competition and collaboration to expand coffee markets and maintain high coffee prices. Unfortunately, they didn't trust each other enough for the alliance to endure, spurring a price roller coaster as the countries tried to alternately knife each other in the back and jointly control the flow of coffee to prop up profits.

Enter the United States. At the onset of World War II, the nation consumed close to 80 percent of the world's coffee, giving American companies a vested interest in the cost and availability of beans. Furthermore, the U.S. foreign policy apparatus felt a need to maintain political allegiances with neighbors to the south, where German settlers had long been central to the coffee industry. In 1940, mostly to deter Nazi sympathies in Central and South America, the U.S. government signed onto the Inter-American Coffee Agreement to stabilize both coffee prices and coffee-growing governments.

When the Nazi threat of World War II was replaced by the communist threat of the cold war, the United States agreed to the International Coffee Agreement (ICA), wanting to ensure that just enough money dribbled into developing world economies to deter a swing toward big-C Communism. The ICA and its implementing organization, the International Coffee Organization, were fueled by a rare convergence of interest among governments, coffee producers, and coffee buyers, all of whom saw an opportunity to control the flow of coffee, maintain prices, and promote a level of political and economic stability. And with the power of the U.S. market behind it, the ICA actually worked. As sociologist John Talbot notes in his fine book on the coffee commodity chain, *Grounds for Agreement*, the ICA was probably the most effective of all Third World efforts to regulate, and benefit from, the sale of the nations' own commodities "due to the strength of the coffee producers. One measure of this success was the ability of the ICA to dampen the wild price swings caused by the tree crop price cycle."

But the ICA was doomed, in part by its own success in creating a strong voice for producing countries rather than consuming corporations, in part by changing geopolitical circumstances. By the 1980s, Ronald Reagan became president, the Berlin Wall fell, the cold war fizzled out, and the United States felt less pressure or inclination to modify its free-market ideology. In Africa and Southeast Asia, countries that weren't parties to the agreement were producing more coffee and offering new coffee-buying options. Furthermore, Nestlé and the other large transnational conglomerates were rapidly dominating all aspects of the coffee supply chain, pushing independent exporters and roasters out of business. With a chance to both push down prices and reduce the risk of unpleasant political consequences, their support for international price agreements faded. Things were definitely not looking up for small coffee growers. And to top off the situation, America's demand for coffee was dropping.

Although a more fashionable public is consuming coffee in a more public fashion, Americans actually drink considerably less coffee than they did fifty years ago. In 1960, Americans downed 38.8 gallons a year, nearly one-quarter in the form of instant coffee, which works out to about three cups a day. According to the USDA, coffee drinking steadily declined until, by 2000, Americans consumed only twenty-two gallons a year, or one-and-a-half cups a day, one-tenth of which was instant.

What happened to coffee? The short answer is RTD, or ready to drink, beverages. People really did believe that things went better with Coke—and bottled iced tea, flavored water, and an ever-changing mix of other drink options, all luridly and relentlessly promoted. According to *Euromonitor International*, "Retail consumption of coffee faces threats on many fronts, including increased consumption of foodservice hot drinks, U.S. consumers opting to drink healthier hot drinks like tea, and growing interest in RTD beverages which now include iced teas and energy drinks, in addition to traditional soft drink options."

And then, seemingly out of nowhere, came a coffee deluge, and from an unlikely source, Vietnam. There's a prevalent belief that the

World Bank was responsible for turning Vietnam, previously a small producer of low-grade robusta coffee, into a mega-player on the world market. But factual backup is hard to come by. "I looked for evidence that the World Bank was somehow involved," reports John Talbot. "But even though I'd have been glad to blame them, I couldn't really find any. The World Bank is a convenient villain for a lot of things, but this is one of those cases where a story gets repeated and reported, and you hear it so much you figure it must be true."

Talbot suggests an alternate scenario. In the 1980s, Vietnam initially received some assistance from Eastern European countries, which were looking for a source of cheap coffee. This dovetailed with the Vietnamese government's goals to relocate people to the country's highlands as well as to find a more lucrative export crop than rice. In the mid-1990s, when the price of coffee on the world market rose, "it just got out of control. People flocked to the region and planted a lot of coffee."

It is true, however, that the World Bank began to extend development loans to Vietnam in 1994; and some experts continue to blame the bank. "Five years after the World Bank loans to Vietnam resumed, the country saw its largest increase by far in coffee," Nina Luttinger and Gregory Dicum note in *The Coffee Book*. "Two years later, as prices were hitting rock bottom, one of the bank's principal economists was quoted in the *San Francisco Chronicle* as saying 'Vietnam has become a successful producer. In general we consider it to be a huge success.'"

There is also speculation that Nestlé and other transnationals may have helped create a glut to reduce the price of coffee from its somewhat improved 1997 rates. If so, the plan worked brilliantly. In the space of five years, Vietnam went from insignificance to major player, quadrupling its output and eclipsing Colombia as the second-most-prolific coffee producer after Brazil. In 2001, Vietnamese coffee flooded the market, and the price of coffee plummeted. Robusta, which had sold for $1.80 per pound in 1994, was selling for as little as seventeen cents in London; arabica, which had sold for up to three dollars per pound in 1997, was selling for forty-three cents in New York.

This disaster for small farmers was exacerbated by consolidation of the coffee industry. As Talbot describes it, "By the early 1990s, four major manufacturers and about eight major trading companies controlled a majority of the coffee flowing into, being processed, and being consumed in the major markets of North America, Europe, Japan, and Australia. Four TNCs [transnational corporations] now account for well over 60 percent of total coffee sales across all major consuming markets." But for coffee-growing regions, this windfall for Nestlé and its ilk came at a high price. In "Can Great Coffee Save the Jungle?," a June 2004 article in *Smithsonian* magazine, journalist Katherine Ellison decried "a race to the bottom that has trampled many of the world's twenty-five million small coffee farmers, throwing millions out of work and off their land and leaving families impoverished and malnourished."

But a saving trend, one that Starbucks both grabbed and precipitated, also developed. In 1999, the USDA began tracking a new form of coffee consumption: gourmet. By 2002, of the daily 1.64 cups per capita, one-third was gourmet, and a lot of that was Starbucks, meaning high prices, higher profits, and a whole new style of coffee consumption. In other words, Howard Schultz didn't ride a wave; he succeeded in an undertow, creating both a cultural phenomenon on Main Street and an economic marvel on Wall Street.

Together, the Vietnam surge at the low end of the coffee sector and the Starbucks revolution at the high end define the modern coffee era. Dominating the low and vastly larger end are the transnational corporations and trading companies, an oligopoly with a stranglehold on the mainstream coffee industry. And on the high end, where barely twenty years ago a small and select cadre of connoisseurs savored the pleasures of fine beans and café society, a newly visible and rapidly growing coffee market has emerged, with Starbucks in the lead. Suddenly there's a two-tiered coffee system—and a new field of contention in the economics and ethics of the coffee chain.

A number of interactive websites let you take a crack at allocating your coffee dollars along the supply chain. And chances are, your preconceived ideas are wrong. According to Oxfam's *Make Trade Fair* website, only 2 percent of the cost of a jar of coffee goes to farmers, while 3 percent goes to exporters, 6 percent to shippers, 64 percent to roasters, and 25 percent to retailers. In *The Coffee Book*, Luttinger and Dicum break down a coffee dollar as farm labor, seven cents; growers, four cents; value added in producing country, two cents; transport and loss, eight cents; roasting, grinding, packaging, and distributing, sixty-eight cents; and retailers, eleven cents. The message is clear: the greatest share of money we spend on coffee goes to the roasters and retailers in the consuming countries; the least amount goes to farmers in the countries of origin. And each time the beans change hands, some money changes hands as well, all the way to your purchase.

The coffee chain begins with a plot, estate, or plantation of coffee plants. What grows on the tree, though, is not a bean but a cherry that starts as a little white flower and ripens into a deep red or, in a few cases, a vibrant yellow. The beans, usually two to a cherry, are the seeds at the center of the cherry. Once the cherry is picked, it goes through a milling process in which the beans are separated from the pulp, sorted, dried, and bagged before they are shipped to the roaster.

The path from coffee cherry to coffee cup may involve a few parties or many. But here's the basic chain:

- Farm worker or farmer
- (Possible middleman)
- Processing mill
- (Possible middleman)
- Exporter
- Shipper
- (Possible importer)
- Roaster
- (Possible packager)
- Retailer
- You

In countries such as Brazil and Ethiopia the government controls several steps in this chain, although, since the death of the International Coffee Agreement, governments have had less power to affect the supply of coffee and the market price. In other cases, especially where plantation robustas and lower-grade arabicas are involved, many steps may be under the direct or indirect vertical control of a transnational corporation. Large import houses such as Neumann, Volcafe, and Ecom have close ties with the big four coffee-roasting transnationals on the receiving end. They also maintain a controlling interest in the exporting operations in producing countries. The exporters, in turn, may own mills, which may employ middlemen or "coyotes" (the latter term often implies exploitative dealings) to buy coffee from farmers. The result is a tightly woven chain of power and pricing that disadvantages the small farmers. To reduce the potential for exploitation and keep more money at the farm, advocates for small farmers work to maintain as many farming and processing steps as possible under the control of the farmers, often through the formation of cooperatives.

Starbucks, for its part, has tried to create a kinder, friendlier vertical integration. It encourages small estates and cooperatives to improve the quality of their coffee and harvest and process it under environmentally and socially sustainable conditions. The company has also pioneered standards to ensure transparency at the exporter level. "It's lots of paperwork both for me and for the farmers," one exporter in Costa Rica laughingly acknowledged; and because Starbucks signs more contracts directly with farmers, the exporters do stand to lose some of their business. As of 2006, just over 50 percent of Starbucks' total coffee purchases were produced under C.A.F.E. Practices, with some portion of the rest still going through the larger import-export operations. From there coffee goes to the Starbucks roasting facilities in Kent, Washington; York, Pennsylvania; Carson Valley, Nevada; and Amsterdam in the Netherlands, all to become Yukon or Gazebo blend or be roasted as a single-origin offering.

Starbucks' other major innovation on the chain is, of course, the one we see: the addition of the cafés at the retail end. This extends vertical integration of the process under one company, from farm to you. That's where the culture and the coffee are branded and where the profit margins are added. Markups on the roasting and retail end may seem excessive until you consider that retail also necessitates labor, real estate, and utility costs that generally far exceed the cost of the product. Starbucks would have those same costs whether the coffee were first-rate or low-end dishwater. But by having excellent coffee, and by creating a desired atmosphere and at least the illusion of luxury, Starbucks is able to charge more per drink than many competitors—and get it. Starbucks coffee ceases to be a commodity once it's bagged or brewed. That's where the big money is made, not on the farm.

In all cases, farm workers who own no land are the lowest, least protected, and most poorly compensated link in the process; and they are in even worse straits if they are migrants, as many are. For the coffee they pick, harvesters are paid by weight, unit, or day or by some combination of the three. Some countries have established minimum wages and regulations for working conditions; some have not. Some cover migrant labor; some do not. In the overwhelming majority of cases, picking coffee is still seasonal subsistence work that leaves the laborer in poverty.

Coffee smallholders lie at the heart of better-grade and gourmet arabica coffees. The smallholder family probably does some of its own harvesting and may (1) sell the coffee to a middleman or coyote, who in turn sells it to a processing mill; or (2) sell the coffee to a processing mill; or (3) belong to a co-op that owns a mill, to which the family brings the coffee; or (4) in the case of larger or more sophisticated smallholdings, own its own mill. Each transaction takes a little cut out of the per-pound price. The fewer transactions made, the more money the farmer keeps, which is why those interested in fair trade prefer dealing with small cooperatives and eliminating some of the middle steps. Also, exchanges involving middlemen can be murky, and people who want their coffee origins to be clear and the financial dealings to be transparent are better served by fewer steps.

Once the coffee reaches the mill, the mill either exports it or sells it to an exporter. The exporter delivers the coffee to a shipper, who transports it either to an importer on the other end or to the roaster. But before most beans get to where they're going, the paper chits that vouch for their existence are traded, bought, sold, and resold many times over.

If the Starbucks annual meeting seems like a Las Vegas floorshow, the floor of the New York Board of Trade commodities exchange (NYBOT) looks like a casino; and my guide through the spectacle is no stranger to the game. His name is Willard Hay, but everyone calls him Dub, and he's Starbucks' senior vice president for coffee and global procurement. His face is round and smooth, his genial manner layered over strong opinions. Before coming to Starbucks, he handled coffee commodities for UBS PaineWebber; and his résumé lists stints at both Nestlé and Procter & Gamble. I prod him: "Were they really different from Starbucks?"

"There," he said, "it was all about money. And only about the money. This is about the coffee, and the values."

"Do you really believe that?" I ask.

"Yes. Most definitely. Yes, I do."

Most of us, if we think of commodities at all, may have some vague image of hog futures or pork bellies traded at the Chicago Mercantile Exchange. NYBOT, on the other hand, deals in commodities—sugar, coffee, cotton, cocoa, and orange juice—that arrive in the United States through east coast ports. The coffee traded here is arabica, almost all of it from Central America. The traders buy their seats for a cool 250,000 dollars. Although the old trading floor has since became history, when I visit in 2006, coffee is still traded via the "open outcry" or "shout out" method. Which means that the room is loud.

The exchange is on the seventh floor of the tall glass NYBOT headquarters along the East River in lower Manhattan, and you can hear the din from way down the hall. Throw open the swinging double doors that lead into the room, and wham! Think of all those Wall Street movies. Where the walls meet the ceiling, there are huge screens of glowing red and green numbers, filling the entire circumference. Those numbers are the world's economic condition codified into the data of plus and minus: currency exchange rates, lead indicators, stock prices. And the room is packed, mostly with men, all of them screaming.

Like the casino it resembles, the commodities market is at heart a gambling operation. No matter how simple the language or good the teacher, I just don't have the Rosetta Stone that decodes the mysteries of coffee futures. Basically, however, the exchange deals not in coffee but in paper—contracts stating that a certain amount of coffee will be delivered at a certain future month, generally at a specified price.

Market analysts with a strong knowledge of the industry predict prices for the different coffee delivery periods: March, May, July, September, and December. They establish a benchmark C market price for each period; in 2006, it hovered from a per-pound low of $0.9395 to a high of $1.30. Then price differentials are determined based on bean quality and the reputation of the source. And traders buy and sell against those prices. If it's December and you buy a contract for the March period at the currently predicted March price, and then the March price goes up, you stand to make some money because you've bought at the lower price and can sell at the higher price. But if the price goes down, you've bought at a higher price and have to sell for less or hang tough and hope the price changes again. And then you have to deal with the vagaries of drought, flood, war, pestilence, the World Bank, and hedge funds.

Official know-it-alls swear that a commodity's price is set by the laws of supply and demand: if you have more buyers than sellers, the price goes up; more sellers than buyers, the price goes down. In the past, C market pricing has somewhat reflected that reality. Talbot notes that, until the 1980s, "the major participants in coffee futures trading were importers and roasters, who used it mainly for hedging, or protecting themselves against sudden price changes." He adds that, when futures contracts are used as intended to cushion coffee buyers and sellers against market fluctuations, "the total futures volume would be expected to be about two times the volume of physical coffee traded, assuming that the buyer and the seller in each purchase both hedged their positions."

But as hedge and index funds increasingly play the commodities market, the pricing of coffee loses touch with actual coffee conditions that determine real value. These days, the contract for each lot of coffee is traded many times over by speculators trying to turn a quick profit based on criteria that have little to do with actual changes in the world's coffee supply. According to the president of NYBOT, only 1 percent of transactions result in the shipment of bags of coffee from a supplier to a roaster or a manufacturer. Stefan Wille at the Coricafe exporting house in Costa Rica explained using a hypothetical example: "A hedge fund might hear that a different government is taking over in Brazil, assume that will reduce the flow of coffee, and the price will go up. Meanwhile, people who understand coffee know that there's going to be a large harvest, and the price really should be going down."

Where once the coffee used to drive the paper, now the paper drives the coffee. "It's ridiculous," Wille says, sort of laughing when I ask him how he makes the speculative decisions for his coffee. "It's a question of stomach and mind together. Sometimes I just ask my kids, should I buy or sell? And the result is just as good."

The one bright spot is that, thanks to computerization, smaller exporters and even farmers in origin countries now have an easier time staying on top of trends. As Dub Hay notes, "It used to be that only traders had access to the fluctuations, but now the farmers have access too. I've been to small farms in rural areas and they are wired into the trading process. They don't have to take someone else's word for what's going on."

Still, you'd have to see it to believe it. On the trading floor itself, each commodity has a pit shaped like a mini-amphitheater. Smaller screens track the trading relative to the basic C market price, showing the third, second, and last price for each period, plus the high and low. On three raised levels, lots of white guys, mostly young, gesture and scream, motioning away from their bodies for "sell" and toward themselves for "buy." Unlike their counterparts on the Stock Exchange, they're not in suits; comfortable shoes and zippered windbreakers sporting trading-house logos are the prevailing couture. Traders stand

and scream and wave their arms wildly, while their colleagues man the phones, checking in with buyers and sellers. Dub points out the pecking order: the more prestigious your position, the higher your level in the pit. Those on the top tier are closest to their phone lines and runners and thus have an advantage in speedy communication. Likewise, the more prestigious trading houses have their phones closer to the pit along the aisles that radiate out on all sides. Across the circle from where Dub and I are standing, two traders get into a screaming match and look to be headed toward a fist fight, prompting intervention from a floor monitor. Dub rolls his eyes and laughs, "Happens all the time." In the center, at the bottom of the pit, four recorders strain to hear and record all the transactions that tumble over each other in unruly riot so that each can be duly noted, as the complicated rules require.

"It's a young man's or woman's game," Dub tells me, although women are seldom seen on the floor, in part, he suggests, because they're not as easily heard. He introduces me to Paul, who is in his late fifties, one of the rare traders to survive beyond his youth on the trading room floor. Paul has seniority for sure and is teaching his son the ropes. "People think working 9:15 to 12:15 is the life," he tells me, "but when closing time comes, I'm beat."

I can see why. It seems impossible to extract the necessary information from the din, process it, and act on it, all within seconds. And mistakes can be costly. The coffee is traded in lots of 37,500 pounds, the equivalent of a full container or truckload. Any one-cent fluctuation means 375 dollars. As Dub and I watch, a hundred lots are sold in a single transaction at a three-cent differential—more than 112,000 dollars speculated in moments.

Now that electronic trading has replaced outcry, there's little left to watch but a computer screen. A more decorous game, perhaps and, who knows, maybe a few more women. But the same fortunes and lives are still at stake.

Starbucks, like many gourmet roasters, buys almost no coffee on the exchange, considering it of lesser quality than the company demands. The big coffee multinationals, however, have plenty of traders working in their behalf, trying to snare coffee at the cheapest possible price. Like Wal-Mart, their goal is always low prices—and those prices have no floor. But unlike Wal-Mart, the coffee corporations share few of their downward dealings with supermarket consumers. When coffee from Vietnam flooded the market and drove down the prices of all coffee, the consumer price hardly wavered from its upward trend. Yet there was no safety net to keep the per-pound prices at a level on which the farmers could survive, and coffee growers started to go under.

As the situation deteriorated, organizations such as Global Exchange and Oxfam began demanding more help and higher prices for coffee farmers. The struggle they joined—and brought to Starbucks' door—is an old one. Concerns about coffee farm workers and growers reach back more than a century. In the 1850s Eduard Douwes Dekker, a disillusioned public servant, resigned from the Dutch East Indian civil service to protest the abuse of Javanese workers on Dutch colonial coffee plantations. He vented his outrage in *Max Havelaar, or The Coffee Auctions of the Dutch Trading Company*, published in 1859 under the pseudonym Multatuli (Latin for "I have suffered greatly"). It castigated colonial regulations that forced farmers to grow coffee and tea instead of rice, a practice he described in what may be the book's most frequently quoted passage:

> The Government compels the worker to grow on his land what pleases it; it punishes him when he sells the crop so produced to anyone else but it; and it fixes the price it pays him. The cost of transport to Europe, via a privileged trading company, is high. . . . since, after all, the entire business must yield a profit, this profit can be made in no other way than by paying the Javanese just enough to keep him from starving. Famine? In rich, fertile, blessed Java? Yes, reader. Only a few years ago, whole districts died of starvation. Mothers offered their children for sale to obtain food. Mothers ate their children.

Writing in the *New York Times Magazine* in 1999, Indonesian author Pramoedya Ananta Toer calls *Max Havelaar* "the book that killed colonialism." Toer suggests that, just as *Uncle Tom's Cabin* fueled the anti-slavery movement, *Max Havelaar* provided ammunition for liberals in the Netherlands to demand and win reforms in colonial policy. Those reforms, however, have taken a very long time to appear.

After the 1960s, as a New Left culture swept both Europe and the United States, newly liberated Third World colonies strove for an economic toehold; and there was a resurgence of interest in the

relationship between producers in the developing world and consumers in the global north. The mix of political interests was leav-
ened by a growing cadre of environmentalists and organic food
activists. Some of these sixties activists found their way into the specialty coffee sector. When Paul and Joan Katzeff started out as coffee
roasters in Aspen, Colorado, in 1969, they didn't know any other
roasters. "I later discovered there were a few," Paul later recalled,
"Peet's in Berkeley, Capricorn in San Francisco, and McNulty's in
New York City. What was different about Thanksgiving Coffee was
that I put my coffee roaster right in the center of my coffeehouse and
roasted coffee in front of people. That had hardly ever been done
before. I had no thoughts about building a long-term business. I had
no idea that coffee would capture me."

In the mid-1980s, three food co-op managers from New England
quit their day jobs, raised 100,000 dollars, and started Equal
Exchange, the nation's first fair trade company. Their mission was
"fairness to farmers—a closer connection between people and the
farmers we all rely on." Circumventing U.S. trade regulations, Equal
Exchange started out by importing Nicaraguan coffee to support the
new Sandinista government. Initially, its survival seemed tenuous:
the founders were trying to combine a business model with a decidedly progressive, nonprofit mission. But they endured and in 1991
established themselves as a fair trade specialty coffee company.

Meanwhile, more than a century after Eduard Dekker's death, the
Max Havelaar Foundation in Switzerland became the first organization to offer and promote certification for fairly traded coffee to
advance the livelihoods of workers in countries of origin. Fair Trade
Labelling Organization International followed in 1997 and now has
twenty-one affiliates worldwide. Although Fair Trade has environmental standards and offers a premium for organic coffee, it is unique
in its focus on fair pricing and democratic control at the farmer level,
which it promotes by dealing solely with cooperatives, many of them
quite small. The producers pay a five-cent-per-pound fee to support
the certification process, but those who meet the certification requirements are guaranteed a minimum price for the sale of their coffee: initially, $1.21 plus a social premium of five cents per pound. Fair Trade
maintained that minimum regardless of any downward or upward
fluctuations in market price, eventually raising it by five cents in 2007.

TransFair USA was established in 1998 with support from a
number of progressive organizations, including Global Exchange.

Although fair trade coffee covers just a fraction of the coffee bought in the United States (just over 3 percent of all coffee and 7 percent of specialty coffee), the amount has grown from 76,059 pounds in 1998 to 64,774,031 pounds in 2006; and the black and white "Fair Trade Certified" logo has become part of the ongoing dialogue about what values farmers and consumers should expect in a coffee cup.

"Fairly traded." "Shade-grown." "Bird-friendly." "Organic." These labels tug at the conscience of the U.S. coffee maven in her hunt for the ethical bean, and each label implies its own set of standards. And then there are the certifiers of these labeled traits: Fair Trade and TransFair USA, Rainforest Alliance, the European-based Utz Kapeh (recently rebranded as Utz), not to mention Starbucks' C.A.F.E. Practices and a network of verifiers.

Even big transnational corporations such as Nestlé and Kraft are claiming warmer—and definitely fuzzier—coffee-buying practices. In 2004, a group including Nestlé, Sara Lee, and the big trading houses began work on something called the Common Code for the Coffee Community (also known as the 4Cs). This international initiative to set baseline uniform standards also includes governments and nongovernmental organizations (NGOs), though Paul Rice, president and CEO of TransFair USA, dismisses it as "bogus. Make that totally bogus. It's to be expected, though. Higher-priced sustainability models have made inroads in the market, in partnership with strong brands. This is the counter-attack of the industry dinosaurs." Noncorporate actors participate in such initiatives because they can't afford to ignore them; but as one participant from a coffee-growing country dryly noted, "It's a case of keeping your friends close, and your enemies closer. We have to monitor what they're doing."

This web of initiatives has roots in two camps of conscience: social justice and environmental sustainability. While Fair Trade was focusing on the plight of the farmers, Rainforest Alliance was tackling forest destruction. The transnationals' demand for greater technification, as they call it, and faster yields has resulted in rapid clear cutting and increased environmental risk. Rainforest Alliance, Conservation International, and other environmentalists want to counter this trend and avoid the consequences of soil erosion and habitat destruction.

These two trajectories—labor and environment—have found intersecting but by no means identical constituencies in consuming countries. While the market for fair trade coffee continues to expand, environmental sustainability and organic consumption have generally drawn a larger and trendier following. Organic farming began in the early twentieth century as a reaction against chemical farming. The term first appeared in 1940 in a British book, *Look to the Land*, and soon thereafter in works by American organic gardening prophet J. I. Rodale. In the United States, the organic movement got a tremendous boost from Rachel Carson's *The Silent Spring* and the environmentalist outrage that book inspired. As evidence of environmental degradation has become indisputable, sustainability has emerged as a popular issue; and in 1992 it became a policy at the United Nations Conference on Environment and Development. Since the 1990s, organic farming in the developed world has grown about 20 percent a year.

As the market for organic food has expanded, the number of certification programs, both real and bogus, has proliferated. More than 65 percent of Fair Trade Certified coffees are organic, and the Smithsonian Migratory Bird Center promotes a bird-friendly certification that combines "shade-grown" with organic criteria. Yet even though the USDA and a number of international organizations have set out fairly straightforward criteria for what constitutes "organic," certification remains a Wild West show; and coffee producers suspect that a number of so-called organic certifiers are merely cashing in on a lucrative niche. "Many of the groups are leeches," Betty Hannstein Adams, a farm owner in Guatemala, told me, and her opinions reflect a common view. "One farm near me borrowed coffee borer insect traps so they could fool the inspectors, and the inspectors didn't know enough or care enough to catch them. Also organics is a very narrow lens. You can grow your crop without pesticides and still use a process that contaminates the river—and they don't care about that. They also don't care about how farm workers are treated or how much farmers are paid."

A small gourmet roaster concurs. "I've seen organic certs come out of places where I know it's just not possible," he said, "and I'm thinking, how did that happen? As the market grows, we need to do more due diligence."

It's worth remembering that sustainable coffees comprise barely 2 percent of the total world market, and not all of these sustainable coffees are certified. Furthermore, certification doesn't always pay. In *The Coffee Paradox*, published in 2005, two European academics, Benoit Daviron and Stefano Ponte, graph and compare the benefits that accrue to farmers from organic, shade-grown, Utz, and Fair Trade Certified coffee. The study covers both lower- and higher-grade coffees. The researchers conclude that, of the initiatives promoted by

NGOs, only Fair Trade Certified coffee, which deals exclusively with small grower cooperatives, consistently delivers a significant premium to growers; the additional monies accruing to farmers from Fair Trade sales in the United States grew from 44,114 dollars in 1998 to 16,970,608 dollars in 2006. Utz is still too small to be significant and doesn't guarantee premiums, and shade-grown and especially organic coffees are much more likely to command a higher consumer markup than to provide consistent financial benefit for farmers. Furthermore, Daviron and Ponte suggest that the certifications themselves have become commodified, value added for roasters and retailers that isn't necessarily reflected in the farm price.

What sets Starbucks apart in this mix of standards and certifications is an initial screen based on bean quality. In its early days, the company was one of a pack of small specialty roasters that viewed coffee purchasing through the lens of quality and taste. A teensy part of the overall coffee industry, these roasters often started by purchasing coffee through exporters and importers and then branched out to find small lots of quality coffee, sometimes from small farms. "Originally when I bought coffee for Starbucks, we were only buying from Bay Area importers," said Jim Reynolds, who holds the lovely title of roast master emeritus at Peet's Coffee. "We weren't as selective—it wasn't available, and we weren't big enough. But when I came to Peet's, it was a bigger company. I had the advantage of knowing who Mr. Peet was buying from. It opened a new window of opportunity. We look for new sources, and often they find you. They recognize you're good quality and pay good prices. We're not just a one-time customer: if the quality is good, we'll buy reliably. Our Guatemala coffee is from a specific estate where we've been buying coffee twenty or thirty years."

As Starbucks, under Howard Schultz's ownership, grew, went public, and grew some more, it outstripped all other purveyors of gourmet coffee. As it did so, it began to expand its coffee-sourcing as well. By the time Rainforest Alliance and Fair Trade were starting their certification programs, Starbucks was the largest corporate coffee company with an apparent interest in ethical sourcing; and both environmental and social justice nonprofits started to press the company on those issues.

Like its early upscale and discerning customers, Starbucks was initially more inclined toward environmental priorities, an attitude that eventually led to the first preferred provider program and C.A.F.E. Practices. These initiatives were just getting off the ground when the Vietnamese coffee hit the international market. And it's hardly surprising that Global Exchange and other activist groups, casting around for a way to dramatize the plight of coffee farmers, should focus their gaze on Starbucks. In 1999, Global Exchange launched a campaign to demand that Starbucks purchase Fair Trade Certified coffee. Activists started picketing Starbucks stores. By the time the Seattle protests rolled around, the Left was hearing and proclaiming a new message: Starbucks helps to impoverish the world's coffee farmers.

Ever conscious of its image, Starbucks began buying Fair Trade Certified coffee. Although these purchases constituted just a small percentage of the company's total coffee budget, they were still a large percentage of the total Fair Trade coffee on the market. By 2006, Starbucks was the largest purchaser of Fair Trade coffee in North America, although predictably it still didn't buy enough to satisfy its critics. But the company's next step probably had a far greater impact, for it transformed pricing in the gourmet coffee sector and saved many coffee farmers from ruin.

Confronting the fallout of the Vietnam coffee disaster and the devastation it was causing in origin countries, Starbucks decided to create its own program to assist struggling coffee suppliers. Sue Mecklenburg, who started out as the company's first director of environmental affairs and became vice president for sustainable procurement practices, recalled that Starbucks was experiencing rapid growth and had just begun a preferred supplier program for its best coffee growers. "That's about when the coffee crisis hit," she said, "and Mary Williams, who was running the coffee department, knew it would not be sustainable for us to grow like we wanted to grow, with high quality coffee, if the farmers couldn't survive."

At that pivotal moment, when the C market price for arabica stood at barely fifty cents, Starbucks decided to offer its regular suppliers multiyear contracts at fixed rates between ninety cents and $1.35—two and three times the market rate and often equaling or exceeding the rates guaranteed by Fair Trade. "Starbucks always paid over C market prices, and when the C market was high enough, that was fine for farmers," explained Mecklenburg. "But when the market dropped, there was a decision to move away from the C market prices and help farmers stay in business. It's all part of the same thinking—that the people who supply your business need to be sustainable if you're going to be sustainable."

Mary Williams is something of a legend in coffee circles, one of the rare women to reach the highest echelons of roast masters. Scott McMartin, who still works in the coffee department, started out under her tutelage in 1992:

> Specialty coffee was a relatively new concept back then, separate from the commercial grade arabicas sold on the C. We had to pay incredibly good prices for good quality so farmers would see producing good coffee as a good long-term investment. When the market tanked, we were working directly with coffee farmers. These farmers had been partners, and provided us good coffee; we absolutely had to stand by them. At fifty-five or sixty cents a pound, even ten cents above that, they couldn't invest in their farms or keep quality up. So we abandoned the differential model and offered an outright price. The outright price basis took away the downside risk the market was creating. It was a pretty conscious choice to keep suppliers healthy.

The consequences were significant, and systemic. As the floor was falling out from under the mainstream coffee industry, Starbucks single-handedly set a floor substantially over the prevailing price of premium beans, essentially forcing other buyers who wanted top beans to raise their purchase prices as well. "Starbucks did something quite new, rolling in those costs for long term sustainability," observed Konrad Brits, a trader based in Great Britain. "And they're far, far better than Nestlé, whom we call Satan. The largest transnationals have thousands of brands, and are generally reprehensible." At a time when all certified coffees had a market share almost too small to count, Starbucks changed the financial equation for the growers of gourmet beans.

"I remember talking with Mary at a conference she and I attended, it was even before the coffee crisis," said Jim Reynolds of Peet's Coffee. "She was saying, 'We've got to get away from this C market index.' And when she created the fixed price contracts, it really set a model for others."

Yet this pivotal initiative was not widely publicized by Starbucks or acknowledged by the progressive community. I harvested this piece of the narrative in the coffee fields of Central America. "Starbucks became the Costa Rican coffee ambulance," exporter Stefan Wille told me. "Lots of the farmers I deal with wouldn't be here today if it weren't for them."

4 | Go Sell It on the Mountain

On the hillsides of Costa Rica, farmers talk about their fields as though their coffee plants were human. They wait for the day when their trees are "fully dressed" and the beans lie red and lustrous along the branches. They shade them from the sun with canopies of banana trees and worry about how to revitalize them after they've been "stressed" by the harvest. "Look, here's my baby," said one of the Sanchez brothers, caressing the shiny leaves of a small Geisha plant growing along a contoured path on the La Candelilla family farm in the country's Tarrazú region.

The Geisha, an old arabica varietal treasured for its refined elegance and aroma, has finally returned to these mountains. It's making a comeback after falling out of favor in the 1980s and 1990s. In those years the shade trees were cut down and big, fast-ripening beans were planted because Nestlé and Procter & Gamble demanded quantity rather than quality. Today this farm is free of chemical pesticides, and the soil is tested several times a year. "Before there was a one-size-fits-all approach to fertilizer," Ricardo Hernandez told me. "Now there's more precision. We add only what the soil needs."

For which we can thank Starbucks.

This isn't the whole story, but it's a recent chapter in the coffee saga, a historical potboiler that begins on farms in the developing world and ends up in our morning cups. The epic acquires its power not just from the specific acts of people and nations but also from the interwoven narratives of exploitation and empire. In the mountains of Guatemala, this legacy of colonialism and grueling inequality lingers—in the German names of the larger farm owners, in the European faces on the board of the Guatemalan coffee organization ANACAFE, in the deferential manner of indigenous farm workers who struggle to turn their small holdings into a marginal living. About a third of the country's 60,000 smallholders belong to Fedecocagua, a federation of 45 cooperatives and 140 smaller organizations of farmers. During my visit, Fedecocagua marketing director Gerardo Alberto de Leon returned from an ANACAFE meeting in a rage. "These three Europeans on the board said we need the Americans to finish the wall between Mexico and the U.S. so that our farm workers can't escape over the border and get higher wages," he fumed. "And then one of them said the problem was that we're educating our indigenous population, and once they develop skills, they don't want to work on the farms anymore. Can you imagine? It was like going back 100 years. I couldn't believe what I was hearing."

But at least this time, Gerardo was present at the meeting, able to text-message the astonishing remarks to his colleagues and challenge the old powerbrokers. During the past ten years, smallholder and indigenous representatives demanded a larger voice and a vote in the coffee corridors of power, and Gerardo's leadership is proof of their progress. That, too, is part of the latest chapter of the coffee story; and Starbucks has increasingly become a part of the tale, embroiled in the realities of the world coffee trade and embroidered into the narrative.

How Starbucks developed its concern for, and relationship with, coffee growers is a matter of some contention. Starbucks would like you to believe the company did so for reasons of high principle; Global Exchange and other advocates of fair trade believe the company was pressured by proponents of global justice. As one activist remarked, "they don't move any faster than you push them." The truth probably lies somewhere in between. Whatever the motive, Starbucks has claimed the high road in its dealings with coffee farmers, raising prices, forging relationships, and improving lives.

Yet to what extent has the company advanced a new order of equity and environmentalism? Or is this merely another strand of an old story of exploitation? These questions are hotly debated. Progressive organizations jump at the opportunity to challenge the Starbucks version, sometimes to the advantage of poor farmers in struggling nations, sometimes to their own advantage. As a long-time activist wryly noted, "I wish we were going after Starbucks right now. We raise a lot more money when we do."

In October 2006, when Starbucks invited me to join two foreign journalists (a food writer from Brazil and a freelance photographer from Japan) for a three-day tutorial and tour of the company's agronomy center in Costa Rica, I decided to see for myself. This little media show was intended to tout Starbucks' approach to coffee growers, and the company had apparently assembled our quirky cast to test out its material before facing the big-city press. Leery about being spoon-fed a Happy Meal, I added several days to my trip, hoping to compare the official Starbucks version with the experiences and analyses of others.

I didn't have to wait long for the story to grab me. Rodolfo Murillo Bogantes, my charming seatmate on USAir Flight 1773 from Charlotte to San José, spoke only marginally better English than my Spanish; but when I told him the purpose of my trip, he beamed. "I work at Cooperativa Victoria near Grecia, the oldest coffee coopera-tive in Costa Rica. Come visit," he urged. When I mentioned the S word, he laughed. "Starbucks?! I just got certified under Starbucks C.A.F.E. Practices."

Unbidden, Rodolfo, a coffee co-op program analyst who also owns under an acre of coffee plants, proceeded to tell me, in fractured English and some detail, what he had done to comply with the C.A.F.E. Practices, the latest in a series of coffee buying standards that Starbucks has been revising and refining since 1998. He described sev-eral years of effort, which included learning from Starbucks agrono-mists how to clean up and protect the little river that runs through his tiny farm. "I don't use pesticides," he told me. "We can't have any trash near the water. And you need to provide safety equipment for people who work with you."

Before we lost each other at customs, he gave me the phone num-ber of his friend Carlos Mario, who also comes from Grecia and who works for Starbucks. But I didn't have to track his friend down; the next morning, he was the first person I met when I walked into the Starbucks farmer support center.

Starbucks opened this agronomy center in 2004 when it estab-lished the C.A.F.E. Practices. Its location reflects Central America's critical role as a supplier of premier beans, and Costa Rica's more restful political history and superior infrastructure make it an ideal regional base.

The center occupies a modest suite on the third floor of a low-rise office building in Escazú, a suburb of San José, where gringos abound, signs of construction are everywhere, and crossing the street is a death-defying act of faith. The office vibe is casual: desks are close together, and the staff is close-knit. Director Peter Torribiarte, who comes from a coffee-growing family in Guatemala, is lanky and loose-jointed, with manners so naturally graceful that I only noticed and admired them in retrospect. Like him, the majority of the staff members seem to come from north of the class divide and are cosmopolitans, moving easily between languages and countries. Starbucks claims that the company spends roughly four hundred person days a year visiting coffee farms, and the people in this office make many of those visits.

On our first morning, Torribiarte, along with staff agronomist Carlos Mario and Jessie Cuevas, the manager for coffee quality, poured and PowerPointed my two journalist colleagues and me toward basic coffee literacy, focusing on the dual tracks of coffee quality and community relationships that constitute the company's desired public persona. But if Starbucks detractors are cynical about the company's values, the staff of the agronomy center isn't. Carlos Mario and Jessie may be loyal employees of the Starbucks Coffee Company, gracefully discreet in their comments; but during the time we spent together, I learned that their commitment is as much to their compadres as to their paychecks: their families live in the region, and their lives are intertwined with coffee.

At present, the center assists farmers in all the regions that supply Starbucks coffee, although a second support center is on the drawing board for East Africa. And because Starbucks has decided to help a broad swath of regional farmers improve coffee quality and farm sustainability—not just the farmers who are its current suppliers—the center is barraged with coffee samples. Thus, our little group's education started from the grounds up. Jessie and her colleague Fernando roasted small batches of five different beans: Costa Rican, Nicaraguan, and, to honor the Brazilian food writer, a Bourbon coffee from Brazil. They set out trays with samples of beans in both their green and roasted states, along with small glasses. In standard Starbucks style, the beans were arranged from the simple to the more complex, and the taster walked from one sample to the next along a high table. In other coffee-tasting venues, the tasters remain stationary while a rotating table spins the beans from one person to another.

The ritual is performed with reverence. Our hosts placed fresh grounds in each glass, then poured boiling water (ninety-six degrees Celsius) over them. "You don't want to let it boil too long," Fernando cautioned, "or the water loses oxygen, and that changes the taste of the coffee".

Soon the grounds rose to the top, forming a crust over the liquid. "They say you can smell 10,000 shades," said Jessie. "Now break the crust and invite the smell in." Using small spoons, we struck through the crust, pressing our faces close to the glasses and fanning the steam toward our noses, just as my grandmother used to coax the spirit of God from her Sabbath candles. Then we skimmed the foam in a quick, shallow motion. (Or at least that's how Fernando did it. I was less adept.) Finally, we ladled up big spoonfuls of the hot liquid.

And we slurped. The process is neither dainty nor quiet. The goal is to loudly suck in the coffee, creating a lusty spray that sends the flavors to every part of your mouth. It's the equivalent of the swilling motion that wine tasters favor. Different parts of the mouth receive different qualities of the bean, the upper mouth evaluating body and richness, the throat measuring acidity. Then, once you've savored, you spit the rest into a convenient spittoon.

As we tasted, we talked: "How would you describe the body of this one, the aroma of that?" "How does it differ from the last one you tasted?" This was my second tasting; and if I concentrated very hard, I could tease out differences between one sample and the next, or at least between the first sample and the fourth. But much as I love coffee, my coffee palate is stupid. Some people may easily identify "undertones of chocolate" or "bright hints of caramel," but I have to struggle to find them. Jessie and Fernando, however, go through this ritual maybe 1,500 times a year, sometimes twenty times a day.

Getting one's palate to recognize and remember so many different samples is like getting to Carnegie Hall: it requires practice, practice, practice. Jessie learned "to cup" when she worked for a well-known Costa Rican exporter, whose clients included Starbucks; and she speaks with affection about Jim Reynolds, Peet's legendary coffee buyer, who helped her hone her skills. Reynolds started out at Starbucks when the company was just a few Seattle stores and followed the original founders to the Bay Area when they acquired Peet's. "I'm sixty-eight," he told me, "and the younger generation evaluates coffee a lot differently. They describe coffees almost like wine: fruit flavors, all kinds of off-the wall-descriptions. We talked about good acidity, kind of chocolaty or winy perhaps, but you didn't find things like pine needles falling on . . . I don't know what. I think they're trying to impress by using as many adjectives as they can. There's nothing wrong with it, but it's only useful to the person describing it."

I asked him what was important in teaching someone to evaluate coffee. "Here's what Mr. Peet taught me," he responded. "Keep an open mind. Don't fall in love with a coffee; just evaluate what's in the cup. Don't be intrigued because you liked it in the past or went to this country. Tasting is comparing; evaluate the sample with others from same origin, and then compare it to past examples and different regions."

How does Jessie decide what's good? "I have my own taste," she answered, "and then there's the Starbucks profile." She noted that these don't always match. Each company or brand, she explained, cultivates a unique savor. "Starbucks coffee is richer than the run of the mill. It has more complexity, more layers."

For all coffee companies, both low and high end, the challenge is to produce consistent blends, batch to batch and year to year. If you like the taste of Maxwell House (heaven forefend), you want your next container to taste like your last. But the mainstream roasters also have a wide range of beans that can be substituted to approximate the same result.

At the high end, substitution is harder; yet consistency in taste and quality is central to the product. Starbucks, along with other specialty roasters, is challenged to produce reliable signature blends while offering a spectrum of unique single-origin coffees. The demand for beans is expanding along with the corporation, and Starbucks staff is always on the lookout for new sources. Currently, it's investing time and energy to facilitate a comeback of the Nicaraguan coffee industry, decimated in the 1980s when American-backed Contra soldiers pillaged rural communities, murdered citizens, and chased farmers off the land. The Nicaraguan beans we sampled showed promise. Only a few weeks before my visit, that country's English language *Nica Times* headline had proclaimed, "Starbucks Hot on Nica Coffee," with the article noting that the domestic coffee industry hoped to advance its beans from a Starbucks blend ingredient to a full-fledged single-origin offering. Still, the industry has challenges. "There's no mill; there are no roads," Torribiarte explained. "And Peru is another country with some great coffee, but not much infrastructure to support it, making it harder to do business there."

But for Costa Rica and Guatemala, Starbucks has been a pivotal player. Just how pivotal was brought home to me later in the week by the deputy executive director of ICAFE, the quasi-governmental Costa Rican Coffee Institute. "More than a decade ago, Costa Rica decided to focus on the quality coffee market," Adolpho Lizano Gonzales told me. "Search for those markets was quite difficult. Then Starbucks arrived. It's buying almost 68 percent of the crop that is being exported. That proves the effort has been worthwhile." He smiled. "And second, it has made other buyers of quality coffee and good practices come here. They said, 'Well, if Starbucks came, there must be something there.'"

That 68 percent figure means there's a lot of beans in one basket, but no one seems particularly worried. "Starbucks basically ended up outbidding the European roasters," said one local specialist. "If they suddenly pulled out or collapsed, there'd be a readjustment period, of course, but we'd probably regain that market. And the Japanese are also buying more coffee, and their purchase price is just as good." Meanwhile, the Costa Rican coffee industry seems eager to embrace Starbucks' presence, the higher coffee prices it's brought to the region, and the C.A.F.E. Practices it promotes on the farms.

C.A.F.E. Practices anchors the Starbucks approach. It's "an incentive based performance system that gives purchasing preference to coffee suppliers that provide green coffee grown, processed and traded in an environmentally, socially and economically responsible way." The documents, available online, are something of a surprise, itemizing twenty-eight criteria that farmers, processors, and suppliers must meet to become "preferred" or "strategic" suppliers. Strategic suppliers (those with highest compliance to the standards) are paid an extra premium, receive priority in purchasing, and are frequently offered multiyear and/or exclusive contracts.

Call it the Starbucks version of fair trade. Yet C.A.F.E. Practices did not spring from the mermaid's forehead, fully formed and ready to battle evil. Rather, this accretion of consciousness and experience began in 1998, when Conservation International, a small but well-established nonprofit focused on biodiversity and conservation, contacted Starbucks about a coffee project in the Chiapas region of Mexico. Amy Skoczlas, now Conservation International's vice president for conservation investments, recalled the first tentative steps toward building a working relationship:

> The head of our board contacted Howard Schultz, and we had about a year of informal conversations about the environmental issues. At our first presentation to them, we took a map of the coffee-growing regions where we also work and said, "Look, we share the same real estate; our concerns also overlap."
>
> We were working on a small conservation coffee project in Chiapas. The growers were in a key biological cloud forest region and already growing coffee in a very sustainable way. Our intent was to support the community so they wouldn't have to technify and tear down the forest. They needed a market that bypassed the middlemen who were taking an exorbitant amount of their profit, and they needed technical assistance to improve their quality and their yields.

Starbucks didn't buy coffee from conservation organizations, but Starbucks vice president Sue Mecklenburg and several others decided to offer a 50,000-dollar grant and some technical assistance. "We were firm we wouldn't sacrifice our quality for environmental correctness, but if the coffee was good enough, we would buy it from the cooperative and bring it to our customers," said Mecklenburg. "And in a year, it had improved so much that we could buy it."

She still smiles when she recalls the first trip that Conservation International and Starbucks took to Mexico, three staff members from each organization, right after Hurricane Mitch had swept through the region. "It was physically a challenging trip. We really bonded, and it created a lot of trust," she told me, laughing. "And we were somehow like-minded. There are lots of people there like me, with nonprofit backgrounds, and [Conservation International] had worked with a lot of businesses. It set the foundation for a very good relationship, and we set some good rules to help us be good partners."

The venture was a success. She said, "If you go to this dusty little town now, you'd see what a difference it makes if you buy several million dollars worth of coffee every year. Over five years you move from a town where the only hotel has only cold-running water to a second hotel, to farmers sending their children to high school instead of grade school, to a diversification of shops—it's quite a remarkable transformation. And after a few years we said this project is really good, let's do it in five countries, and we signed a second memorandum of understanding."

Skoczlas at Conservation International credits Mecklenburg for making that success possible: "Sue was really the driving force. My impression is that Sue opened up dialogue with diverse stakeholders and made huge progress. Anyone who deals with corporate social responsibility knows it's about having the right individual in the right place at the right time. It takes a passionate, inspired individual to change things."

Starbucks liked the program and wanted to expand it; but its coffee buying, climbing toward 300 million pounds a year, was outstripping its capacity to proliferate the project in its current form. According to Mecklenburg, "Conservation International said to us, 'Why don't you try to build these environmental and social standards into your buying guidelines?' " That suggestion evolved into the preferred supplier program and became C.A.F.E. Practices in 2004.

Coffee quality plus economic equity and transparency are prerequisites for doing business with Starbucks. In addition, suppliers are graded on social responsibility and two categories of environmental practices that cover coffee growing and processing. The eight social responsibility standards cover minimum wages and overtime pay, prohibitions against child labor and forced labor, access to education and medical care, safety standards, and freedom of association, including the right to join a union. The environmental standards protect water, soil, shade canopies, and wildlife and discourage the use of chemicals. All criteria are broken down into specific measures; and manuals guide participants through the process, which is evaluated according to a point system. Preferred suppliers must achieve a 60 percent compliance level in each of three sections. Strategic suppliers must score a minimum of 80 percent.

Much of the debate about the merits of C.A.F.E. Practices and other corporate standards focuses on the question of whether or not the process incorporates independent certifiers or verifiers. Progressives often claim that Starbucks' efforts lack independent oversight; but in 2002, as the program was in transition, Starbucks contracted with Scientific Certification Systems (SCS) in Emeryville, California, to help develop its new standards. SCS provides certification, audit, and testing services for agricultural products and a variety of industries, working with government agencies and nonprofits as well as corporations. In the SCS offices, with a dazzling view of San Francisco

Bay, I spoke with Ted Howes, director of corporate social responsibility and supply chain programs. His work with Starbucks began with meetings in Costa Rica and Guatemala, followed by a stakeholder feedback session in Seattle in early 2004. He said, "We collected comments from a wide range of people, from Fair Trade, Rainforest Alliance, suppliers for coffee globally, farmers. Conservation International was very involved at that point as well. They all provided written feedback about where the standards could be improved or weren't appropriate. It's a process to get experts in their fields to provide you with the best standard possible. And that's the way all standards develop globally."

Howes waxed enthusiastic about Starbucks as a client and a partner: "There are companies that talk the talk, and there are ones that walk the walk. And Starbucks is a company that walks the walk. That's been a pure joy for me. That being said, they're a very demanding client, and that's fine. They expect a very high level of service and performance. And we appreciate that because it gives us an opportunity to shine."

He acknowledged that SCS is not an independent verifier, explaining that "it would be a conflict of interest for us as the developers of the standards to act as a certifier, the actual inspector on a farm-by-farm basis. That would not fulfill the test of independence. We cannot develop a standard and then certify against that standard." What SCS does do is to make sure that third-party inspectors have the capacity and experience to conduct independent inspections and to train them and oversee their work. One criterion is a verifier's independence: "What are their current relationships with farmers? Are they an ongoing certification entity? That takes us a long way in terms of independence issues. And they aren't paid by Starbucks; they're paid by farmers or suppliers, just like for any other certification."

As it turns out, Rainforest Alliance provides many verifiers for Starbucks' standards as well as its own; and as both sets of standards have evolved, the organizations have adopted some of each other's priorities, including an added emphasis on social factors. According to Howes, social audits, which he calls "more art than science," are more difficult to implement than environmental ones. Inspectors are assigned to interview 15 percent of the workers on any one site. "The obvious and most basic guideline," said Howes, "is that workers are not interviewed in the presence of management and ideally not in the presence of their co-workers. . . . A social audit is definitely a fact-finding mission, one to be compared with the interviews and documents from management. So it's a tripod—the documented evidence, verbal evidence, and anecdotal evidence." He added that plenty of farms fail to make the cut for C.A.F.E. Practices, usually because of minimum-wage and child-labor flaws.

This process may not equal independent certification as some progressive nonprofits define it, but all complaints in the field related to excessive rigor and documentation rather than laxity. There was nary a suggestion that the process lacked integrity, only frustration because SCS overseers sometimes came to different and more stringent conclusions than did frontline verifiers. This reaction probably suits Ted Howes: "There are a lot of misunderstandings about C.A.F.E. Practices out there, and that's unfortunate, because this is a program of great rigor, and we feel comfortable standing by it. I would like to go on record that it is a higher standard. When people claim lack of independence, it's because they don't understand what the program's composed of."

While Starbucks buys coffee from farmers who don't meet C.A.F.E. Practice standards, it is trying to move all its suppliers into compliance. The goal is to acquire a greater amount of coffee each year from strategic and preferred suppliers, thereby becoming less dependent on farms that don't meet the company's criteria and relying less on traders, exporters, and importers whose sources cannot be easily verified. By the end of 2005, almost a quarter of all Starbucks' coffee purchases (nearly 77 million pounds) were made under C.A.F.E. Practices; in 2006, purchases under the program exceeded the company's goal of 150 million pounds and accounted for more than half of the coffee it bought.

To see what this means in practice requires a visit to the field. On my second day in Costa Rica, our entourage traveled about ninety minutes south of San José to Tarrazú, one of the country's four main coffee-growing regions, where perfect altitude, a beneficial microclimate, and volcanic soil yield a prized coffee. It was a breezy October day, and the hilly winding road made me wish I'd remembered to take a Dramamine.

Audrey Lincoff from Starbucks headquarters in Seattle had come down to Costa Rica for this little press jaunt. She's waifishly thin, funny, tense, and tough, with a passion for running and sports cars.

Oddly, her journey to the heart of Starbucks had paralleled mine: when I went to Seattle to demonstrate against the WTO, she had just started her first Starbucks job as a regional marketing director. A few weeks before the demonstration, she had paid her first visit to headquarters, learning the ropes and figuring out the organizational culture. "I remember being there late one evening, after a bunch of meetings," she related, "and I saw Howard Schultz walking along the hall. It was deserted, and he looked kind of quizzically in my direction like, 'Who is this person?' There are people who always have to make themselves known to the boss, but I made up my mind I wouldn't be one of those. I just smiled, and went on with my work."

She got to know Howard soon enough; in 2001, she moved to headquarters as director of public affairs. Her protectiveness about the company sometimes got on my nerves, but I understood it. After all, I had been a union public relations director; and I, too, had shielded my organization from any perceived media threat and had crafted a party line. The truth was, we shared a bond; we were quirky, secular Jewish women of a similar age who didn't see the world as neatly as might have been convenient. We didn't always have the same point of view, but we liked each other. In 2005, she was promoted to vice president for global brand communications and became guardian of the new social responsibility catchphrase: "Good Coffee, Good Company." But she kept me in her portfolio, and we continued to debate and discuss. We were pleased to have each other's company.

Peter drove us in his SUV. As the Japanese photographer snoozed, Audrey and I took in the small towns clinging to the curves of the hillside. Pastel paint peeled from the low, worn buildings; but the towns were alive with skanky dogs, rickety trucks, and an air of cheerful commerce. After a wrong turn or two, we reached the gates of Cooperativa Tarrazú, a cluster of industrial buildings on the edge of the small town of San Marcos.

The common assumption is that coffee grows on large plantations like bananas and sugarcane do. While that's true in some places, the fine mountain coffees treasured by connoisseurs and popularized by Starbucks tend to come from smaller holdings, especially in Costa Rica. Because it lacked mineral resources and a large, exploitable, indigenous population, Costa Rica escaped Spain's worst atrocities and gained independence early, in 1821. Despite a bumpy advance into democracy, it developed a fairly benevolent culture that includes national health care and a literacy rate of 93 percent. It has also encouraged small farmers. According to ICAFE's Adolpho Lizano

Gonzales, in Guatemala, with its large, oppressed Indian population "it was easier to have a *latifundia* [a huge farm traditionally owned by aristocrats and cultivated by slave or indentured labor] because you had the workforce assured." On the other hand, "Costa Rica gave you free land so long as you used it for coffee. If you wanted a piece of land, it was 'how much can I work?' not 'what can I afford?' and that's why many of the farms are relatively small."

Today there are more than 65,000 coffee producers in Costa Rica; and although the country does have some large and powerful coffee farms, more than 90 percent of growers have farms that are smaller than three hectares (seven and a half acres). There is also a strong culture of cooperatives, where farmers pool their resources to process their crops, thus eliminating a string of middlemen and retaining more profits at the cooperative and farmer level.

Coopetarrazú, founded in 1960 with 228 members, has grown to a membership of 2,445 farm owners, including more than five hundred women. The women were not in sight on the day we visited, an absence that echoed throughout my travels. We met with the president of the board and with Carlos Rivera Chavarria, short and substantial, hired as the cooperative's general manager in 2002. His charisma required no translation; and despite the presence of the Starbucks brass, he and the board president spoke frankly. They were explicit that this cooperative had politics and a mission: "to bring back to the growers the control of the commercial activities surrounding the Original Tarrazú coffee [and] to stop the unfair business practices of the big economic forces involved in the commercialization of coffee."

Fair Trade and Rainforest Alliance had already certified the co-op. "Changing from synthetic maintenance to organic is difficult," Rivera explained, "but we're trying. This region has the highest incidence of gastric cancer, and pesticides are a significant part of that." Now the co-op was working toward C.A.F.E. Practices certification as well, which would add an extra five-cents-per-pound premium to the Starbucks purchase price. A number of member farms already qualified, Rivera said, and the co-op could have created a special processing protocol for that coffee but decided to hold off until all the farms in the cooperative were up to standard. "We didn't want to create an inequality among our members," he told us. Long-term principle was holding its own against short-term profit.

Our group moved off to look at the mill.

There are many nuances in coffee production, but almost all arabicas are processed via the "wet method," which coddles the beans to bring out the best flavor. Although we were visiting early in the season, when most of the cherries were still green on the branches, we followed the trail that the harvest would eventually take. The cherries are hustled to the mill on the day they are picked to avoid fermentation, which at this point in the process destroys the flavor. At the top of the plant, near the road, they are poured into little carts, each measuring half a *fanega* (roughly fifty pounds). A numbered wheel keeps track of the amount of coffee per farmer, and the coffee is spot-checked, the first of many examinations it will undergo. Then the cherries are emptied into large siphons, leading to machines that separate the beans from the pulp. The depulping machine needs to be adjusted to exactly the right abrasion level to remove the pulp without injuring the beans. The end result is usually two beans, each encased in a thin, hard, green shell called parchment or pergamin and covered with a slimy layer of mucilage. Then they're washed and sorted.

In the old-fashioned process, which I saw at other mills, the beans rush along in water channels like a fast-moving tan slurry and then rest in fermentation tanks for anywhere from twenty-four to thirty-six hours. The downtime loosens the mucilage and allows the traumatized beans to "de-stress;" knowing how long to rest each variety of bean is one of the fine points of the process. The cooperative, however, had replaced the old tanks with mechanical washers. "The old method used to be all a question of art, dependent on the knowledge of one guy," Peter Torribiarte told us. "If something happened to that guy, it was trouble." Learning the new technology took time, but it was worthwhile. The cooperative reduced the water used in the process by 90 percent, and that water is cleaned and recycled. In addition, the discarded pulp is now used as fertilizer and the parchment as fuel for the drying process, reflections of the new environmental awareness encouraged by Rainforest Alliance and C.A.F.E. Practices.

At this point, the bean has a moisture content of 50 to 60 percent; it must be dried until the moisture is reduced to between 12 and 13 percent. At the co-op, the beans, still in their parchment, are tumble-dried for a day or more. At other mills, they are spread out on large drying patios for up to twelve days and raked at regular intervals to assure even drying until they are ready.

When the beans are about to be shipped, the parchment is usually removed, revealing a green bean wearing a transparent silvery negligee of seed covering. These precious beans are then shaken through screens that sort them by size and another contraption that sorts them by density. Those that survive as first quality are destined for the Starbucks roaster and your mermaid cup.

Those beans are also key to the farmers' survival. "Our goal is not to suck up to Starbucks," Rivera asserted, "but to provide good coffee for a long time. We need to move from survival to improvement. Those who don't know coffee measure it by the price per pound. It's better to measure it by the change they are creating." He added, "Poor people have a right to dream. Costa Rica is what it is. It's not like the more developed countries, but we can dream, we can improve, we can shine."

That spirit also animates La Candelilla, an estate a short distance away, where nine Sanchez siblings and their families have combined their plots to create a ninety-nine-acre property. We are met by representatives of seven of the families and a spread of coffee and homemade desserts. In 2005, La Candelilla received one of Starbucks' Black Apron awards for producing a stellar coffee. The farm used the 15,000-dollar prize to buy computers; and we have been brought here, in part, to celebrate the recent signing of a three-year contract with Starbucks for purchase of the estate's entire coffee stock. It's charming public relations, to be sure, but the hosts don't seem the least bit deferential to the Starbucks staff. Rather, the relationship reflects an ease, especially with Carlos Mario, whose agronomy skills have helped many farmers calibrate their soil and find alternatives to chemical fertilizers and pesticides. This farm also has a micro-mill, intimately small, which features the traditional drying patios. But it's the coffee fields that draw us, and they are lovely.

Imagine a wavy hill of plants, surrounded by other hills. Each shiny-leafed tree takes from three to five years to mature, remains productive for fifteen to twenty-five years, bears profusely in alternate years of a two-year cycle, and yields one to one and a half pounds of coffee beans per year. Each acre on the average family farm has 400 to 1,000 trees.

The fields look almost casual in their order, the coffee trees shaded with banana fronds and poro, a tree species transported to the region so long ago that it's now considered native. The plants are nestled in a natural ecosystem, where the shade trees protect the maturing cherries and also yield timber, fruit, and other sources of income while providing habitat for animals and migratory birds.

In defiance of a previous decade's fashion and folly, this farm was never "technified" or mechanized. In the 1990s, before the explosion in demand for specialty coffee, ICAFE succumbed to market pressure from the big transnationals and promoted a set of practices aimed at bigger beans and higher yields. One particularly misguided initiative replaced existing coffee stocks with a strain known as Costa Rica '95. "It was a very high producer," recalls Peter Torribiarte. "The beans were big and fat; it was more resistant to pests and produced higher yields on a smaller curve. But they hadn't done sufficient research. And after a few years, the coffee got stressed out. It tasted fine for a few years, but then the crop rapidly deteriorated."

To promote rapid ripening, farmers were urged to cut down the poro trees and replace them with eucalyptus, which are notorious for sucking up water and eroding soil, further weakening the quality of the fields. And the promotion of chemical fertilizers, pesticides, and insecticides to control coffee borers and fungus created health risks for growers and pickers while poisoning soil and stream. The technification programs exacerbated the Vietnam glut, degraded coffee quality, and severely threatened growers' survival.

But not all farmers acceded to these pressures. At La Candelilla, Marco, one of the brothers, stood his ground. "I said no." He smiled—mustached, reedy, and relaxed among his coffee trees. "Since I left school, I guess, I've never done what anyone wants me to do. I said, 'I'll keep my shade trees, I'll work the land by hand with a machete, and I won't use herbicides.'"

His brother chimed in, "Then, when conversations came up about the shade trees, and Costa Rica '95, we had an example of how to do it differently. You have to retain your common sense and keep a balance."

Costa Rica '95 is no longer planted, and the country has revised its strategy for cultivating Starbucks and other high-end growers. When the gourmet coffee market gained momentum, Marco's stubbornness gave La Candelilla the edge.

As we stood among the rows of plants, the brothers talked about the changes that our new coffee-drinking habits have brought to the farms. What intrigued me over and over again, throughout all my visits in Costa Rica and Guatemala, is growers' newfound awareness of how care in the fields affects taste in the cup. It's a sad consequence of the historic north-south coffee relationship that many farmers once had no idea about what kind of coffee their beans produced. With most of the good coffee exported as green beans to be consumed in the global north, locals seldom got to taste their own best beans; among coffee-growing countries, only Ethiopia and

Brazil are also major domestic consumers of fine coffee. Almost all of Costa Rica's coffee—roughly 90 percent—is exported. Lesser-quality beans are retained for in-country consumption, many of them roasted with sugar. Valeria, translator for the Brazilian food writer, is Costa Rican and often gives tours for visitors. She told us, "People are always asking, 'Does this coffee go to Starbucks?' But I myself have never been to a Starbucks or even seen a Starbucks store."

Starbucks is finally aiming to change that equation, at least by a little, by opening retail stores in origin countries. As of 2007, there were 132 Starbucks stores in Mexico and 13 in Peru, which have been quite successful. And with an eye on Brazilians' devotion to coffee, Starbucks opened its first store in São Paulo in December 2006; by mid-2007, the country had four.

"Opening stores in countries of origin completes the circle," Torribiarte says. "It will be different than the neighborhood stores in the States because people here know more about coffee. Many of them are involved with its production in some way. They're more sophisticated about it. We believe coffee should promote a social conversation, and that conversation is expanded when you can talk about a specific origin."

I'm reminded of the old, and eventually abandoned, campaign to draw Saturn owners like myself into a strained relationship with the manufacturer and other Saturn owners. The company profits from the resulting brand loyalty. The approach is certainly suspect, although, truth be told, unless you can prove it hurts either the person at the beginning of the chain or the person at the end, it's hard to prove harm. What's really exploited here is a basic tenet of conscious consuming—the illusion that, by purchasing an item or service, you are linked to others with your level of knowledge.

But there is real sophistication at work in the developing world in the new cupping skills that Starbucks and other premium roasters promote with in-country coffee agencies and farmers. Companies such as Thanksgiving Coffee, a fair trade roasting company now based in California, have been sharing their cupping skills for decades. Starbucks, however, has used its resources to expand the effort. "We only used to know it was good if someone told us so," said one of the Candelilla brothers. "Now we can recognize our own coffee. By learning to cup, we've learned what combinations of agronomy practice and milling make for better coffee. If the beans are overripe or over-dried, all the small mistakes, now we know the result. And so we can change it and make it better, and do better in the market."

A few days later, when I went to visit my airplane seatmate Rodolfo at CoopeVictoria, this story unfolded in greater detail. CoopeVictoria sits amid rolling farmland in the hills northeast of San José. It's a large complex that includes an administration building, stores, a clinic, and two industrial facilities—one for sugarcane, the other for coffee. Founded in 1943, the co-op now has more than 3,000 members. This mill is in no way a showplace; it's a *beneficio*—a factory, large and a bit gloomy—where the workers wear hardhats and a serious attitude. Through a web of colleagues, I'd corralled a great young freelance journalist, Ben Witte, to translate and share observations. Rodolfo proudly showed us around the factory, ending with his favorite loft-like room at the top, the only room to escape modernization. This is where the sorted beans wait in comfortable, low, wooden containers to be packed into burlap bags for transport. We ran our hands through the beans, breathing in the distinctive smell of burlap commingling with the unique, slightly sour smell of green coffee. "You think of the smell of roasted coffee," Peter Torribiarte had told me, "but for me, this is the smell of my childhood; this is the smell of coffee for me."

Toward the end of our tour, Rodolfo took us to a small set of rooms tucked on the side of the plant: a tasting kitchen. Five mill workers were huddled intently over a row of miniature roasters under the supervision of coffee master Juan Gerardo Arturo Roman, learning the taste of what they produce.

Wearing a loose green and white checked shirt over his substantial frame, Juan Gerardo looked like a mafia don on his day off. He was coaching the men on how long to roast their samples and how to determine exactly when the beans are done. "My great-grandfather, my grandfather, my father, they all grew coffee. I learned to roast and to taste from my father," he told us. Like Jessie at Starbucks, he thinks that tasting is "just practice," although he believes that, to do well at a profession, you need to have something "in the blood. If you don't really like it, you don't do it well. If you don't like being a doctor, you'll kill the patient. To be good, you must like coffee. I used to work at ICAFE, and the person who replaced me drinks tea." He chuckled. "How can he say what's good? I say, if you don't like coffee, get out of here. For more than thirty years, I've been drinking twenty cups a day, and I enjoy them all."

According to Juan Gerardo, the men at the cooperative are easy to teach. "They have a stake in it; it's part of their lives. Ask yourself, 'Where does a good cup of coffee begin?' You have to go back and know the entire process, the different beans, the different roasting that they need." He recalled, with some bitterness, that, until a decade or two ago, only foreigners ran the coffee business. "There were no Costa Ricans. My father learned about coffee quality from an English boss, and he went and taught his brothers and all of us. It's my personal crusade that all who work in coffee can distinguish its qualities."

His laugh was loud, his gestures large, his opinions acidic. When we asked about Starbucks, he admitted he'd been curious enough about the company to visit the mother ship in Seattle and meet with its coffee experts. In his opinion, they know "muy poco"—very little—about roasting. "The story is that they learned in Italy, where they don't have great quality control and roast the beans very dark. Costa Rican beans lose their special characteristics when you roast them that way," he complained. Juan Gerardo sees this is as a tremendous waste of high-quality beans; but Jim Reynolds, Jessie's tasting mentor from Peet's, would disagree. "Peet's, like Starbucks, is a dark roaster," Reynolds explained. "When you buy best qualities, you can roast them darker, and it develops a certain flavor. If you roast it light, you don't have to buy that good a quality. Guatemala Antigua, for example, when it's roasted dark, you get acidity and spiciness in the coffee but also a toasty flavor that dark roasting gives. We wouldn't roast this way if our customers didn't like it."

Juan Gerardo might have doubts about Starbucks' dark roasting methods, but he has nothing but praise for the company's impact on the country. "They're excellent for Costa Rica," he told us. "We used to have excellent quality in the 1970s and '80s. Then the huge multinationals started to push for quantity. Now thanks to Starbucks, we can go back to quality: we have quality control, houses for workers, water standards."

"But don't you have any complaints about Starbucks" I asked hopefully.

"Sure," he laughed. "The farmers are complaining all the time. Starbucks is super-demanding. And the first year is really hard. All those environmental conditions. All that paper."

Like a number of people we interviewed, Juan Gerardo noted that policies and practices used to be informal and unwritten. If the guy who knew them left or died, no one else understood the protocols.

But Starbucks standards demand a complete paper trail, a big pain in the neck, but it does allow workers to duplicate results and maintain consistency. "Someone might pay a little more once in a while," he said, "but Starbucks pays well and provides long contracts, and then the farmer has security. Once the farmer meets the criteria, we hear no more complaints."

Before I left Costa Rica, I went to visit Robert Murillo's coffee farm. Dusk and drizzle enveloped the loveliest vista of my journey. Covering less than an acre, the holly-green coffee plants held strings of green berries along their branches. Oranges, tangerines, soursop, and guava grew alongside, and a canopy of banana trees shaded them, protected in turn by the sheltering mountains. We lingered a long time in the field before turning back for dinner.

The coffee story in Guatemala was more complicated, and I had no Rodolfo on the plane to launch me joyfully into my subject. Instead, I had a book, one recommended by a trade unionist at the AFL-CIO's international Solidarity Center. *Silence on the Mountain: Stories of Terror, Betrayal, and Forgetting in Guatemala,* by human rights activist Daniel Wilkinson, concerns the long struggle over land ownership in the coffee regions and the alliance forged by European owners and the military against the exploited, indigenous workforce. Wilkinson's narrative begins: "All I knew when I began was that a house had burned down. And not just any house. This was the house of the patron—the *casa patronal*—on a coffee plantation named La Patria."

Guatemala unfolded for me along with the book, as I followed Wilkinson's very personal quest to discover the truth behind the silences that obscure the country's recent murderous past. Central to the story was the U.S. role in toppling Guatemala's president Jacobo Arbenz in 1954. Arbenz had instituted much-needed land reform, attracting our government's misguided anti-Communist wrath and American corporate anxiety about U.S. coffee interests. What ensued was a succession of brutal military dictatorships and a thirty-six-year civil war, brought out of the shadows, in part, by the work and words of indigenous leader and 1992 Nobel Peace Prize winner Rigoberta Menchú. The details in Wilkinson's book were often horrible, but the writing was beautiful; and each night, his search framed my day's experience.

My trip to Guatemala was hard to organize. Contacts didn't pan out, an arrangement with a prospective traveling companion and translator fell through, and the folks at Starbucks failed to recommend farms to visit. Finally, I got a few breaks. The marketing manager at Fedecocagua (the Federation of Coffee Cooperatives of Guatemala) responded to my e-mail and helped me coordinate my stay. Several nonprofit staffers and activists contributed sociopolitical insights. And through a variety of sources, I was able to contact three owners of midsized farms: Betty Hannstein Adams, who was the mother of a friend of a friend; Don Felipe Guzmán and his wife, Maria, whom my colleagues at Fedecocagua warmly regarded; and Fernando Fahsen, who was recommended by Rainforest Alliance.

But I still wasn't prepared for Guatemala. At the time I arrived there, the peace treaty of 1996 was ten years old; yet as I met with owners of *fincas* (larger farms) and small farms, and spent time with Fedecocagua staff members and indigenous coffee smallholders, the legacy and silences of the country—those themes at the heart of Wilkinson's book—clamored for my attention.

One of the first things I noticed about Guatemala City was that the war there wasn't quite over. Guards and guns were everywhere. My lovely little hotel on a side street of Zone 10 had a private security guard who cradled an automatic rifle. So did the bodega down the street and the restaurant on the far corner. So, it seemed, did almost every building and business. Cars were securely gated in; likewise the people. As a confirmed urbanite, I'm usually nonchalant about safety issues, but Guatemala City was a whole different ballgame. I was emphatically warned about walking or driving anywhere alone.

In Guatemala, contemporary danger is rooted in longstanding colonial tensions and a recent history of violence. Guatemala is still a very poor country; and during the fighting in the 1980s and 1990s, many impoverished workers left the land and headed for the city, creating a new urban underclass. Simultaneously, a dangerous new drug trade began to flourish, aided by endemic corruption. This thriving drug trade had links to U.S. immigration policy; many of Guatemala's drug dealers and gang members had grown up in the United States. When police in, say, Los Angeles busted up street gangs, they turned over members to U.S. immigration personnel, who then deported them to their countries of origin. Thus, many young men who had left war-torn Guatemala as small children were suddenly returning to a country, and to a language, they no longer remembered. Dumped into Guatemala City, they began dealing drugs and fueling all kinds of crime.

Guatemala City was a bit grim; but once I left it, I realized that the country was beautiful. Every road I took wound steeply up or down from one vista to the next. I had been lent a house in Antigua for a few days, and from the balcony I could see the stones of the old church next door and the green slopes of volcanoes. Sometimes, in the quiet, I could hear the volcanoes growl; and on a farm visit I saw a spume of smoke belched against a blue sky.

Little villages rested along surprisingly decent roads, and each had a tiny grocery store and often a machine shop. Small trucks sold produce, and small outdoor grills served roadside meals. Tin-roofed homes snuggled together like a collection of ramshackle trailers, each with a woodpile, lots of busy chickens, and the occasional goat. Behind them plots of coffee climbed the hills.

On one of these roads, near Lake Atitlán, is Finca Santo Tomas Pachuj, the coffee farm and nature preserve of the Fahsen family, where Fernando tends to administration and his brother Federico tends to the land. Throughout the Americas there are growing numbers of government-certified private nature preserves, an effort to protect ecosystems from further degradation. In exchange for maintaining private property according to stringent ecological standards, owners can support the venture with crops and ecotourism. As it happens, those environmental standards are also congenial to growing high-grade coffee; and many owners of midsized farms are active participants in the program.

These farms also have other things in common. They range up to several hundred acres, considerably more than the ten or so acres common to the average smallholder. Although the owners all have homes in Guatemala City, they spend much of their time at the farms, making the lengthy journey to the land each week during the harvest and frequently throughout the year. All of the families I met had owned their land for at least three generations (the Fahsens for five), and all the farms had at some point been subdivided among family members. Yet these owners are in a complicated position. Whiter and far more affluent than the smallholders and indigenous workers, they are nevertheless not politically aligned with the biggest farmers or the colonial vision. Instead, they are working to redefine themselves, and their workforce, against the pressures of their history.

Originally, all three farms had *colonos*, indigenous tenant laborers who lived on the farms, a system established by Spanish colonialists and adapted by subsequent generations of domestic and European owners. Each tenant family was entitled to a house, a small plot of land, and some payment in exchange for labor. Many of the workers came from families whose own lands had been expropriated in the 1870s to create the big coffee farms, and they were coerced to work for the new owners.

In 1952, Jacobo Arbenz's labor and land reforms promised these long-exploited workers the security of their own land rather than tenancy at an owner's whim as well as opportunities to organize unions and cooperatives. But in that cold war decade, the United States was quick to see a Communist in every reformer. The CIA helped overthrow Arbenz, and Guatemala's political right replaced him with a military dictatorship. The military and the farm owners quickly restored the old power system, kicking leaders, unionists, and other troublemakers off the farms. They bullied the remaining indigenous workers back into submission, fueling a guerilla resistance movement and nearly forty years of civil war. The coffee farms became a battleground. The military targeted communities it believed were supporting the guerillas, often instigating unspeakable acts of torture and destruction. Meanwhile, the guerillas took vengeance on coffee owners suspected of colluding with the government, acts that led, among other things, to the homestead fire that opens Wilkinson's book.

The civil war's peace treaty signaled a cessation of hostilities rather than a victory. It brought about just enough reform to maintain relative tranquility but created few significant shifts in the distribution of wealth or power. As the revolution petered out and minimum wages and labor laws were reestablished, many farm owners—occasionally unable to comply with those laws, and frequently unwilling—terminated the traditional workforce living arrangements and forced the remaining colonos off the farms. True, the system was paternalistic and exploitative and had long needed transformation. But the colonos were also attached to the land they had worked, sometimes for generations; and their labor had given them housing, basic food rations, and other necessities. Eviction threw families into chaos. In some cases, owners turned a portion of the land over to the colonos, giving them the opportunity to become smallholders. Other colonos established new villages in the region. Some went back to work as hired wage laborers on the farms they had once called home. Today, the relationship between the Europeans and the wealthier Ladinos who own the fincas and the indigenous families who work on them remains unsettled, with both sides trapped between traditional and modern ways of interacting.

Betty Hannstein Adams and her son Walter run Finca Oriflama, half of the original farm that Betty's grandfather established in 1923 and maintained with colonos. In 2007, only the mechanic, foreman, cook, and beekeeper lived on the property. The farm employed forty-eight permanent workers from the area, and the owners were constantly struggling to balance old needs with new sensibilities. "We don't employ children under the age of fourteen," Betty told me, "but sometimes a mother will come and tell me her oldest son would like to work; it means more money for the family. And we thought about providing child care, but the mothers wouldn't bring the babies to it. They'd rather bring the children to the fields, where the five-year-old can watch the one-year-old and they're with the family."

According to Betty, foreign agencies' inflexible position on children in the fields isn't always warranted. Her opinion reminded me of a conversation I'd had several years earlier with Stephen Coats, director of the U.S. Labor Education in the Americas Project, formerly the Guatemala Project. In 1995, US/LEAP uncovered labor violations on some of the Guatemalan farms from which Starbucks got its coffee and embarked on a campaign to pressure the company to adopt a code of conduct. After several years, Starbucks did adopt a code, which eventually mutated into C.A.F.E. Practices. Child labor was one of the issues, and Coats had found himself in the odd position of urging Starbucks to adopt a more lenient standard rather than an outright ban in order to acknowledge both cultural traditions of child raising and economic necessity.

Each of the owners I spoke to also mentioned the cultural challenges of building a new relationship with workers. Felipe and Maria Guzmán were the only owners I met who still have a small number of field workers living on the estate and who continue to ensure certain basic necessities while trying to create some changes. "I told one of the men he can't let his wife carry both the baby and the heavy load; he needs to help," said Maria Guzmán. "And we try to convince them not to have so many children. But it's tradition, and it's hard to convince the girls not to marry at sixteen."

There are also still occasional incidents in which indigenous workers mount an occupation of a farm, and rogue harvesters still steal coffee from unguarded sections of the estates. Despite the fact that Fernando Fahsen's father was a renowned expert on Mayan culture and even though the community thought well of the family, forging a stable workforce remained Fernando's greatest challenge. The part of the farm he inherited never had infrastructure for colonos (the same was true for Betty); and of the thirty-four workers whom he originally hired from nearby communities, only two were left. "The workforce is our Achilles heel," he told me. "If you don't have colonos, there's no loyalty. We need permanent workers. We need to motivate them, pay them well, and make them feel loyalty, that we are all fellow workers. So we decided to make a system to be more productive; we created teams, and we employ a core of workers all year, doing harvesting and maintenance."

The Fahsens provided transportation to and from the three surrounding communities to the fields so that workers didn't have to walk so far. They also provided some additional perks, like paid time to chop a measure of estate wood for personal use. And they offered workers special training at ANACAFE, the country's coffee agency, then placing these trained workers in management positions. They've schooled the workforce in the benefits and requirements of sustainable agriculture, replacing chemical fertilizers and pesticides and, with some difficulty, trained workers not to leave garbage in the fields. But the effort was yielding better coffee and higher prices. And along the roads, there was a new phenomenon: workers on bicycles instead of on foot.

Fernando said his workers want him on the farm because "when we're here, they feel protected. They can do the work, but they need someone to care for them." His father has suggested that the need for leaders is ingrained into Mayan culture. In Fernando's words, "we have more skills, we've been to university, we can find solutions easier. We need to train them, and share that with them."

"I hate the term *padrón*," he added, grimacing. "They're always trying to be nice to me, to make sure I pay them at the end. They don't have to do that. These people don't trust, and why should they? They don't even trust each other. I'm trying to change that way of being. We're all Guatemalans, all workers for the same company, which is like a second home, and which provides us all a living, so we all have to take care of it."

I heard these juxtapositions, ambivalent and contradictory, throughout my visit as decent people searched for better ways to blend old legacies with new realities. But of course, that effort was only half the story. Like the other farm owners, Fahsen walks a tightrope: he must address historic injustices in the fields while navigating the demands of an unstable and ever more complex coffee market.

The crash in coffee prices created much hardship. "When the prices fell in 2000–2001, we were almost gone," said Fahsen. For the past eight or nine years, Betty Hannstein Adams has been operating at a deficit, a fate the Guzmáns escaped by planting rubber plants, which provided a second income stream when coffee prices failed. Now the Fahsen farm augments its coffee income by producing honey and hosting ecotourists. For all of these owners, sustainable farming practices and specialty coffee have become part of their survival strategy. All three were certified by Rainforest Alliance; Betty's farm and the Fahsen farm were also certified under C.A.F.E. Practices, although only Fahsen was currently selling to Starbucks.

The office at the Fahsen farm looked like a cabin at summer camp, even down to the pine tree on the sign by the door. Inside was a map of the property and a long desk along one wall. A bathroom adjoined, and there was a covered patio out back, where a worker entered payroll figures into a ledger. There was no electricity, and the phone was hooked up to a battery.

Wherever I went in Guatemala, farmers pulled out the paperwork that verified their goodness and talked about certifiers and their check-lists. Fernando produced several notebooks. He said that Rainforest Alliance shows up every year ("you've always got to be ready") and Starbucks comes every three years ("a little better because it gives you time to make changes"). Although outsiders tend to dismiss both groups as soft on social issues, Fernando said work conditions are the first thing that buyers check: they confirm minimum-wage standards and interview workers to ascertain how they feel about their treatment. He pointed out the railings around the mill porch, which Rainforest Alliance made him add to prevent falls; the organization also wanted him to encase chains on the machinery to protect fingers. He noted that Starbucks led the way on demanding water conservation and cleanup. "They're more scientific," he observed. "We must document and measure everything. And we have to explain it to the workers as well. The certifications have changed us."

Fahsen had a soft spot for Rainforest Alliance. Like many farmers I met in Guatemala, he saw its certifiers as pests who showed up too often and nitpicked about too many things; but he also saw them as caring and the relationship as personal. Betty Adams echoed this assessment. "They deal with both welfare and environment," she told me, "but they're not in the business of telling farmers how to produce their crops. They're really on the farmers' side; they don't want us to fail."

With Starbucks, the relationship was less personal, the contact less frequent, and the motivation somewhat more suspect. Everyone understands that Starbucks is getting rich, while the farmers are just getting by. Yet in the wake of Hurricane Stan, which devastated the region just before the 2005 harvest, Starbucks was the only entity to extend tangible aid. Stan buried entire villages in mudslides and killed 669 people in Guatemala alone, many in the communities around Fahsen's farm; it also damaged and blocked the only road through the property. "The people were scared to come to work," Fernando said. "It may prejudice your story, but I have to tell you, we belong to Rainforest Alliance, Starbucks, ANACAFE, the association of nature preserves, the government, and when Stan hit, Starbucks was the only one who offered us money, not supplies, but the actual funds we needed to repair the roads."

Like his fellow farm owners, Fahsen credited Starbucks for having increased the overall market for specialty coffee and for having paid decent prices early on. But though Starbucks had recently paid him $1.45 a pound for coffee, the company wasn't currently his biggest or his best-paying customer. The Japanese were buying more coffee at higher prices, up to $1.65 a pound. And through one of the big exporters, Fahsen had been discussing a contract that could reach two dollars a pound. With a record harvest and his trees showing signs of another good harvest the next year, he felt as if his hard work was finally paying off.

Fedecocagua's marketing director, Gerardo de Leon, and its general manager, Ulrich Gurtner (known as Ueli), are less certain about the latte revolution's payoff. Fedecocagua's members are cooperatives that represent smallholder coffee growers, most of them indigenous, many of them former colonos and farm workers who managed to hang on to a plot of land. When I walked past the armed guard and the buzzers into the organization's offices in Guatemala City, I felt instantly at home. Fedecocagua is, in Gerardo's words, "a cooperative of cooperatives." It promotes collective action as a way to create power for small farmers who previously had none. Fedecocagua was formed by nineteen cooperatives in 1969. Today the organization has forty co-ops and 140 smaller farmer associations. Together they represent more than 20,000 smallholders, close to 80 percent of them indigenous. Fedecocagua is also one of the largest and most successful Fair Trade groups in Latin America.

Gerardo arrived at Fedecocagua in 1981. At a height of about five-foot-one, he and I stand eye to eye. His face is round, his voice a bit weary, not a surprise given that he's up at 4:30 A.M. every morning. "That man's a workaholic," Ulrich told me later. "When he went on vacation, he didn't stop working or writing e-mails. I just deleted them. He needs to know he's more valuable to us alive than working himself to death."

Gerardo has basically grown up in Fedecocagua, and he takes it very personally. Born in 1962 in Guatemala City, he worked as a house-boy to help his family survive. "We were very poor," he told me, "but at least I went to school. I saw that people in this country need to work very hard to get something in life. I felt if I could just help people in the countryside get a basic education, we could make a difference. And eventually I came to Fedecocagua when I was nineteen or twenty. At that time we had just 7,000 smallholders and twenty co-ops—and only fifteen or so were in good shape."

Thinking about Wilkinson's book, I asked about the impact of the civil war. As always when I asked this question, there was a pause, then a restrained answer, the details spare: "The cooperative move-ment resurfaced at the end of the sixties. First, there were savings co-ops, different things, and then it moved into coffee production. The Catholic church organized some, and the left organized some." He paused again. "It was hard for everyone to survive. A lot of the guerillas felt cooperatives belonged to the government. And the gov-ernment thought co-ops were Communist. We were in the middle; we just tried to show everyone that we are working for workers."

In 1973, he recalled, a group came from the Netherlands with an agenda out of *Casablanca*. "They brought money, not only to buy cof-fee but more for us to arm our members—a social premium, they called it." The Dutch group wanted to support the guerillas against the government forces. But that was out of the question. Fedecocagua was trying desperately to stay out of the fray. Besides, said Gerardo, "How could we tell our members, 'This is for the coffee, and this is a premium to buy weapons'?"

One European who has worked in the NGO community in Guatemala for many years sees the impact of the long civil war in other ways. "I have a really strong idea about this," he told me. "I don't know whether I'm right, but I think in rural communi-ties, people are not into organizing themselves, even in small community organizations. There are about twenty-five small co-ops or federations outside of Fedecocagua; each of them has a member-ship from fifty to one hundred. They're not self-sustainable, they do not pay a full-time manager, there's no bookkeeper. The military government actively promoted division, not to organize or be organized."

I still don't really know what deals Fedecocagua made or what price it paid for survival, but it must have been both cautious and brave, and very tenacious. Not only did membership grow, but its staff members have since become expert marketers. As a result, its capacity has soared: the organization is now the fourth-largest exporter of coffee in Guatemala, ranking just under the transnationals that cater to the coffee giants. And there's widespread agreement that the organization has wrested some political power for smallholders, thanks in large measure to Ueli's intervention.

In Gerardo de Leon's office, two pictures hang side by side . One is a studio shot of Ueli with his father and his son. "I keep that photo in my office so people know that, even though Ueli is a European, we have a relationship of trust and respect," Gerardo explained. The other photo shows the ANACAFE board, whose preponderance of white faces reflects western European (in particular, Germanic) dominance of the Guatemalan coffee industry.

Ueli, tall and bespectacled, is the not-so-secret agent in their midst. In 1984, he went to work for the Guatemalan export house Waelti-Schoenfeld, an affiliate of Swiss-based Volcafe, one of the world's largest commodity trading houses. He quickly suspected that the company, which supplied large quantities of coffee to Nestlé and Maxwell House, was moving beans in a way that circumvented existing quota systems, to the detriment of producing countries. Within four weeks, he had proffered his resignation, though he remained for another two years when the company promised to clean up its act. He finally left in 1986, when a management change brought some of his nemeses to power.

By 2006, Ulrich was in his eighteenth year as general manager at Fedecocagua. Both he and Gerardo call the decision to hire him a strategic move, one that forcibly unlocked the doors of ANACAFE and the coffee establishment. "In 1988, we got some funds to hire Ueli as a consultant, and then he became general manager," Gerardo said. "When we went to ANACAFE with our own European, everyone hated him. We voted for Ulrich because he'd been part of Volcafe. He knows how rich people work, and he doesn't like it."

Ueli told the same story: "The people here know that my being Swiss has value because they don't try to cheat me the way they'd try to cheat Gerardo. Of the people in export, 70 or 80 percent are foreign, maybe 30 percent rich Guatemaltecos. In the end we're the reps of the indigenous. We were able to force representation for Fedecocagua because they didn't know how to say no to me."

Why did he do it? "I come from a labor family," he explained. "I learned always to help the weaker ones. My life has had more growth, and more warmth—and I'm happy. I'm glad to do this job."

With Ueli as the wedge, Fedecocagua was able to pry the doors open; and now it has a number of allies on the ANACAFE board. One is Don Felipe Guzmán, one of the farm owners I interviewed, who has worked hard to ensure that smallholders are fairly treated in the board's deliberations. Gerardo himself was appointed to the ANACAFE board as the Guatemalan president's delegate in 2000 and has been able to hang on to his seat, despite occasional political flaps.

Despite the odds, Ueli and Gerardo have managed to eke out a working relationship and a friendship and to build an organization. The federation's staff members range widely in race and class; and although women are underrepresented in the leadership, those on staff are vibrant, outspoken, and smart. Onelia Fernandez, who coordinated my visit, had just completed her degree in business administration and helped to keep the office on an even keel. Adolfo Monterroso, who accompanied me on some of my visits, was taking his sixth or seventh round of English classes (sponsored by Fedecocagua), and we gleefully enlarged each other's vocabularies—for instance, discussing whether the word *ripe*, as in beans, can also be applied to women, and with what implications. A sense of community seems to sustain the staff as Fedecocagua navigates the perilous shoals of a changing coffee market.

Still, not everybody has good things to say about Fedecocagua. "A lot of people not affiliated speak badly about them," said one observer. He continued:

> Gerardo and Ueli are very capable, but they can have a nasty side. The complaints are around two issues. There doesn't seem to be a high level of transparency on the business side; its not always easy to know that my coffee will be sold as organic or fair trade at x price and I'll get back y. The other thing people react to is Fedecocagua has a kind of goal to be everywhere, and be in charge everywhere, and for a lot of people that creates bad feeling. They're not willing to give any space to anyone else. A few years ago we tried to build a coordinating body of twenty-plus organizations, and Fedecocagua was constantly complaining about "Why did we need something other than them?" It took us a lot longer to move forward. And I know it doesn't have to be that way. In

Nicaragua, several organizations of vastly differing sizes have managed to work together. They even sell each other's coffee.

These grievances exasperate Ueli and Gerardo, who live, eat, and breathe Fedecocagua and fret over its health like protective parents— albeit with dogged good humor and an ever-present touch of irony. Ueli suggests that the criticisms, especially those about transparency, are based on a lack of understanding about the nature of the organization, where the prices paid to individual cooperatives and farmers are calibrated to benefit the collective as well as the individual. "At Fedecocagua, the big cooperatives are subsidizing the small ones and helping them in different ways to bring their coffee at the same price levels of the world market," he protested. 'Fifteen cooperatives deliver 60 percent of our coffee volume, twelve cooperatives 15 percent, and fifty-seven cooperatives 25 percent! And if you looked closely, you'd find that Fedecocagua supports its poorer cooperatives much more efficiently with much less development money than the NGOs do."

Then there are the added pressures of the market. "I say give me really free trade," declaimed Ueli, striding across the room like a British actor with a Swiss accent. "Everybody talks about free market, but they never mention that free traders are making their own rules. I'm convinced if we had access to a really free market, we'd produce more coffee with better prices. But what we have now is twenty people who all know each other making the rules. It's this little circle, and they set the rules, and their own quotas, and if we make enough noise they'll throw us a bone."

It's true that the controllers, new and old, are a tightly knit group. In Guatemala, coffee producers are quick to point out that the chief Starbucks buyers come from the big coffee export companies and are presumed to retain close ties with those entities. Furthermore, everywhere I went, I heard that Peter Torribiarte, head of the Starbucks agronomy center in Costa Rica, comes from a large coffee-growing family in Guatemala. A member of the Torribiarte family put the Fahsens in touch with Starbucks, and Torribiarte's father sits on the board of CAFCOM, a Guatemalan export house that also happens to be the largest exporter of Guatemalan coffee to Starbucks. People speak warmly of the family, especially Peter's mother, who worked to aid widows of the civil war. But few believe that CAFCOM's key role is a coincidence, and some suggest that it compromises Starbucks' avowed commitment to transparency.

There are, indeed, difficulties in achieving transparency through-out the Guatemalan supply chain. Costa Rica has comparatively more government oversight: all mills are registered, and safeguards prevent certain egregious forms of price gouging, making it easier to trace cof-fee from point of origin to export. Not so in Guatemala, where coyotes still play a large role in buying and selling coffee. Traditionally, coy-otes bought coffee from independent smallholders, often in rural locations where transport was difficult, paying farmers for the day's harvest as they came home from the field. Prices were lower than market average but offered convenience and ready cash. More recently, however, coyotes have become part of the drug-money laun-dering chain, offering higher-than-market prices, tempting farmers to abandon previous sale commitments, and sometimes seducing co-op members away from the collective to seek a higher per-pound price as individuals.

In addition, several export houses that deal with large transna-tionals have been caught trying to make direct deals with coopera-tives that are part of Fedecocagua. For instance, an export house tied to Nestlé tried, and almost succeeded, in wooing away a cooperative with promises of better prices and a health care center. "They didn't notice that there already was a government clinic not 150 meters away," Ueli recalled, his voice exuding frustration. "And the cooper-ative eventually realized they were being lied to. It's outrageous. They want to go around us to make deals with our member groups, without dealing with us, as though we didn't exist. It's as though we went to a Starbucks store and started selling another brand of coffee right there in the store." He and Gerardo are increasingly concerned that emerging bifurcations between the old transnational giants and the new world of specialty coffees and certifications will leave their members in purgatory, waiting for rewards that never come.

Think it's hard to figure out the nuances of "shade-grown" versus "organic"? "Fairly traded" versus "Fair Trade Certified"? Starbucks versus Rainforest Alliance versus Utz? Now imagine being a small farmer or a cooperative that has to comply with a mess of certifica-tions and agencies. Sometimes all these good—and less than good—intentions seem to be paving a road to hell.

Boutique bird-friendly labels don't hurt, and some organic labels don't help, but mostly these stamped-on phrases are statistically insignificant. In Costa Rica and Guatemala, the key players in certification and verification are Fair Trade, Rainforest Alliance, and Starbucks, with Utz a distant fourth. Many organic farmers received their certifications through these major players with the hope of generating additional per-pound premiums.

Like many estate owners and cooperatives, Fedecocagua has struggled to comply with the certifiers' regulations. It's spent roughly 300,000 dollars to help member co-ops meet various standards, close to 100,000 dollars of that sum going to twelve cooperatives working to comply with C.A.F.E. Practices. The investment was huge.

"Our samples had been going to Seattle since 1995," Gerardo said, "but they never, ever, bought any coffee from us." Finally, after he commented on the matter in a speech at the Specialty Coffee Association of America conference in 2003, the company bought some of Fedecocagua's coffee, but only a little.

"At first it was just changing to meet the standards that was a problem," said Gerardo. "The harvest was okay; but once the coffee was harvested, there were the water requirements, the worker regulations, getting more space to store coffee, we had to improve facilities. And it wasn't a real relationship, they just gave us the forms." A lot of forms.

"It's a difficult process," the administrator at the Acatenango cooperative attested as he spread out the log books that farmers have to sign when they bring in their coffee. "The cultures are different. There's too much paperwork; often the grandchild will have to write for the grandfather. It needs money and organization to do all this, and then if they don't buy what they said they'd buy, the farmers lose confidence."

In fact, Fedecocagua's confidence was sorely shaken by its 2006 experience. Although the co-ops produced 32,000 bags of coffee (roughly 152 pounds per bag) under C.A.F.E. Practices, Starbucks only bought 5,000, citing quality concerns. To help member cooperatives sustain the losses, Fedecocagua bought the remaining coffee at Starbucks prices. "We bought it from the farmers at $1.40 a pound, so they were okay, and we paid the difference between that and the lower price for which we sold it on the market," said Gerardo. "It was a painful disappointment."

He thinks that the Fair Trade principles are authentic, perhaps the only label that consistently makes a difference for small farmers. "But," he said, "I'm very angry with all of them sometimes. In the case of smallholders, the demands are not always reasonable. Our lives are in the harvest of these trees. Sometimes we just need to get the berries picked, and people just need jobs, so we pay the minimum, and if you pick more, you get more." His comments echoed the words of all the farmers I met.

He had other complaints as well: "And then sometimes the certifiers are like robots. Let's say I have organic coffee on part of my lot, but I also grow some vegetables that aren't organic, so then they can't certify the coffee as organic. It's just a predicament."

Costa Rican exporter Stefan Wille related a similar story about a different set of certifications. "Everyone has a different interpretation of the indicators. I had one grower who had a plot of coffee and then forty-five hectares of natural forest," he said, "and the first verifier didn't qualify the coffee as shaded, because the coffee itself wasn't shaded. But then the supervisor came and said that since the farm had a natural farm, the only thing that should be done to make it better was to create biological corridors to link different plots of forest habitat to each other. But that meant cutting down some of the coffee, and for a small farmer, that's a big sacrifice. .... . I finally asked my friends at Starbucks, 'Are you growing shade, or are you growing coffee?'"

Fedecocagua was frustrated enough to create a video presentation that explained its concerns, which I watched in a darkened meeting hall. I saw farmers from four or five cooperatives describe the hardships of conforming to the various standards. One cooperative decided to forgo certification because it wasn't bringing in enough money and was dividing members. A member from another co-op spoke about how hard it was to provide required health care in a country with such a tenuous health system.

This was the ultimate irony: despite all the bad things the Left has to say about Starbucks, it, along with Rainforest Alliance and a number of other NGOs, has become the toughest enforcer of environmental standards in the coffee fields. Coffee trader Konrad Brits told me, "One of the farmers in Nicaragua told me that through C.A.F.E. Practices Starbucks supports the single largest environmental initiative in the country. I just hadn't thought about it that way. I have farmers in Nicaragua who wouldn't be on their farms if it weren't for Starbucks. They have tiny farms in a tiny and poor economy. And because of the prices Starbucks pays, the farmers are eager to buy in."

The Fedecocagua video left me feeling depressed and uneasy, and I expressed my discomfort to Gerardo and Ueli. Surely, I argued, the standards embodied in the various codes, while difficult and costly, would ultimately benefit the community. Surely all the small-holders would be better off with health care, with clean water, with their lands protected from chemicals and clear-cutting. Surely there must be another strategy for dealing with the burdens these standards place on the smallholders.

The Fedecocagua leadership sees the story differently. "We spend a lot of money, a *lot* of money, to get all those certifications," lamented Gerardo. "They who have the money want us to bear the cost of doing these things, with no guarantees that they will buy from us in the end. Believe me, at end of the day, I would like it to be different. We all want to see clean water, green mountains, being with our families in better conditions. Everyone has those desires, just like the First World, just like the developed countries. But for us in the Third World, at the end, the smallholders are looking for better prices; if they can get as much from the coyotes as from the Starbucks program, then they'll do that. In the end, they have to feed their families."

In more peaceful, less racially polarized Costa Rica, many farmers have a different attitude. "I like the Starbucks way of doing business," ICAFE deputy Lizano told me. "They work within the market, but they don't play politics, making money based on the business. We have a *dicho*—a saying: 'There are different ways to kill a flea.' I like their way. It's good business practice, not the normal absorbing and slaying way."

In Guatemala, however, it's far easier to see the economic dominance of the global north as continued oppression, with the old colonialism of physical occupation replaced by the neocolonialism of economic subjugation, a system by which wealthy *blancos* make the rules that the native population must follow. Even if the rules are beneficial, the underlying equation remains. Those who make the rules get rich; those who follow them get by. The bloodshed may have stopped; but behind the silence, resentments continue to fester.

Fedecocagua has an additional challenge: it's an agent of collective action in an era of individual entrepreneurship. It had to fight for Fair Trade status because it didn't neatly fit the definition of small cooperative. And Starbucks, for all its benevolence, prefers relationships with small estates or cooperatives, where transparency is simpler, quality more consistent, and the power relationship less complex. Although Starbucks believes in helping those at the bottom of the chain, it likes to define the parameters; and Fedecocagua has created some power of its own to challenge company rules.

The question is not merely one of power but also a matter of perception. By creating an effective united front, the smallholders and cooperatives in Fedecocagua have changed their image. They're no longer just struggling farmers with heartwarming stories who can be branded along with the coffee. This image bias affects not just Starbucks but small progressive roasters. "The frustrating thing about co-ops is that they have operating expenses," lamented Peter Guiliano, purchasing director at Counter Culture Coffee in North Carolina and a longtime follower of Central American politics. He acknowledges that dealing with large third-tier configurations such as Fedecocagua and its Nicaraguan counterpart is a hot topic among specialty roasters. "We might pay $1.50, but the farmers might only get seventy or eighty cents," he told me. "How do you address the inefficiencies in democratic cooperatives if we sometimes see them wasting money? And then there's the issue of nontransparency, and leaders driving really nice cars, and living in big houses. It makes you wonder what sort of structure you're participating in."

Although cooperatives are generally egalitarian and accountable, Guiliano, like Starbucks and many others in this niche market, is drawn to smaller cooperatives, where it's easier to provide financial management assistance and there is less incentive to mix lesser-grade coffees with higher grades. "Increasingly," he said, "I'm attracted to small, dynamic, indie coops of fifty farmers—or farmers that have larger farms." So like unions around the world, Fedecocagua is caught in an odd no-man's land where it has limited power to fight the big transnationals but where it's also been stripped of the cachet and respect that once accompanied the mission of combining energies and resources for the common good rather than individual profit.

Ultimately, the question centers on agency. There's lots to be said for one-on-one relationships where the company and the farmer or small cooperative form a direct connection that builds warmth and trust. The partnership has the added benefit of an engaging story line that can be sold to the consumer along with the beans. You can go to Starbucks or your progressive independent coffeehouse and perhaps read about the farm that supplied your morning brew. And you can see the glowing photographs of smiling farmers, those descendents of Juan Valdez, inviting you to savor the beans picked by their hands.

But building political power so poor and indigenous people can help set the rules is not part of the picture, is not part of the brand, and apparently is not part of what Starbucks—or we—are buying.

5 Moving Up on Eighth Street

Starbucks opened 599 stores in North America in 2003, one of them on Southeast Eighth Street in Washington, D.C., barely three blocks from my front door. The buzz started long before the first cup was served. A few weeks earlier, the Payless shoe store had anchored a tired block of downscale businesses, which included a Popeye's, a check-cashing store, and a 7-Eleven where wary Pakistanis and Ethiopians served cops and drunks in roughly equal numbers. Now the ubiquitous green mermaid was about to take up residence.

Twenty years ago, few tourists used to venture east past the Capitol, the Supreme Court, or the Library of Congress; so few knew that there was actually a residential neighborhood called Capitol Hill. Though plenty of white Washingtonians knew it existed, most wouldn't venture there, frightened by media crime reports with a black subtext. That's why, in 1995, aided by a housing slump, Alec and I were able to afford a home just ten blocks from Congress in one of the largest historic districts in the country.

With tree-lined streets and lovingly preserved brick and stone row houses, my new neighborhood retained the scale and feel of an urban village. At Eastern Market, the last survivor of several similar markets first erected in the 1870s, I often got a personal greeting from Mrs. Calomiris and Mr. Paik, owners of competing produce stands, along with a complimentary banana tucked in with my red-leaf lettuce. The cheese man dispensed free samples, and the bakery offered giant sugar-coated fritters to nibble while I shopped. On weekends, the area around the building and the schoolyard across the street were transformed into open markets, with produce and artisans predominating on Saturday and a flea market taking center stage on Sunday. I often bumped into neighbors there, gossiping over the peaches or waiting in line to enjoy blueberry pancakes at Market Lunch. The grungy décor and fried food hearkened back to the fifties, while the vibrant racial mix celebrated millennial multiculturalism.

But change was in the air. After years of stagnant and then gradual growth, housing prices were skyrocketing, and construction was everywhere. New townhouses were on the market for more than 750,000 dollars. A deteriorating public housing project just south of the freeway was being replaced by new Marine Corps dorms, enlarging the historic corps headquarters at Eighth and Eye streets. New federal office buildings were predicted for Navy procurement, bringing thousands of additional workers to the neighborhood. Eighth Street itself was slated for a makeover, with new trees and fancy streetlights. And now a Starbucks was coming.

Over on Tenth Street, we all speculated. Was the Starbucks rumor really true? Would our houses, worth less than 200,000 dollars eight years ago and 500,000 dollars today, become even more valuable? Would those magic words, "only three blocks from Starbucks," command previously unimagined selling prices? And given that we neighbors were mostly progressive, the kind of people who worked at the Library of Congress, taught in the D.C. public schools, and populated do-gooder nonprofits, did we believe that having a Starbucks was a good thing? We wavered between avarice and anxiety as we mulled over the fate of a neighborhood that was rapidly outclassing our incomes, not to mention those of our less affluent neighbors down the street. In our minds lurked the specter of the "Starbucks effect": higher prices, higher taxes, homogenization, deracination, and overwhelming commercial traffic. In other words, gentrification loomed.

English sociologist Ruth Glass coined the term *gentrification* in 1964. She had been studying various London districts as they began to get richer, as *abandoned* changed to *desirable* and cheap lodging became more or less expensive. "Once this process of 'gentrification' starts in a district," she wrote, "it goes on rapidly until all or most of the original working-class occupiers are displaced and the whole social character of the district is changed."

While there are various explanations for gentrification, it's generally a safe bet that undervalued but historic urban districts won't stay poor forever; and the track they follow from shabby to chic is remarkably similar, no matter where they're located. The old neighborhoods at the city's inner core, abandoned in the middle of the twentieth century by whites fleeing to the suburbs, become home to poorer communities, often populated by African Americans or recent immigrants. Then, sometimes decades later, sometimes sooner, artists, bohemians, and political activists move in; for them, the lure of cheap rent or more space outweighs reputed danger and discomfort. These newcomers are generally from white and middle-class backgrounds and have more discretionary income than existing residents do. They create a lively subculture, often involving arts, crafts, and food, perhaps even a coffeehouse. These subcultures are usually gay-friendly and sometimes draw gay homesteaders with some money to invest in renovating their homes. Property values start to inch upward. This tends to be good for homeowners, who suddenly see their property values rise, but pushes out long-term renters as owners upgrade their properties or sell to new homebuyers or speculators. Then the young professionals arrive and finally everyone else with money and a taste for classy urban living.

Although my neighborhood began to gentrify in the 1970s, the pace of change had been gentle. Unlike some neighborhoods, ours retained a mix of black and white residents, of artists and public servants. A stubbornly downscale streak lingered along Eighth Street and at Eastern Market, where area residents resisted efforts to gloss up the market's façade and replace vendors with more upscale and, in our minds, useless sellers. Even Murky Coffee, previously Stompin' Grounds, previously Roasters on the Hill, retained its rakish air and relaxed service.

So what would the arrival of Starbucks mean? As the *St. Petersburg Times* wrote about one of its own gentrifying Florida communities, "Starbucks' arrival could mean a turning point for the neighborhood. The Seattle chain has a reputation for bringing high traffic and commercial development adjacent to its stores." Stephen Ludlow, director of a London real estate website (ludlowthompson. com) told the *Observer*, "Once an area has its own branch of Starbucks, All Bar One or Pizza Express much of the explosive period of capital growth is largely over." What would happen in our case? Was Starbucks riding the wave of the neighborhood's rising economic status; or was Starbucks the wave itself, ready to drown the community in gentrification? Or would its arrival make no waves at all?

Conflict often accompanies Starbucks to a new location, and residents of many neighborhoods have taken political action to prevent or at least mitigate the Starbucks effect. In 2004, Illinois governor Rod Blagojevich even signed a law aimed specifically at the effect. "We now have a bill," he said, "that will make it so that when Starbucks comes or your neighbor starts improving his or her home, you don't have to fear that your property taxes will rise so high that you can no longer afford to stay in the neighborhood." Economic development, it seems, can cut either way; and sometimes it's hard to tell where Starbucks will fall. As an Associated Press story noted in November 2001, "The story of Seattle's Central District is the story of many urban areas across the country. The good economy of the '90s and the deliberate efforts of residents like [DeCharlene] Williams, who founded the Central Area Chamber of Commerce, helped eradicate crime. Businesses like Starbucks moved in, and many blacks—once corralled into the Central District by racist red-lining policies of banks, insurance companies and real-estate firms—found themselves moving out."

Like any issue that intertwines economics and race, this one is complex. When Starbucks moves into economically or culturally upscale locations, everyone is happy (except cranky bohoes). In white middle-class and striving neighborhoods, there are seldom problems or protests. Then lower-income neighborhoods of color, desperate for more amenities, demand inclusion: they deserve a gracious coffee haven as well. At this point, white political activists and artists begin to see the chain as predatory and worthy of opposition. Thus, just when a Starbucks finally opens in a neighborhood of color, white activists start protesting—which can cause a world of misunderstanding.

Although black and Latino neighborhood organizations are frequently at the forefront of opposition to Wal-Mart invasions in their communities, dissenting voices often clamor that poorly paid jobs are better than none and that predatory economic development is better than empty storefronts or vacant lots. The Starbucks case has certain parallels. The largely African American Anacostia neighborhood across the river from us in D.C. eagerly awaited its first Starbucks, slated to open in the neighborhood Safeway. As one of the advisory neighborhood commissioners told the *Washington Post*, "We're wondering what is it about our neighborhood, that everywhere else people are whining that they have too many Starbucks, why can't we get even one?"

In fact, our Eighth Street store was part of Urban Coffee Opportunities (UCO), a joint venture between Starbucks and Magic Johnson Enterprises, owned by the former Los Angeles Lakers basketball star, to bring upscale coffee to lower-income neighborhoods. UCO is also a partnership between Howard Schultz and Magic Johnson, forged by mutual admiration and a shared belief in the transformational powers of basketball and entrepreneurship. Some suggest that a venture like UCO is meant to bathe upscale Starbucks customers and the company in a virtuous feel-good glow, but these stores are also often eagerly awaited in neighborhoods where amenities are scarce.

I caught up with Magic in Charlotte, North Carolina, at the grand opening of a UCO Starbucks store on a tired strip of Wilkinson Boulevard between the airport and downtown. "I used to go to Starbucks for hot chocolate," he told me, "and I was standing in line thinking, 'Why am I driving thirty or forty minutes outside my community to get it?' So I went to Howard Schultz, and he jumped right on it. Everyone thought minorities would not commonly invest three or four dollars in a cup of coffee. But it's not just a great cup of coffee; it's a meeting place. We don't have meeting places in our communities, and we don't have job opportunities. Starbucks provides both. And it attracts other retailers. People come in behind you because they know we attract foot traffic."

Looming over everyone else in the room, Magic chatted up local politicians and answered questions from the press. Area residents, including several workers from the adjoining Wal-Mart, stood outside for several hours to hear Magic speak, mollified with free coffee, Frappuccinos, and pastries. A few lucky ones even got inside and had basketballs, jerseys, and other memorabilia signed by the star. Kids in braces grinned into cameras, and several Starbucks baristas walked away with signed work aprons. Not one of the residents was worrying about gentrification. "This is an area that needs economic development," a county commissioner told me. "It will be many years before gentrification happens here."

But the issues weren't as clear in my D.C. neighborhood. Some residents wondered how the Urban Opportunities designation squared with the breathtaking ascent of local real estate prices and our whitening racial profile. It wasn't clear what the Starbucks effect would be.

And then one afternoon, there it was, open and ready for business. As Alec and I took our Sunday stroll toward Eastern Market, we were waylaid by the unmistakable aroma of brewed coffee competing with the penetrating odor of Popeye's fried chicken three doors down. Lured by curiosity and the promise of a free sample, we entered.

It was training day. A lively young African American woman with unruly dreads and an irresistible smile was coaching a grinning but nervous team of baristas on the arts of espresso making and working the cash register. "You can have whatever drink you want," the young man behind the counter told me. "It's free today while we learn how to do everything." That was just fine with our fellow caffeinistas, a palette of colors and ages—moms with kids, teens with Frappuccinos and lots of whipped cream, everyone in good spirits.

It turned out that our Starbucks was also in the process of gentrifying a low-wage workforce, not necessarily by paying them enough to vault into the middle class but by augmenting their skills and upgrading their tastes. The unconventional local agent of this transformation was Tawana Green. A twenty-eight-year-old African American high school grad from D.C., she started working for Starbucks in 1999—that famous Battle of Seattle year. With a warmth and energy that match her smile, Tawana could be a poster child for the Starbucks company vision. "I've been on my own since I was seventeen," she told me, "started work right out of high school, and eventually I went into retail where I could work with people. When I left Whole Foods, I saw an ad for Starbucks, sent in my résumé, went to a few open houses, and they called me back. I wanted to be somewhere where I'd meet lots of different people, and this was it."

Most people that I've encountered or consulted consider Starbucks to be one of the best, if not *the* best, employer in its class. When the Eighth Street store opened, workers' starting salary—$7.50 an hour, plus tips—exceeded D.C.'s required minimum wage. More impressive are the Starbucks benefits: workers are offered a generous health, life, and disability insurance package for which they contribute roughly forty dollars per month. The company also offers a 401(k) plan with a matching program; Starbucks Bean Stock, which reflects the company's annual success and is allocated among all employees according to hours worked; and discounts on the company's public stock. These benefits, available to all employees who work twenty hours a week or more, are almost unique in the world of retail and, indeed, in most of corporate America. And as a perk, workers get a free pound of coffee every week.

For the most part, young workers consider a job at Starbucks miles above a job at McDonald's, Pizza Hut, or KFC. Nevertheless, it's a low-wage, retail business best suited to those looking for part-time or fill-in work. No matter how good you get at being a barista, the job won't give you the means to buy a house, raise a family, or even rent an apartment or make payments on a car—unless you get promoted. Yet quite a number of baristas, including Green, do rise up the ranks. According to Starbucks, approximately 67 percent of assistant and store managers were internal promotions, as were 54 percent of district managers and more than 70 percent of regional directors.

The potential for advancement was one of the factors that lured Green to Starbucks. Her rise from shift supervisor to store manager has been deliberate, both on her side and the company's, in a process that involves constant training for ever-increasing responsibilities. Most important to Green, Starbucks has people who help new hires survive. "My first store manager was Felice Torre," she related. "On my second day working at the busy Dupont Circle store, he says to me, 'Okay, girl, close the store.' He believed in me and trusted me." Her mentors have been Korean, German, Venezuelan, and African American, although she notes that district managers and regional directors have been less racially diverse. She sees a future for people like herself at Starbucks, where the vice president who runs the Urban Coffees division is an African American. "I think we do pretty well," she said, "It gives me hope. It makes me feel like I can do it."

There is a hint of messianic vision among Starbucks workers, which has filtered down through management and ultimately comes from Howard Schultz himself. He continues to write and talk about how "a company can grow big without losing the passion and personality that built it, but only if it's driven not by profits but by values and by people." In 1990, as Starbucks grew from an extended family into an empire, its mission statement became a way to tie the larger entity to the values that had defined the smaller. "I've met Howard twice," Tawana said, easily referring to Schultz by his first name, as do many of his employees. "He came to talk at the leadership conference, and he told us, 'We take care of the partners, the partners take care of the customers, and the customers take care of the business.'"

As manager of the new Eighth Street store, Tawana initially got to hire fifteen workers, twelve of them new to Starbucks and many from the local neighborhood. She said, "When I ask people why they applied to Starbucks, they often say they've been a customer, and the partners look like they're having fun, and it's an upbeat environment, and I tell them, 'Well, here's how we get that environment. Treat each other with respect and dignity is principle 1; profit is number 6. Sure, we aim to be the best coffee retailer, but it's people first.' "

Nevertheless, from the point of view of worker advocates, the Starbucks approach has a few very big flaws. The company tries to avoid the entire issue of workers by simply calling them something else. Tawana Green carefully avoids the word *employees* in favor of the company's preferred term, *partners* ("that's because we own stock in the company"), quickly correcting herself the one time the *e* word slips in. But a number of Starbucks workers in Canada and the United States are cynical about that terminology, and union efforts in both countries have met staunch company resistance. As Schultz's book makes clear, Starbucks thinks benevolent management should make unions superfluous. Such attitudes chafe me like an itchy sweater. Although the labor movement's flaws make me crazy, I still embrace the basic principle: workers have a right to independent democratic representation, no matter what their management prefers.

This is not to say that the present situation is always bad for individuals; it's certainly worked well for Green. "My goal is to provide a great place to hang out and also give back to the community," Tawana told me. "I'm not saying it's easy. You have to be a really hard worker. But here I am, twenty-eight, with a high school education, and I'm a store manager with a piece of the company. Where else could I get this opportunity? It doesn't get much better than this!"

Almost a year later, things seemed to be working out for the neighborhood as well. Even Murky Coffee, which might have paid a price for Starbucks' success, seemed to be thriving, its stools and chairs stuffed with customers. Nonetheless, signs of a second wave of gentrification were apparent on the street, with newly painted signs announcing a spate of recently opened restaurants. And Starbucks was plenty busy.

To see how it was really going, I decided to spend an entire day at the store, from opening to closing time. With staff prep time at both ends, that turned out to be 5 A.M. to 9 P.M., with no time off but plenty of coffee breaks. So one dark August morning in 2004, I forced myself out of bed at an ungodly hour and trundled the three blocks to our still-dark Starbucks.

5:10 A.M. Unlike many late-summer mornings in D.C., a fresh breeze was blowing. Morning traffic was just beginning to pick up. Tawana walked up the street with a Coke in her hand and a lit cigarette in her mouth, wearing a black Starbucks sweatshirt and off-white cotton pants. She, too, savored the change in the weather. "I know I should quit," she said, as I eyed her cigarette. "My husband and I both want to try." She doesn't mind the early mornings too much. "Early in, early out, and it's cool to watch the world wake up."

5:20 A.M. The newspaper delivery man showed up with the *New York Times* and the *Washington Post*. "Tawana is one of my favorite managers," he confided, "always on time, always courteous, one of the best."

After Tawana let him into the store, she loaded up the coffee machine and put on some music in the still darkened store. The coffee (today's blend was Light Note) is determined by the company-wide coffee-week calendar, the music by whatever spirit moves her. "First, something to wake me up, with a percussive beat. Then I move toward jazz and blues as the day wears on," all of it good in the Starbucks tradition. Her assistant was late. She put out the milk and the half-and-half and moved fresh pastries (delivered earlier that morning) from racks onto shelves. As the traffic outside increased, she checked the bathrooms, donned her green Starbucks apron, and turned on the store lights.

In these last seconds of quiet, I sat still and took in the store's familiar décor, its comfortable chairs and small merchandise displays. I was reminded of what journalist-activist Naomi Klein has described as the branding phenomenon: what's on sale is not just a product but an image and a lifestyle. Klein hates the replicated nature of the stores and what she sees as a cynical manipulation of the consumer. And I know what she means; this isn't an authentic Italian coffeehouse; it's not a home-grown neighborhood institution. It is, however, authentic Starbucks.

And surprisingly, on its own terms, that ambience works. Jon Markman, a stock analyst and publisher of *Stock Tactics Advisor*, describes it as "the white collar equivalent of the tavern next to the auto plant, where Frankie behind the counter hits us with a shot of Wild Turkey and a Bud draft on sight." This analogy only sort of works since even well-paid auto workers rarely order top-shelf Wild

Turkey; yet as I was watching, lots of Starbucks customers, even the non-rich, glibly demanded four-dollar cinnamon spice lattes and their ilk. But Markman's comparison does hold true in another way: like all good bartenders, the early morning Starbucks crew knows its regulars.

5:40 A.M. The first customer through the door was Perry Jackson, who, as it turns out, runs the boot camp at my gym. She always orders a *venti* (twenty-ounce) cup to keep her going all day, usually a mild coffee (though sometimes she orders a bolder brew) with cream and twelve (that's right: *twelve*) sugars. "It's something comforting, that suits my personality, and I love coffee," she said. She stops on her morning jog between home and the gym. If she has clients, she might return in the afternoon for a java chip. "I'm consistent and committed."

Another early bird ordered a double espresso and lemon pound cake. Apparently, he's just as consistent as Perry because Tawana already had it ready as he walked through the door.

6:00 A.M. A woman entered carrying a purse decorated with the words "Love, Peace, Life, Hope, Joy" and toting an Old Navy shopping bag and a black bag. She was middle-aged, blond, and seemed normal enough until it became evident that she wasn't. She launched into her life story: the abusive husband, the divorce, the miscreant daughter on drugs . . . on and on like an endless stream. She stayed and stayed and stayed, like the Ancient Mariner who "stoppeth one of three."

Tawana told me that crazy folks are rare and said the store hasn't yet dealt with anything extraordinary. "We try to embrace them; they're still customers. And if someone's unhappy with their drink, we make the drink over or offer them something else."

Another morning regular, who works at the Marine Corps' Quantico base, thirty-five miles south, confided that she prefers the Eighth Street store to the one on Third for just this reason: "It's because of the people. Here, they care. There, they get your drink wrong and it's, whatever."

6:30 A.M. The first short lines formed, and the first Frappuccino was served. Frappuccinos became more popular as the day progressed; caramel was particularly in vogue, especially among African American customers, although the entire Frappuccino line seemed to be a hit across races and generations.

One woman, more sedate than most, in a long skirt and navy hose, opened up the cardboard hot-coffee sleeves and lined them up on the serving bar, "My community service for the day," she quipped.

7:00 A.M. From 7 to 8 A.M., I did a demographic survey: forty-five men, forty-four women; forty-one whites, forty-eight people of color, most of them African American. Age distribution seemed to be weighted on the thirties and forties, a bit lighter on both ends. Soy milk seemed to have a small following among African American women.

8:00 A.M. The stream of customers ebbed and flowed between 8 and 9 A.M., sort of like unexplained traffic jams do. For a while six women waited for drinks around the bar, with another six on line. Two laptops materialized, in addition to mine. Two moms, each with a child in tow, joined the mix.

A few days later, a barista at a suburban Starbucks asked a breast-feeding mom to cover up, prompting two dozen mothers to stage an in-store "nurse-in" that was gleefully reported in the local media. But many Starbucks watchers report that the stores are viewed as mom-and-stroller-friendly and serve as regular mid-morning meeting places in many neighborhoods.

9:30 A.M. The comforting murmur was broken by the long arm of Starbucks business: Kenny Fried appeared. He's the Starbucks public-relations guy for the region and was sent to check up on me. In general, the company was quite accessible; but like their employment protocols, their approach to me was "cooperate and control." The PR department didn't like to leave me to my own devices; and I was given a string of solicitous minders who arranged a preferred path for me and then followed in my footsteps, although usually they were friendly and often graceful.

Kenny Fried, contracted from a local PR firm to deal with media in the D.C. area, looks like the slightly rumpled and distracted midlife suburban dad that he is. He is clearly a fan of both Starbucks and Schultz, without being an acolyte, and his attitude about his role is mercifully relaxed.

We had first met a few months earlier, when he was sent to monitor a set of interviews at a store in Bailey's Crossroads, Virginia. I had interviewed the regional and area managers—both blond women in their mid-thirties, casually neat. Red-state types, I thought; but the people I was meeting often surprised me, defying stereotypes and labels. Elaine and Martha were no exceptions.

When I first asked what they thought about unions, they gave one of those standard answers about how unions were once needed but are no longer necessary and certainly not at Starbucks. But, I persisted, if you have companies like Wal-Mart constantly pushing down the wages and standards, how does a good company like Starbucks survive when others in the sector offer so much less? And how are you going to deal with it? And what about the bigger picture beyond Starbucks? Is Starbucks going to become the voice of working people in the public arena?

One of the women said that her husband used to work at a unionized supermarket; his wages and a union loan had provided the down payment for their first house. And, yes, as they mulled it over, they felt that perhaps there was a problem if there was no voice for the larger family of working people so that others could have the benefits that Starbucks offered. And Wal-Mart was certainly a bad company, with a negative impact on wages and benefits in the larger community—one that made it more difficult for companies like Starbucks to maintain their high standards.

When the women left, Kenny confessed that he, as well as his seventy-five-year-old mother in New Jersey, both loved shopping at Wal-Mart. "I know they're terrible," he confided. "But I just love going there, and I love a bargain. And my mom, she's even more liberal than I am, and she knows better; but now that she's retired and the department stores are more expensive, it's her entertainment. She can go to Wal-Mart and spend twenty dollars and come home with a bunch of stuff."

I had given him a friendly hard time about that revelation. As a resident of an upscale, politically liberal suburb, I contended, he could easily afford the breadth of retail options available in his neighborhood. So when we met again on Capitol Hill, he was eager to resume the conversation. He reported that his wife had stopped shopping at Wal-Mart but that he and his mom were having a harder time breaking the habit. Kenny himself remained torn on the issue. He admitted to being the "ultimate consumer" who perpetually shopped for discounts and coupons, gleeful when he got the sixty-dollar sneakers for sixteen dollars, proud of his persistence and shopper savvy.

A young woman with a baby stroller sitting near us leaped into the conversation. She used to live in North Carolina and patronized

Wal-Mart all the time, but she stopped when it refused to carry RU-486, the morning-after birth-control pill. She then did some research and found out how terrible Wal-Mart was and stopped shopping there. Now, she told us, she usually goes to Target. Every time she buys something at Target, she sends a letter to Wal-Mart telling them how much she's spent and reminding them that they need to improve if they want her business. She has a personal list of demands: stock the pill, treat workers fairly, end discrimination. She's decided she'd rather spend extra money at places like Starbucks if the workers get health care and the company is okay. She got her info on Starbucks through an environmental newsletter, and she buys Fair Trade coffee.

10:30 A.M. After Kenny left, I struck up a conversation with an eavesdropping artist. He told me he goes to various Starbucks stores but is at this one today because it's near his mechanic and he's having his car fixed. He has a love-hate relationship with four-dollar coffee, especially since he's been in a twelve-step debtors' program. "Since I drink decaf and skim, I'm not even a purist," he mused. "Still, it's hard not to get caught up in the culture of it. It's like, politics is such a sham so might as well have another cup of coffee."

11:45 A.M. One of my neighbors showed up. I explained why I was there, and he joined me while he drank his coffee. A young African American woman, coming in for a Frappuccino, riffed on how she only lets certain workers prepare certain drinks, pointing out who makes the best passion teas and who fixes double lattes the way she likes them. "Now S., at the beginning, his Frappuccinos had all these ice chunks in them, but I whipped him into shape."

S. worked with Tawana at her previous store and has been at this store with her since opening day. He's preparing for promotion to shift manager. Soft-spoken, thin, and shy, he punctuates his responses with a deferential "Yes, ma'am." "They do take care of you," he told me. "I give 20 percent of every paycheck—10 percent for benefits [health, pension, and so on] and 10 percent for stock."

I noted that most young people wouldn't set aside that much money and asked for his reasons. He told me he had taken a high school class on personal economics and that the teacher was really good. He eventually wants to open his own business (a common aspiration among the employees) and sees this as an opportunity to save money and get ahead. Tawana's hard, he said. "She'll drive you to make you better. She demands the best from you. Some of the partners can't take it, or take it the wrong way, but I take it as motivation."

As to working conditions, "from one to ten, I give it a fifteen. The pay is better than my friends make, and we get tips. They come out to about a $1.00 to $1.25 for every hour worked, which is quite a bit. My friends get nothing, no sick days, no vacation days."

He started at $7.50 and after two years now makes $8.50. If he's promoted to store manager, the pay would be about 50,000 dollars a year. "But it's not just about the money. Money does help, but I love it." He said that, although his family was disappointed that he hadn't gone on to college, they were cool now because he's paying his own way and will be able to go back to school.

I asked him what he'd learned during his tenure at Starbucks. He told me, "If I go anywhere, I can describe what coffee I'm drinking, and I know how to act. I can be a leader."

2:00 P.M. Tawana joined me during the afternoon lull. The store's first anniversary is coming up in September, and the store has done extremely well in its first year. She said that if Saturday and Sunday are strong, this will be its best week ever: more than 20,000 dollars in coffee drink sales—even more when you add food. The store's been topping predictions, which is why she now has an assistant manager.

I asked about the original fifteen workers. A year later only three still work at the store. Two of the others have been promoted and are working at other stores—a victory in a system in which managers are evaluated, in part, on how many of their subordinates advance to better positions. The other ten have left or been fired. One of the young women went back to college. Another worker's mom was really sick, and he was also not so happy with the job. Another also didn't take to the work, and one young woman moved back to North Carolina. Tawana characterized the past year as "smooth, no big revelations. The beginning was a little rough, but I've been sane, I haven't jumped off a bridge, I have no regrets."

In many ways, her shining path at Starbucks is no different from other corporate ladders. But she thinks there are distinct advantages to being with a company that pulls, pushes, prods, and watches its people. "To me, the opportunities are great," she said. "We're growing so large, we now sometimes need managers and assistant managers from outside. You have to be aggressive to succeed; I tell my partners, 'No one will give you anything.' There are a lot of other people out there with bachelor degrees, so you have to be hungry."

And she really loves her store. "It's sometimes hard work," she acknowledged. "You get busy, and you have to be there for your partners. I want them to be able to say, 'Tawana was the one who took me to next level.' It's like having a baby, your own, you're raising it. And when I do get promoted and someone else takes over, I can say, I opened that store over there."

4:00 P.M. A younger set of customers drifted in, mostly in their late teens and early twenties. Caramel Frappuccinos and strawberry crèmes seemed to be their drinks of choice, almost always in large sizes.

The new assistant manager clocked out. He said his first week has gone fine. He's had previous retail experience and said the eight weeks of training at Starbucks is the most he's ever gone through, but it was pretty good.

5:15 P.M. Two cops came in, partners—one African American, one white. The white guy looked like your classic cop, and I couldn't resist asking him whether this was his usual stop. "No, I don't usually go for this stuff, but my partner brought me in, so I thought I'd try something." He ordered a caramel Frappuccino. "It's not just because I'm a cop, but I prefer Dunkin' Donuts. Now that's good coffee."

5:40 P.M. A little pickup scene emerged, pairs of girls, pairs of guys, eyeing each other, sometimes chatting. The store soundtrack had changed to something a bit more up-tempo, with a more insistent beat than the earlier jazz selections. By 6 P.M. all the tables were taken. A lesbian couple flirted at the table next to mine.

6:20 P.M. There was a short line again. The barista was trying to give away a leftover wrong drink. "Free latte on the bar," he called. There were no takers. "Hey," he said, "is there something about *free* you don't understand?" A young African woman in traditional garb picked it up. "You didn't spell it right," she quipped. She said she's not actually a coffee drinker but she's bringing it home to the babysitter, who'll be thrilled.

7:00 P.M. The store was quieting down. Now most of the folks coming in were strangers to the neighborhood, on their way to a band concert at the Marine Corps barracks down the street. A young African American was in the corner with a caramel macchiato, one of two other people still occupying seats. He was a regular Starbucks customer, having his regular Starbucks drink. He'd moved to D.C. from Chicago about six months ago and said he often comes to this particular store. "I like the coziness and these comfortable chairs where I can look out the window. I don't like crowded and trendy ones, and this one has an Afrocentric feel. Also, if you go to the same

Starbucks enough, they know what you want." He'd also had a regular Starbucks back in Chicago, but "it didn't have a nice feel like this one, not a place I wanted to linger."

He noted that, when he was growing up, coffee wasn't very popular. "Starbucks popularized it," he asserted. "I did not drink coffee when I was younger, Starbucks helped me figure out what I liked and what I didn't."

8:00 P.M. Another workday was ending, the store winding down toward its 8:30 closing. Three people worked on the closing crew. One went out and put locks on the outside furniture so it wouldn't migrate overnight. The crew cleaned the bathrooms, replacing toilet paper and towels, bagging garbage, mopping floors. They checked all the displays and tidied them up.

8:30 P.M. The doors were locked, although people kept trying to open them as long as the lights were on. The final closing routine took another forty-five minutes of hard work. The money was counted and put into the safe. The pastries were wrapped. The empty plastic food delivery flats were stacked near the front door for the pre-dawn delivery. All the equipment was washed down. The half-and-half and milk carafes were washed out, refilled, and refrigerated for the morning crew. All the stations were restocked and made ready for the next day. The powdered base for the Frappuccinos was mixed, the whipped cream dispensers washed and refilled with heavy cream, and both were placed in the small refrigerators in the drink-making station. One woman almost had a nasty accident slipping on the floor between the back room and the store. Later, another worker almost took the same spill. But finally cleanup was over.

9:15 P.M. Everyone hurried to get home to their families or to their Friday night dates. The alarm was set, the lights turned off, and everyone hustled out the door. The store was dark again, ready for tomorrow.

Almost three years after the Eastern Market Starbucks opened, Tawana left to manage the Liberty Starbucks across from the Navy Memorial downtown. It was just down the street from the courthouse, an odd-shaped, triangular corner in a historic brick building topped by a gold-domed turret. The move wasn't exactly a promotion, she told me, but a lateral change to a busier location that she thought might offer additional opportunities for promotion up the ranks.

The transition between Tawana's departure and the new manager's arrival at Eastern Market was bumpy. Ideally, there's a two-week overlap between store managers; but the Liberty store needed Tawana right away, and the new manager couldn't start for several weeks. So Eastern Market had an interim manager, which didn't go well. Some of the employees flaked out; others didn't bother to show up at all. It took several months of concentrated effort for the new manager to get the store back in order.

Meanwhile, Tawana had trials of her own. One of her staffers had a family tragedy and was out for several months, "and I was already short-staffed, and it was just incredibly stressful."

Soon after her move, I stopped at her new store. Starbucks was offering free coffees that day, in one of its sporadic publicity moves, and the place was a madhouse. Because of its odd shape, Liberty isn't well suited for crowds, and the line snaked out the door. Inside, the staff looked slightly panicked as the slow-moving stream of customers got progressively more ill-tempered, demanding mixed drinks rather than the regular coffee specified by the promotion. But when I stopped back later in the afternoon, calm had returned. "They really didn't think this promotion through very well," one of the workers acknowledged. Indeed, a number of the year's freebie offers had created more negative than positive buzz. Mostly they were overwhelmed by their own popularity. One coupon lent itself to replication over the Internet, creating a flood of demand, until Starbucks finally canceled the offer—to a chorus of cyber-hisses. Tawana's store, however, was on an even keel, the staff reflecting her energy and attitude. If I stopped by when she wasn't working, the baristas smiled when I asked after her and treated me well.

Things were harder on Eighth Street as both company and store evolved. Even before Tawana left, our Starbucks had lost the plush, comfy purple armchairs that used to frame the tables by the window. Without the chairs, the space, which had previously looked welcoming and occasionally crowded, suddenly looked cramped, more like a corner of the school lunchroom. Then, as company policy changed, the bins of coffee beans were replaced by shiny vacuum-packed bags. A big square oven for the new breakfast sandwiches stood where the beans had once been; the sandwiches were fine, but the oven gave off an acrid smell, which sometimes enveloped the store. The music was still good, although sometimes a bit loud for conversation.

The new manager was also working hard to put a team together. The young man who had been saving for his future was long gone; he had vanished from the landscape, and I was unable to locate him again. There were a few great additions. A lively and efficient young woman anchored the morning shift, bantering with customers, keeping up with the drink orders, always remembering my dry cappuccino. And Denoris Hill, a young worker whom Tawana had hired in the months before she left, decided to stick around and see what would happen.

One of the things I like about Starbucks is that it takes risks and gives people chances. Denoris, not yet eighteen when he was first hired, had come to Starbucks after being turned down by dozens of other retailers. He was young and needed a break—both of which he covered up with bravado. But Tawana thought he might make it and paired him up with another worker, who taught him the ropes and became his mentor. When that worker left, the assistant manager took over as what Denoris describes as a kind of "father figure." Denoris doesn't use the benefits package (he's still covered under his parents' health plan), but the flexible hours mean he can continue with his schooling and find time to compose music. Six months or so into his employment, he was promoted to shift supervisor. "Honestly, I can't say how long I'll be here," he told me. "But I love it. It's less stressful than anywhere else in my life, less stressful than home, less stressful than school." For Denoris, Starbucks is both workplace and "third place," and his presence felt like a success for both him and the company.

As for the neighborhood? On a block already home to Blockbuster, 7-Eleven, and Popeye's, plus a firehouse and a regular handful of street people, we now also had a Thai restaurant, an Indian restaurant, an environmentally friendly dry cleaner, and a gay-themed gift shop, none of them national chains. Plus a large, new Dunkin' Donuts, not precisely a symbol of gentrification. For the time being, the old and the new, the downscale and the modestly more upscale were all coexisting. Starbucks, it would seem, was hardly a change for the worse.

6 The Cross-Dressing of Coffee-Counter Culture

There's often a flurry of opinions, pro and con, about the potential impact of an urban Starbucks on its neighborhood. But there are also people—surprisingly many of them—whose passions extend beyond a single store to the very idea of Starbucks and all its earthly manifestations. Who would have thought that a glorified coffee shop could cause such a stir?

Starbucks believes it has reinvented coffeehouse culture by providing an affordable luxury for the discerning masses while being a good citizen in the community and the world. According to its opponents, however, Starbucks has colonized and irreducibly branded coffeehouse culture as its own. These views, each arguably half-right and half-wrong, compete on websites such as *http://starbucksgossip.typepad.com/* and *www.Ihatestarbucks.com*, in the strong language of love and hate, virtue and vice. They also coexist in our common economic and cultural imagination: the warm and fuzzy small enterprise, a nostalgic throwback to a better time, versus the large and predatory corporate venture that's simultaneously essential and menacing.

But there's one giant problem with the progressive coffee house analysis. Despite the Starbucks onslaught, independent coffeehouses are not only surviving but proliferating. Statistics indicate that, compared with the pre-Starbucks era, small coffeehouses are more numerous today and exist in many more geographically diverse locales.

According to Mintel, a market research firm in Chicago, there were 9,500 coffeehouses in 1998, fewer than 2,000 of them Starbucks. By 2005, however, there were 13,849 non-Starbucks coffeehouses, plus 7,551 Starbucks. Despite an increase in Starbucks' market share, independent cafés showed increased sales right alongside the Starbucks expansion. But to survive, independents have needed to be at the top of their game. They require a devoted local following, great coffee, good management, a decent location, knowledgeable counter staff, and an endearing counterculture—or at least a reasonable mix of some of these characteristics.

Sandwiched between two universities in Pittsburgh's Oakland neighborhood, the Kiva Han coffeehouse and Starbucks glare at each other across Craig Street like two boxers in opposite corners of the ring. John Mutchka bought the Kiva Han café in 2002, when it was eight years old, taking over from the first owner, who still maintains a roastery of the same name and supplies the café with its beans. When Mutchka became the managing owner, Kiva Han was a typically eccentric and somewhat grungy independent, although, he says, its inception owed as much to the success of early Starbucks as to counterculture coffeehouses. Mutchka actually trained at a Starbucks in a Barnes & Noble to see whether he liked the work. "I learned how to make drinks and about customer expectations," he said. "They gave good in-house training, and I had a great manager."

One reason for America's interest in coffee entrepreneurship is that coffeehouses are fairly inexpensive to open. According to *Badgett's Coffee Journal*, an industry newsletter, in 2003 it cost between 15,000 and 20,000 dollars to open a coffee cart, 50,000 to 60,000 dollars for a permanent kiosk, and 120,000 dollars for a sitdown coffeehouse. For a small business, that's a modest sum. But opening a business is one thing; staying in business is another. Small Business Administration figures show that new small businesses face big survival odds; two-thirds are still around after two years, but only 44 percent survive for four years.

Still, thanks to Starbucks, an increasing number of people are placing their hopes on a coffee future. In 1994, the year the Craig Street Kiva Han opened, David Heilbrunn cautiously debuted his first Coffee Fest, a trade show for independent coffeehouse owners and aspirants, with classes in all aspects of the business and an exhibition hall brimming with coffee-related merchandise. These days, the show, held several times a year in the United States and expanding into other countries, regularly draws 3,000 participants. "People saw it as the get-rich scheme of the 1990s," said Heilbrunn. "They saw Starbucks and felt they could open up a coffee shop and be successful."

John Mutchka, however, also had an alternative economic vision. The son of a university janitor in a small coal-mining town, he trained as an applied anthropologist with a background in development. When he bought Kiva Han, he envisioned a "sustainable model for a service-based industry owned by its employees," perhaps even a cooperative. He told me, "My firm belief is that every business should be owner-owned and operated and that the government should be supporting and subsidizing businesses to do that."

In many ways, Mutchka's saga is the story of an independent coffeehouse with limited resources that is suddenly confronted with a series of unanticipated obstacles. As he was in the process of acquiring the business, both his building and the one directly across the street were sold to a large local developer, who promptly raised rents. And the day-to-day demands of running a business challenged his beliefs. Although Mutchka had budgeted for a two-year loss before the business would become profitable, he was shocked at how disadvantaged small enterprises were in their dealings with suppliers and by how greedy and grasping the vendors seemed to be, as if they were exploiting his limitations. Furthermore, he strongly believed that all employers should provide health care, yet he quickly discovered he couldn't afford the expense. "All my theories about running a business have been scratched," he told me, sighing, but he hasn't given up on the long-term vision of shared ownership.

Mutchka withstood the initial hurdles and won a devoted clientele. But it wasn't long before a rumor surfaced: Starbucks was moving into the vacant storefront on the facing corner. Despite the company's periodic denials, there's substantial anecdotal evidence that Starbucks ruthlessly competes for prime real estate and positions itself near locally owned independent coffeehouses. And because of its size, it can frequently offer a landlord more than an independent coffeehouse can afford. "They're notorious for stealing people's leases," said one expert who, like most industry folks with a negative critique, was reluctant to be quoted by name. "If indies don't own their own property, they're vulnerable."

Mutchka went to see the building owners, but they told him that market forces would determine whether or not he had enough customers to survive. "They're good people, but they're business people," he said. "It's not their position to take a vested interest in individual tenants." Soon two Starbucks guys with tape measures appeared at Kiva Han to scope out the competition, outraging the baristas on duty, who tossed them out. Mutchka decided to stand his ground and compete. "They saw this ratty coffee shop—no color, no plants. My guess is they thought they'd run me out of business." Instead, he and his friends covered the windows so Starbucks workers couldn't see what they were doing and, for 7,000 dollars and a lot of sweat equity, redid the space, adding plants and new counters with elaborate mosaic patterns. After a harrowing few weeks of work, they reopened within two days of Starbucks' debut.

Despite the upgrade, Kiva Han retained the characteristics of a counterculture coffeehouse, with avant-garde staff, local art, and space for community organizations to meet. "We draw the groups because of our staff," Mutchka told me. "I look for people who have a passion for something outside work, like one employee who just loved antique typewriters. And we hire a lot of activists who have ties to Amnesty International and all kinds of groups. We had Dennis Kucinich speak here, and there were 250 people packing the store and the street."

The strategy worked. "I was scared at first," Mutchka admitted, "but then I saw their sterile store, and I thought, thank you, Lord." Early on, someone threw a brick through the Starbucks window and spray-painted the wall with a message: "Starbucks is not welcome here." But as of 2007, both Kiva Han and Starbucks remain ensconced on Craig Street, each drawing its separate clientele; and Mutchka is determined to endure.

If Kiva Han exudes the counterculture vibe of a Pacifica radio station, the 61C Café (named after the bus line that passes its door) is more like National Public Radio. I gladly pass up the Starbucks located two blocks from my parents' house (its *feng shui* is off, and it's dark) and walk the extra five blocks to buy coffee at the 61C. Situated in Pittsburgh's Squirrel Hill neighborhood, on a busy corner with an inviting outdoor patio, the café is the personal venture of Kate Knorr and her partner Gary Kaboly, whose nephew Keith Kaboly oversees day-to-day operations. Knorr, a social worker, had long talked about opening a coffeehouse. Then her mom died and left her a little money, and at just about the same time the storefront became vacant. "That patio was just a piece of grass with a big 'for sale' sign," Knorr recalled. "There were no coffeehouses in Squirrel Hill, the place was a mess, and the landlord wasn't receptive." But when the place didn't rent, the landlord called her back. "That was the decision point. Up till then it was a fantasy, but we had to sign a five-year lease. It was about 40,000 dollars, and for me that was the scariest part. But it was really just a wonderful corner in a wonderful neighborhood."

The store took eight months to open. Knorr got beans from a local roaster, architectural assistance from a friend, and an espresso machine for 6,000 dollars. "We had about 4,000 dollars left when we opened," she told me, "and by the end of the year we made a little money. It took us about five years to make up for the debt of opening it." But 61C was the little coffeehouse that could. More than a decade later, it's a neighborhood fixture, although there are now many more coffee alternatives, including a complement of Starbucks stores.

While the café continues to draw customers, the existence of Starbucks has affected it in other ways. People come into the 61C and order drinks Starbucks-style—in every possible permutation, not to mention grande. Under pressure, the café even decided to serve a Frappuccino equivalent. "When we started to do the blender drinks," Knorr recalled, "we needed some of those large straws, so we ordered them from our paper provider. And when they came, they were in Starbucks boxes. When Starbucks needed bigger straws for their drinks, they were just able to have them manufactured."

Her nephew Keith said that their efforts to order cups printed with the 61C logo were foiled when they discovered that the minimum print order required more storage space than they could ever accommodate. "Starbucks doesn't have to think about that," he lamented. "In a way, I'm jealous. And they charge more for something that's not better." Furthermore, he feels the ubiquity of Starbucks creates a challenge for independents. Students are the café's core clientele; but they change every four years, and the new ones are so used to Starbucks that they may never venture beyond it to an indie like the 61C. "We don't want all the coffee to be Starbucks," said Keith. "Big business is good for cars and airplanes. Leave coffee for small businesses."

Between Starbucks and independents such as the Kiva Han and the 61C, there is a complex interplay at the nexus of economics and culture. For a small but identifiable segment of pre-Starbucks caffeinistas and younger hipsters, the Starbucks iteration of coffeehouse is a metaphor for usurpation, a corporate heist of bohemian culture, a perversion of itself. These protectors of the countercultural flame find Starbucks guilty of taking what they perceive as their own originals, be it coffee culture or music, and repackaging them for bland mass consumption. "I don't consider myself a hipster or proud music junkie," my researcher Stephen Wood told me, as he considered Starbucks' cultural incursions and piracies. "I'm someone who likes honest music and dislikes exploitation, and I feel like branding in the world of art is exploitation. I don't feel like Starbucks is playing an album because they care about the music, like they do at one independent place I go to. I feel that Starbucks is spinning the disc because it best satisfies their aims as an ambient coffee shop chain."

Add to this the emergence of the fair trade movement, with its subtext of corporate malfeasance, and the metaphor begins to get a bit sticky, with an aura of truth. To fuel and validate their ire, the counterculturalists have turned to a growing body of literature about the evils of consumption and branding; and the excesses of the branding profession have bolstered their case. Take Interbrand, for instance. It's part of the Omnicom Group, a global holding company specializing in all kinds of communications; and it seems to be on a mission to brand the world, not merely for riches but for truth, justice, and the American way. As Interbrand's website astonishingly proclaims, "Brands . . . are central to commercial markets and democratic societies. They represent free choice. They also have a profound impact on our quality of life and the way we see our world. They color our lives. They reflect the values of our societies. Global brands act as ambassadors for nations and capture the spirit of an age. Most importantly, strong brands bestow value far beyond the tangible performance of the products and services themselves." This language reflects the counterculture's worst fears: that we live in a world where brands replace ambassadors as instruments of diplomacy and consumers replace citizens as practitioners of democracy.

Howard Schultz, who seems to have lived his life without a moment of anti-imperialist or anti-consumerist fervor, has been alternately hurt, angry, and baffled by the animus his stores encourage. But had he gone to college at Berkeley instead of Michigan, he might have been less surprised by the Seattle protests. In 1969 or thereabouts, the Associated Students of the University of California opened Leopold's Records with the goal of driving down record prices and incidentally creating a venture in which the young and cool sold products to like individuals. Leopold's did rather well, moving into larger quarters and eventually breaking free of the student association to form its own nonprofit board. All was fine until Sacramento-based Tower Records, not at all a nonprofit, set up shop across the street.

At the next riot opportunity (sometime after 1972, witness memories being none too clear), a contingent attacked Tower Records and did considerable damage to the windows, even injuring an employee. The justification was simply that "corporate America was ripping off our culture"—in this case, the music of the 1960s. That destructive act, and many similar ones, were discussed passionately in underground newspapers and in rapidly consumerizing publications such as *Rolling Stone*. No good intellectual conclusion was ever reached, but within a few years Leopold's was gone and Tower remained. This forgotten event, perhaps a metaphoric precursor, was repeated in Seattle in 1999.

Not dissimilar in spirit were the notices plastered onto some San Francisco Starbucks windows in 2003. "The global economy requires a relentless substitution of quantity over quality and shareholder value over human values," read the announcement, which culture jammers (the name ascribed to inventive practitioners of satirical brand desecration) had printed on fake company letterhead. "At our current market level, Starbucks cannot in good conscience guarantee all of our beans meet both our rigorous quality standards as well as our commitment to social responsibility. We are moving over and making room for local coffee bars." But as two Canadian academics, Joseph Heath and Andrew Potter, noted a few years ago, "Having fun is not subversive, and it doesn't undermine any system." Challenging prevailing leftist thinking, they suggest that "what the progressive left needs to do is disentangle the concern over questions of social justice from the countercultural critique—and to jettison the latter, while continuing to pursue the former."

Indeed, the inherited narrative of the counterculture obscures some complicated truths about coffee-counter culture. For most of the people I met at Coffee Fest, Starbucks' success was an incentive, not a deterrent, to create an individual alternative. They were generally inspired not by any counterculture but by the capitalist dream; they were seeking their little corner of market share and sustenance. Furthermore, based on a non-scientific sample of the independent coffeehouses I encountered in my travels, I confirmed that fair trade is not all that high on the café list of concerns. It was certainly not a major consideration at either Kiva Han or the 61C.

Compared to Starbucks, independent coffeehouses almost always provide lower employee pay, fewer benefits, and virtually no opportunities for advancement. Kate Knorr, owner of the 61C, sees her independent as "in between a labor of love and an income-making venture." It provides Keith with a decent salary, a half-time salary for herself, and low-wage work for several others, who start at roughly six dollars an hour. One young woman who has worked there on and off for more than eight years said that, for her, respect for the owners trumped health care; but not everyone has that luxury. Moreover, the employees at independent coffeehouses—café to café, city to city— are almost always white and often economically and educationally privileged. Lots of Starbucks employees also fit that profile, but the chain's workforce is far more diverse.

And to top it off, as I discovered in innumerable cities, independents don't necessarily serve better coffee. When we first moved into our house in 1995, the precursor of Murky Coffee was the independent, and only, coffee bar in the neighborhood, a purveyor of mediocre and unreliable cappuccinos. Then, in 2003, Starbucks came to Eighth Street. Separated from Murky by Pennsylvania Avenue, located on two very different shopping strips, both coffeehouses seemed to thrive. Three years later, there were suddenly four options. First, a block or so from Murky, a Port City Java franchise opened, with sleek leather armchairs arrayed in its picture windows. Then, in the fall of 2006, right across the street from Starbucks, a Dunkin' Donuts arrived, sporting an Italian espresso machine. It was a big two-story affair, far larger than the Starbucks, with an expanded menu and a Baskin & Robbins counter.

One morning in January 2007, my friend Beverly and I took off on a coffee crawl to systematically assess the options. We started at Starbucks, where Denoris said hi and prepared my short cappuccino and a cup of brewed for Beverly. The cappuccino cost $2.70. The drink was fine, but the music was fabulous: Nina Simone, a happy touch for our morning. "I love the Christmas CDs," Beverly confided. "They're such a great mix of old and new, Tony Bennett to Diana Krall." The line moved quickly. Seated behind us was a crew of women who regularly come in after their workout at Curves, the fitness franchise nearby. "Why not go to Dunkin' Donuts instead?" I asked. One woman said she patronizes both, depending on the day and which side of the street she's on, but "Starbucks is more addictive." Another chimed in, "They have better doughnuts."

So Beverly and I bought a Starbucks doughnut, and we discovered our advisor was right. The doughnut we subsequently ate across the street at Dunkin' Donuts was airy and tasteless by comparison. In fact, Dunkin' is less about doughnuts and more about coffee, which accounts for roughly 65 percent of its sales. Back in June 2006, an article in the *New York Times* business section noted that the company sees itself as "democratizing espresso." Beverly's coffee was okay, but no one at my Dunkin' knew what a dry cappuccino entailed. The order earned me a weird look and a $1.99 milky drink that tasted nothing like coffee. The cost may have been democratic, but the beverage was pretty bad. At Dunkin' Donuts, the staff, as at Starbucks, was mostly young people of color. There was one African American woman who'd been there since the store opened, and she was a pleasure and a prize, animated and efficient. She was the exception, though.

Because the stores are franchised rather than owned by the company, individual owners set wages and benefits. Chris Mellgren, who co-owns my local Dunkin', is candid about being in business as an entrepreneur, not for any higher reason, although he tries to make sure that his employees learn skills and that successful ones have opportunities to be promoted. He's happy that he can provide jobs and that he has a product that can be easily donated for charitable events. That's the long and the short of it. On our crawl, Beverly and I observed that, despite the chain's touted upscaling, our store still feels like a 7-Eleven: coffee packages are displayed next to bags of potato chips, and the ventilation system hums loudly. And no customers are just hanging out and talking. In the *New York Times* article, the company's vice president for marketing, John F. Gilbert, told reporter Julie Bosman that customers "have stuff they got to do, and most of what they want to do is not taking place in our stores." True enough. Despite this store's large space, including balcony seating, it's not a place to linger. And we didn't.

Port City Java, roughly two long blocks away, won the award for décor. Almost all the customers were white, mostly women from that side of the neighborhood. It also got the "pleasant" award: stylish, comfortable chairs and sofas in pale green and burnt orange, restful jazz, and a lovely view of historic Eastern Market. But Port City's coffee branding posters gave me pause. The place had plenty of signs for what they call Fairganic coffee, which is both USDA Organic and Fair Trade Certified. But when I asked one of the owners about Fairganic, he said that only a small amount of the store's coffee fits that profile. This is the perfect example of commodifying virtue for the consumer while only incidentally benefiting a few farmers. (Like Dunkin' Donuts, Port City Java headquarters never returned any of my calls.)

The woman curled up in an armchair across from me turned out to be our recently elected school board member, a mocha maven. She said Port City is a good place to catch up on her work. She thought that Murky has the best coffee but has gotten too crowded. She never goes to Starbucks anymore: it's too busy, and the coffee is erratic— sometimes strong, other times watery. Beverly and I found our Port City coffees acceptable but unremarkable. At heart, the store is a Starbucks knock-off, riding the gourmet coffee wave. And my cappuccino cost $2.95.

It was on to Murky Coffee, a block or so back in the direction of Starbucks. The coffee at Murky was the foam on our outing, winning the coffee award hands down. For $2.70 I ordered a classic cappuccino, which came in a real cup. The coffee was deep and rich, and the barista had artistically etched a heart in brown on the dense, white, perfectly silken foam. Beverly is mad at Murky for painting over a mural of the neighborhood, left over from its previous incarnations, in pursuit of a sleeker image. Despite her prejudice, however, she loved her single-origin Rwandan coffee; and her croissant was delicious. All the tables were taken, mostly with student types, and everyone was reading or working. Lots of laptops gave the shop the air of a study hall. A few duos, like us, were conversing.

Once upon a time, the predecessor of Murky Coffee, Roasters on the Hill, actually had a small coffee roaster in the store. The shop was owned by an African American woman, and a quirky, racially diverse staff served the drinks. It was individualistic, sometimes lovable, almost always inefficient and inconsistent. The one guarantee was slow service. As the store morphed into Stompin' Grounds and then to Murky, it kept a changing individualism but finally learned how to operate well and serve great coffee. The staff has remained a shade on the trendy side, bantering, relaxed, with cool hair, tattoos, and arts-district styles—yet both they and the clientele, like the neighborhood itself, seem whiter and a shade more affluent than before. In short, Murky is the quintessential independent, with better coffee than most. And like most independents, the staff is young and independent too. No matter that wages start at $7.50 an hour without benefits: it's a cool place to work, and staff members have chosen to be here.

I've conversed with them about goat's milk and fair trade and have found that several Murky baristas have gone to origin countries to visit the farms that supply the store's coffee.

Murky's coffee supplier is Counter Culture Coffee Company. Peter Guiliano, Counter Culture's coffee buyer, says his company bought close to a million pounds of coffee in 2006, of which 60 percent was Fair Trade Certified. He noted, however, that "we don't sell most of it as certified because we use it in blends with other coffees." In 2006 the price Counter Culture paid for coffee ranged between $1.30 and $25 a pound, with the average between two and three dollars. Most comes from small estates and cooperatives. Guiliano's discussions about sourcing mirrored the language of Starbucks, a company whose policies he generally admires. Like the Starbucks staff, Guiliano has worked to develop personal relationships along the coffee supply chain, although he noted that buying 1 million rather than 300 million pounds is a different challenge. "If you're a coffee buyer who cares, you want to develop the maximum value you can," he said, "but we also have to be mindful of what we can get for it. Almost all the coffee I buy, and all the coffee in the world, is undervalued. I know the best way to fetch premiums, and help the farmers, is for high quality, so I'm very strategic with farmers to improve quality through financial incentives."

One factor that distinguished Murky from the other three coffee-houses on our crawl was that its baristas care about coffee and Guiliano encourages that interest. "I asked one guy applying for a job at Counter Culture why he wanted to work here, and he said he was fascinated about coffee as medium for social exchange. And I thought, yes, that's what Sumatra and Rwanda are about." Guiliano believes that a coffee coming from a specific origin such as Rwanda or a specific estate in the highlands of El Salvador can have an impact that transcends taste because there is an implicit narrative behind the coffee. At Murky, coffee origins are part of the ambiance, much like the free Wi-Fi and the free-spirited, passionately coffee-minded baristas.

Theoretically, origins are also part of the ambiance at Starbucks, although at our local store neither staff nor customers seem to show much interest. Port City Java cares enough to trademark the term Fairganic and prominently claim its implied goodness, yet the store had no obvious dedication to the concept. Dunkin' uses only Fair Trade Certified beans for its espresso drinks, a move announced with much fanfare in 2003. Although only a small percentage of the drinks Dunkin' serves fits that description, Paul Rice of TransFair USA told me that the company is among the top four purchasers of fair trade coffee in the country. The bottom line is that all four stores on our crawl sell some Fair Trade Certified coffee, which is good. Counter Culture Coffee and Starbucks also cultivate relationships with farmers, pay prices above market (and often above fair trade), and operate programs to assist farmers in countries of origin. That's even better.

When it comes to workers, the starting wage is fairly consistent from one store to another: somewhat above the local minimum, varying from $7.00 to $8.50 an hour. Only at Starbucks are workers offered health care and a real benefits package; and only at Murky and Starbucks are employees' personalities promoted as part of the ambiance, with extensive time and resources consistently allocated to staff training.

But what I noticed most on my crawl was the difference in clientele. Port City Java and Murky had higher-end customers, with Murky drawing a more idiosyncratic crowd and exuding an artier vibe. There were no crowds of teenagers at these venues, though they are within a block of a huge junior high school, and not too many people of color. Both were implicitly exclusive: Port City Java by class, Murky by culture. Dunkin' drew predominantly people of color, local fire and police personnel, and people on the run, although, later in the day, the Baskin & Robbins ice cream counter drew a more diverse crowd.

The *New York Times* article about Dunkin' Donuts suggests the existence of a consciously targeted "class war in a coffee cup" pitting highfalutin' Starbucks consumers against the average Joe. In our neighborhood, however, this doesn't seem to be true. Starbucks is not a beacon of exclusivity but a great democratizer. Neither an artisan shop like Murky nor an industrial shop like Dunkin', it broadcasts accessibility to all regardless of race or class, while retaining the music, the lighting, and the ambiance that speak to high-end aspirations. To be honest, I have to say that Murky reflects many of my own cultural preferences, not to mention my coffee tastes, and I could easily make it a regular stop. But despite its flaws, I can't quite abandon my local Starbucks, with its rakish Afrocentric vibe and its determined staff, full of personality, struggling to make good and move up.

In addition to empirical evidence showing the ascendancy of all kinds of coffeehouses, the other flaw in the counterculture analysis lurks in Starbucks' ambiguous status between neighborhood institution and chain store. Since the Industrial Revolution, we have had a system in which the large middle of the market is dominated by mass-produced goods and services. At the lower end of the market, there have always been the entrepreneurs eking out a living at the periphery or under the radar of the mainstream economy: street vendors with knockoff handbags for twenty-five dollars, the guy down the street who knows how to repair your car radiator or fix your leaky faucet, the woman who will mind your kids or sell her homemade pies to the neighbors. At the high end there have always been the entrepreneurs who provide custom goods and services: the guy down the street who can debug your computer or build a custom bookcase, the upscale child care facility or wedding caterer, the one-of-a-kind dress boutique with the four-hundred-dollar handmade bags, the café with designer cakes and coffee.

A small number of today's independent coffeehouses fall into the just-above-informal economy, with owners who eke out a living on the retail margin. But generally coffee bars and designer roasters are niche markets, like purveyors of artisan cheeses, hand-painted T-shirts, and limited-edition sneakers. They appeal to the trendy cutting edge, the exceptionally discerning or demanding, the intelligentsia. They survive by exclusivity, by pleasing a small and loyal following, by keeping their costs low and their prices relatively high or at least competitive.

This is the market that most Coffee Fest attendees dream of, but for Starbucks it's the long-ago past. Nevertheless, the company is loath to admit this truth, and staff members bridle at any reference to fast food. As Schultz told the stock analysts at *Motley Fool* a few years ago, "When I look at McDonald's and Krispy Kreme and Dunkin' Donuts, those three companies do an excellent job, but they are in a different business than we are. They are in the transaction business, fast-food business. That is the antithesis of Starbucks."

But to many people, a chain store is a chain store, despite Schultz's protestations; and communities that fear that their distinctive character is threatened by the relentless march of the brands are sometimes moved to protect their turf. For instance, consider the 2005 set-to in San Francisco's Japantown, where the city's redevelopment authority approved a Starbucks over strong community objections. "Many people in the neighborhood voiced the concern that Starbucks' presence would have diminished the revenues of local small businesses, such as Café Hana, May's Coffee Shop, Benkyodo Diner and Café Tan Tan," reported the local *Nichi Bei Times*. In that case, Starbucks acceded to neighborhood wishes and decided not to sign the lease. "I'm glad that Starbucks is sensitive to the community's issues and concerns," community leader Paul Osaki told the reporter. But Starbucks is generally loath to back down or pull out. Though it recognizes that biodiversity makes for a healthy and sustainable environment in coffee-growing regions, the company doesn't always extend the same principle to the urban and suburban ecosystem. On city streets, Starbucks is the big guy, the Nestlé or Procter & Gamble of coffee retail shops, looking for the big, sun-fattened return while the smaller varietals often struggle to survive.

Travel from Main Street to Wall Street, however, and the picture changes. Here, Starbucks' economic competition is Dunkin' and McDonald's, not Murky Coffee and Kiva Han; and if you compare it to the corporations it most resembles in size and structure, Starbucks seems artisanal by comparison. Even low-paid floor workers know the difference. "Most of my friends from high school, they're working at Popeye's and McDonald's," an employee at my local Starbucks explained, "but I'm proud to work at Starbucks. The customers are more upscale, more friendly. I worked at McDonald's for a minute; it was nasty. I'm not flippin' no burgers."

Starbucks has become to McDonald's what Target is to Wal-Mart, a touch of class for those of modest means while retaining enough savoir faire to appeal to more upscale urban clientele and suburban aficionados. Such cross-dressing—big corporate chain store disguised as a genuine "third place"—also encourages class-based cross-dressing among its employees and clientele, an upscale egalitarianism that reaches across generation and race. Starbucks has created not just a brand but a culture authentic unto itself, which has, in turn, changed the larger culture. This may be the root of its cachet, its ubiquity not just on our street corners but in our popular iconography.

Go online and find a gallery of celebrities clutching Starbucks cups. Go into a store and become a star in your own do-it-yourself production. There are props, a crew, and a cast of thousands—each a walk-on, each a featured player. You can do a one-person show (loner, unbeknownst to passing throng, writes sleeper-of-the-year novel). You can do improv that draws on the talents of fellow actors. Or you can consider the set grist for your own YouTube rant, rave, or send-up. Tony award-winning actress Kristin Chenoweth gets my award for her touching song "Taylor the Latte Boy," which begins with "There's a boy who works at Starbucks" and rises to a soulful chorus: "Taylor the latte boy, bring me java, bring me joy. . . ."

"It's all here!" the Lakeland housing development trumpets in the Sunday real estate section of the *Seattle Times* alongside a photo of two women communing in a Starbucks store. Elsewhere in the same section, architect Brett Zamore promotes his zippy housing design kit and says he hopes to become "the Starbucks of housing." On the editorial pages, syndicated columnist Margaret Carlson calls Pennsylvania "the state that time forgot. . . . It has the lowest penetration by Starbucks of any state I've ever been in." Quality of life, success, modernity. They all equal Starbucks.

But that success can be more than a metaphor. At the Baileys Crossroads Starbucks, located in a Virginia suburb of D.C., manager Kokeb Teferi has transformed her store into a true third place. All day, at any time, the store and its sidewalk, which faces a shopping center parking lot, are packed with Ethiopian and Somali men sharing coffee, political conversations, and chess games. "We go out of our way to make them very comfortable," Teferi told me.

"There were some issues when I first took over," she said. "Most of the guys who worked here had no idea about the background or the culture, so there were language barriers and cultural issues. There could be one person buying for five people, and all five would be standing on line, holding it up. And then there were sometimes conflicts between different ethnic groups." Moreover, Teferi is female in a culture in which women in authority can incur resentment. But in short order, she organized and cajoled the staff and the regular customers into a different way of being, set up ground rules, and created a haven that blends the American host culture with the familiarity of home. "Now when someone from Somalia or Ethiopia is new in town, chances are they'll end up here to make contacts and catch up on the news," she said. In 2002, when a serial sniper was loose in the area, Starbucks ordered the outside chairs to be moved inside as a safety precaution. But the regular customers were so devoted to their habits that they brought their own chairs to the sidewalk and refused to be moved.

As I wrote this book, I kept tripping over what I eventually called "mom stories": tales of colleagues who found a Starbucks haven while visiting their moms. Journalist Ben Witte, my translator in Costa Rica, visited his mom in Pleasant Hills, California, and noticed that a Starbucks had moved into a strip mall down the road. "I've always preferred smaller independent places, sort of my Berkeley snobbery coming out," he told me. "I assumed that people in Pleasant Hill would treat the Starbucks like they treated the nearby Taco Bell or McDonald's, as a place to drive up, dash inside, buy the product, and then hop back in their cars. To my surprise, the place was packed. Every seat was occupied. . . . What was even more surprising was that these people seemed completely funky and interesting. Where did they all come from? This was clearly an 'if you build it they will come' type of situation."

Could it be that we, the counterculturalists with the rebellious hearts who seek to marry democratic ideals with strident individualism, have also been the guardians of arrogant exclusivity? The café counterculture has been, by definition, a bastion of intellectual and class privilege, created to distinguish the superior cool and élan of its habitués. While we may wax nostalgic about coffee shops and lunch counters, the truth is that most of them sold lousy coffee, and they still do.

Propelled by Schultz's vision of a nation parched for better coffee and a pleasant place to sit and chat without pressure to order a meal or a beer, Starbucks polished up its artisanal image and invited in the masses. It branded its coffee as a sign of taste and class (priced accordingly) and took it on the road. Suddenly, racially and class-diverse baristas were serving cappuccinos and icy sweet drinks to a diverse, and very large, body of customers, many of whom had never had access to, or felt welcome in, the cool coffeehouses of the intellectual and Italian ghettos. Now everyone could get a good cup of coffee at the airport. There was a store in Japan with a no-smoking policy. And there were cafés in foreign countries where locals could practice their English and tourists could seize a moment of familiarity amid the whirl of new sensations.

In *The Conquest of Cool* (a very cool book), journalist Thomas Frank dissected the 1960s revolution, noting that it was not only televised but commercialized, a promoter of hip consumerism. That intricate dance continues as the countercultural edge fights establishment brands such as Starbucks while branding itself in the process, a cycle of guerilla raids over the culture divide that has become more frenetic with the advent of cyberspace. The mainstream begets the counterculture, which becomes the mainstream and spawns the next counterculture, each showering us with a new cycle of must-have material or psychic goods.

So, too, with coffee-counter culture. You need only stand on line at the Peet's on Piedmont Avenue in Oakland to declare Starbucks coffee beneath your refined coffee palate. Or you can head up the street to catch a whiff of counterculture grunge and indifferent service at Gaylord's, a veteran coffeehouse that still draws denizens to drink coffee amid slovenly piles of reading material. Or you can cross the street to L'Amyx Tea Bar and drink un-Frappuccino-like red bean bubble tea with its gelatinous black tapioca pearls or sample exotic teas in stylish iron teapots, another cultural blend to smudge the global borders of our minds.

But if none of these appeal, there's always Starbucks. It may not be the Italo-beatnik coffeehouse that once dotted the intellectual enclaves of North America or its edgy independent successor. And it may not be Jimmy's, serving greasy eggs and coffee that's evaporated to sludge on the hotplate. It may not even be Peet's. Starbucks is something else, not always delightful but also not malign. It's the way it is. For now.

7 | When Worker Met Partner

For a year, I kept five lovely little cards on my desk. Each was the size of a standard business card and bore an illustration, awash in gentle color and New Age sensibility, representing a trait that epitomizes the ideal Starbucks partner.

"Welcoming," says one drawn in mock-child style, a picture of a multiracial group of partners wearing green aprons and smiles and surrounded by the word *welcome* in many languages. "Offer everyone a sense of belonging."

"Involved," says another. "Connect with one another, with the company, with your community."

"Knowledgeable," says a third. "Love what you do. Share it with others."

Starbucks managers and partners are encouraged to give each other these cards as tokens of recognition and thanks for upholding company ideals beyond the call of duty. The cards may be hokey; but their messages and, even more important, their existence are meant to serve as an antidote to workplaces that are increasingly transitory and impersonal. It's the kind of symbolism that would probably make your average union leader puke. And that's a problem because, by lavishing even generic personal attention on workers, the company is meeting a need that unions all but neglect.

Unions, it seems, have a great future behind them, rooted in the anthems of the 1930s but tone-deaf to the cultural changes that are shaping new generations of workers. The consequences extend beyond the rise or fall of unions. Without institutions to aggregate the concerns of workers, we lose one of the few tools proven to blunt economic disparity. Moreover, workers lose a singular avenue to participation in decisions that govern the global economy. Individuals may migrate from job to job and country to country in search of a better future, but such opportunities do not lead to improved safety standards or health care for the vast majority of workers, whose options are limited by geography, oppression, or inadequate skills.

Employment these days often seems more like speed dating than marriage: a brief, intense exchange while the clock ticks; then on to the next table or computer station. What sociologist Richard Sennett calls "short term task labor" has become the prevailing model, requiring a high threshold for uncertainty, a talent for flexibility, and a tolerance for constant change. But all this moving around—employees changing, venues changing—wreaks havoc on relationships. Sennett suggests that the new workplace yields "low institutional loyalty, diminishment of informal trust among workers, and weakening of institutional knowledge." How can companies expect loyalty from workers they are able to fire at any time for any reason? How can customers expect consistency, much less community, if the staff is constantly changing? How can employees build relationships with each other when they are part time and transitory? How can they ever gain a degree of ownership over their jobs or any power to confront unfair or unsafe working conditions when they are here today and gone tomorrow?

The ascendant power of brand may be metaphorical, but the descendant power of workers is real. It brought labor to the Seattle protests and, for a moment at least, into alignment with the up-and-coming global justice movement. In the global economy, workers, like coffee, are a surplus commodity, with only specialty workers able to command premiums above the undervalued employment floor. And as unions lose their power to influence the price of labor and governments lose the will to regulate corporations, people who must earn a living are once again in the position of having to negotiate personally with their employers without any real power to do so. To some informal extent, personal negotiation may always be the norm at the local level, where motivational cards can be dispensed, immediate supervisors confronted, and the day-to-day abrasions of the work environment negotiated. But in a world where corporate headquarters set the rules of compensation and culture, it can be hard for the individual employee to have any voice or control over the template of wages and working conditions that define employment.

Wal-Mart, the largest private employer in the United States, with 1.4 million workers, has become a model for how to squeeze the most out of workers from one end of the supply chain to the other, from the sweatshops of Asia to the checkout lines at your local Wal-Mart Supercenter, harming both communities and individuals. The company has racked up an unsavory reputation for discriminating against women, encouraging supervisors to doctor overtime records and pushing its employees to seek Medicaid in lieu of providing proper health care. As one factory owner told Charles Fishman, author of *The Wal-Mart Effect*, "Every time you see the Wal-Mart smiley face, whistling and knocking down the prices, somewhere there's a factory worker being kicked in the stomach."

Starbucks, by contrast, has become a model for socially responsible business practices. It believes it has found a way to build respect and community into a workplace and a workforce that are inherently fluid. Consequently, the annual turnover among Starbucks baristas is roughly 90 percent, as opposed to an industry-wide norm of closer to 200 percent. Responding on AlterNet to an unflattering article about the company, a former Starbucks employee wrote, "They treat their employees surprisingly well. For any business, let alone food service. They give health benefits after two months at twenty hours a week, and don't have discriminatory hiring practices. . . . They give everyone their break at reasonable intervals. . . . If you want to go pick on a big corporation, find one that actually abuses their workers."

What Wal-Mart and Starbucks share, though, is a baseline hourly wage that generally hovers between seven and ten dollars. They also share an antipathy to unions. And as if to obscure the power dynamics of the employer-employee relationship, they've both invented different terminology for their workforce. Wal-Mart calls its employees *associates*; Starbucks calls them *partners*. One might argue that Wal-Mart's goal is to disempower workers, while Starbucks' goal is the opposite; but not everyone would agree.

According to Starbucks, the partner designation came about when it decided to give workers an economic stake in the company through Bean Stock and bonuses in years in which the company excels. But views are mixed on whether average workers would be better off with pension contributions or with more money in their paychecks. Jef Keighley of the Canadian Automobile Workers, which used to represent a number of Starbucks stores in British Columbia, was dismissive: "When you actually start to look at it, it's an absolute crock. Within the hourly staff it would be unrealistic to think that any more than 10 to15 percent of the hourly workforce would be able to qualify for Bean Stock."

While critics disparage the partner terminology as cynical sentimentalism, evidence suggests that Starbucks has traditionally been thoughtful about how it connects with and cares for its employees. Not only did it build in the benefit package, it also has an interesting and evolving system for engaging workers that seems to be based on a two-tier approach: (1) find those with interest and capacity, mentor them, and promote them up the ladder; and (2) provide a relatively benign workplace for temporary and part-time workers. Supervisors are evaluated on both their own performance and the number of their staff members who get promoted. The message is that it's not enough to succeed; your staff should succeed as well. It would be hard to find other companies—or nonprofits, for that matter—with similar criteria.

The company also provides a range of feedback mechanisms, from partner surveys about job satisfaction to a mission review, in which partners can challenge the company for failing to live up to the mission. All of this is easier to commit to paper than to practice, especially as the company grows. Nonetheless, for at least a decade, groups of partners have been engaged in sessions to inform a range of decisions, from environmental sustainability initiatives to benefits priorities. And many feel the company is doing a decent job, certainly compared to the alternative jobs available for hourly workers. A startling 84 percent (101,800 partners) participated in the March 2006 survey, and 86 percent of that number declared themselves to be satisfied. Employees wanted improvements in pay, benefits, and internal promotional opportunities; and the company's 2006 CSR report vowed to take measurable steps to address those issues.

"We're not anti-union. We're pro-partner." That's the Starbucks mantra, repeated by both Howard Schultz and former CEO Jim Donald, among others; but while there's some validity to the latter assertion, the first part stretches credibility. Over the years, Starbucks has faced unionizing efforts by the United Food and Commercial Workers Union, which organized in Seattle in 1987; the Canadian

Automobile Workers, which represented baristas at fewer than a dozen stores in British Columbia; the International Union of Operating Engineers, which organized at the Kent, Washington, roasting plant; and, most recently, the Industrial Workers of the World, organizing baristas, mostly in New York City.

When pushed, the company acknowledges its employees' right to organize, as reiterated in the 2006 CSR report: "Starbucks is committed to following any and all labor laws in a fair and consistent manner. We do not take action or retaliate against partners who express their views about unions or who take part in union activity." The company's behavior, however, tells a different story.

Schultz, like most American executives, takes union activity personally and believes it indicates deep character flaws among both workers and managers. In other words, unionizing means the world is out of harmony. A 2000 article by Liza Featherstone for *Dissent Magazine* observed that socially committed companies such as Ben & Jerry's, Powell's Books, and Whole Foods have all vigorously fought union organizing efforts. It's as if the concept of union representation has vanished as a democratic right and been erased from the liberal agenda. Featherstone quoted Michael Powell, owner of progressive Powell's Books: "You say the word 'union,' and everyone's supposed to feel all squishy. I don't get it. I understand if you're organizing farm workers, or people in Bangladesh. But this is not that kind of situation." The article summarized the feelings of socially responsible employers: "If the people running the show are the ones who bear all the responsibility, and are cool progressive folks, why would workers need a voice of their own?"

Howard Schultz seems to wholeheartedly share this view. When he bought Starbucks in 1987, the United Food and Commercial Workers represented the warehouse, roasting plant, and retail operations in Seattle; but Schultz wanted none of it. In *Pour Your Heart into It*, he wrote that he wanted Starbucks workers "to believe in their hearts that management trusted them and treated them with respect. I was convinced that under my leadership, employees would come to realize that I would listen to their concerns. If they had faith in me and my motives, they wouldn't need a union." The retail store workers decertified the union within months; the warehouse and roasting plant workers following suit in 1992.

Providing benefits for one's employees is certainly not the worst response to a unionization effort; unfortunately, it hasn't been the company's only response. Nor were benefits enough to stave off unhappiness at the roasting plant, where there was a revolving door for managers and a steady stream of complaints, many involving shift scheduling. In 1999, despite both carrots and sticks tossed to workers by supervisors and a personal visit from Schultz intended to allay worker concerns, the International Union of Operating Engineers' Local 286 won an election for a unit of twenty-two technical and machine maintenance workers. From that moment on, the company tried to force them out. Some supervisors attended anti-union seminars provided by the notorious union-busting firm Jackson, Lewis. By the time I first visited the plant in 2004, only two or three of the original members who had voted for the union were still on the payroll, and decertification loomed. When I asked someone at the plant about the situation, he shook his head and, to avoid being overheard, quietly suggested that something must have gone afoul for all those workers to have disappeared from the plant, one by one.

Jeff Alexander, who worked at the roasting plant for five years, was one of those union workers. At the time I spoke with him, he worked as a representative for Local 286; and I met him at the union office in Auburn, roughly fifteen miles and a class divide away from Starbucks headquarters. During my years in the labor movement, I'd visited dozens of local offices, and somehow they were all similar: stocked with furniture that's seen better days and dedicated staff hoping for better times. Union organizing is never easy; and in an era in which individual aggrandizement is rewarded and collective advancement deterred, the work is grueling. There was nothing glossy about Alexander's manner or presentation. But like all good trade unionists, he exhibited a dogged passion for fairness in the face of adversity.

An electrician who had previously worked at a nearby meatpacking plant, Alexander started at Starbucks in 1996, "when it was still small." He earned more than nineteen dollars an hour plus overtime. But then the company changed the shift schedule: now everyone worked four ten-hour days per week without overtime. Some employees worked weekends without additional compensation, costing Alexander and his colleagues more than 10,000 dollars a year in overtime wages. They called in the Operating Engineers.

The organizing effort and its devolution present a classic study of both the power and culture clashes that accompany traditional union organizing in modern America. The union, for its part, assumed it could organize and maintain a unit of twenty-two craft workers in a plant of roughly three hundred full-time employees, although there was no unionization in any of the company's other U.S. operations. Furthermore, the central dispute highlighted the discrepancy between old rules and new efficiencies and sensibilities. Overtime pay is not always cost-effective for a company, and overtime work robs families of valuable down time. In other workplaces—hospitals, for example—the source of conflict is often the opposite issue: forced overtime. Yet in the world of hourly work, overtime pay can make the difference between getting by and making a decent living. For Alexander and his co-workers, losing their overtime hours meant approximately a 20 percent pay cut that they could ill afford.

Schultz's visit to the plant to dissuade the engineers from joining the union is still etched in Alexander's memory: "He told the story of his father and the diaper truck, just like out of the book. 'You know, Howard,' we told him, 'we're not college kids working as baristas in a coffee shop. This is our career. We're in the plant, in an industrial setting—women supporting their families, men for whom this is their job.' We didn't need Bean Stock that you hold onto for five years get the increase in stock value, and give him back the shares. We needed a union pension plan."

The company hired the D.C. law firm of Aiken Gump to conduct negotiations, which dragged on for two long years. Meanwhile, employees who had signed union cards were subjected to both subtle and blatant pressure. The company capriciously changed their work shifts and hired new workers at higher rates. "Some of the other workers even threatened to kill me," said Alexander, "but they weren't fired. Eventually you just get tired." He quit and went back to working at the meatpacking plant until he got the job at the union.

The difficulties Alexander described were echoed by others. "They made it very hard for the Operating Engineers," said one worker. "They promoted new people over them; they wrote them up for everything. One of the guys was a vet from the first Gulf War; he had trouble sleeping because of post-traumatic stress, but they wouldn't give him the shift his doctor said he needed." That veteran's suit against the company under the Americans with Disabilities Act was settled for an undisclosed amount in July 2007.

Worst of all, according to several sources, management ordered human relations personnel to screen potential new hires for any pos-sible union connection and find excuses not to hire them. In this union-friendly town, a place where Boeing was a major employer, applicants were turned away for bogus reasons. I had heard about the screening process early in my research and later asked David Pace, executive vice president for human relations, about it. He emphatically denied the allegation, saying that the company would never have engaged in such a practice. But one human relations staffer resisted the directive on the grounds that it was illegal, and she was fired. She filed a complaint with the National Labor Relations Board, which Starbucks eventually settled for 165,000 dollars.

Of all the problems I explored regarding Starbucks, this was the one that rankled. The roasting plant, despite its generally benign aspect (including the recent addition of an employee fitness center and upscale coffee options in the employee dining area), is still recognizably a manufacturing plant. For about 75 percent of the workforce, the job is permanent rather than temporary. Therefore, relationships with plant management and resulting issues of fairness are critical to employees' futures and well-being. When it came to these workers, far from the prying eyes of upscale and controversy-averse consumers, the velvet glove of employer benevolence enclosed the more traditional fist of intimidation.

According to economist and AFL-CIO policy director Thea Lee, this sort of company response is all too common: "You have a company that has basically decent wages and working conditions and good relations with its employees. The company thinks the union will complicate things and add a level of combativeness, as opposed to a nice, smooth flow. In my view, that's anti-union prejudice." She noted that there are indeed some deficient unions and union leaders. "But at the end of the day, the union's job is not necessarily to make life easier for management. It's to represent the voices of workers."

For a lot of consumers, she said, "it's pretty easy not to get all het up about a nice workplace that doesn't have a union. I hear it with respect to countries as well. Like, 'Did Korea really need trade unions now that wages were rising?' " It makes Lee angry when she hears these rationalizations. "I say it's not really a question of whether you think they need a union or not; the question is whether the workers want a union. If they want a union, they have a right to it, and it's not up to the government or an employer to decide they're better off without one."

The real issue with Starbucks and Whole Foods is not so much the rules of employment but the system of benevolent paternalism: management gets to define what's good for workers. "How's it to work here?" I asked a checker on one of my rare visits to Whole Foods.

"They treat us well," the thirty-something African American woman told me, "We don't have a union or anything, but it's pretty good." I asked whether she'd like a union. "Yes," she replied. "Sometimes it's good to have one, you know, someone who can talk to management for you if something needs fixing." It was a sentiment I also heard at Starbucks, usually in a whisper that couldn't be overheard by the supervisor. That sense of anxious caution, prevalent throughout the company, was one of the greatest arguments for an independent voice for workers.

Schultz, however, has continued to maintain that company generosity precludes the need for a union. In response to the IWW campaign to organize baristas in New York, he sent a voicemail to the New York stores, characterizing the effort as "disappointing and very disturbing. . . . Back in the early days," he told *his* people, "we began offering comprehensive health care coverage and ownership in the company in the form of Bean Stock to full- and part-time employees. . . . Our compassion for one another truly differentiates us."

This was not what the IWW (also know as the Wobblies) wanted to hear. With a zaniness that owes more to Abbie Hoffman than to founder Big Bill Haywood, the union has established its own brand (a cross between 1930s-style working-class hero and Battle of Seattle cool) while branding Starbucks as an evildoer of global proportions. In the process, it has proved once again that a very small crew of individuals can create quite a stir.

There was a time, in the early 1900s, when the IWW actually was an intellectual and inspirational force in the American labor movement. Founded in 1905 by radical industrial trade unionists and anarchists, it had perhaps 100,000 members in its heyday, united under the slogan "One Big Union!" Whereas the craft unions of the time were narrow in focus, with membership mostly restricted to white males, the IWW had a zealous, inclusive ideology of rank-and-file democracy and a revolutionary vision of all workers surging forward against the injustices of capitalism. Among its founders were the legends of labor, the great Eugene V. Debs, Mother Jones, and Joe Hill, of whom nostalgic unionists still sing and dream. From the 1912 textile strike in Lawrence, Massachusetts, to the mining struggles of the Minnesota Iron Range, the Wobblies brought great organizers, a swashbuckling leftist sensibility, and a low level of practicality to labor's organizing struggles. The current IWW Constitution echoes those roots:

> The working class and the employing class have nothing in common. There can be no peace so long as hunger and want are

found among millions of working people and the few, who make up the employing class, have all the good things of life. Between these two classes a struggle must go on until the workers of the world organize as a class, take possession of the means of production, abolish the wage system, and live in harmony with the earth. . . . Instead of the conservative motto, "A fair day's wage for a fair day's work," we must inscribe on our banner the revolutionary watchword, "Abolition of the wage system."

By the 1990s, the IWW had devolved to perhaps a few thousand members worldwide, but the Seattle demonstrations of 1999 gave the group an unexpected boost. The emergence of a new-millennium variant of anarchism on college campuses, particularly on the west coast, dovetailed nicely with the carefully preserved anarchist culture of the Wobblies, creating a ready-made legacy of romance and heroism to march the working class, clad in black T-shirt chic and brandishing computer skills, into the new century. Chief Wobbly Starbucks organizer Daniel Gross joined the union in California. He had grown up in Los Angeles and had attended the University of California at Santa Barbara, where he received a degree in business economics. Then he took some time off to travel in southeast Asia—India, Nepal, Tibet, Thailand, Vietnam. After volunteering for a Greenpeace clean energy campaign in California, he eventually headed to New York.

According to the official IWW narrative, Gross looked for work at Starbucks because of its good reputation and then discovered, to his horror, that the company was really a monster that mistreated its workers. As the story goes, he organized some of his Starbucks barista colleagues at the Thirty-Sixth Street and Madison Avenue store in downtown Manhattan. They went shopping for a union, ultimately choosing the IWW because of its democratic values and low dues structure. Given, however, that Gross was an IWW member before he came to New York, one might posit another story: a dedicated cadre of progressive activists joined the Wobblies and then got jobs at Starbucks with the goal of giving this icon of venal capitalism and yuppie consumerism a black eye.

Organizing a union to represent workers may have been secondary to organizing publicity to revive the IWW and harangue Starbucks. The publicity push, at least, was successful. A small IWW protest at the Dupont Circle store in D.C. yielded a very large article in the *Washington Post*, only two days after a *New York Times* headline proclaimed, "Latte Laborers Take on a Latte-Liberal Business." The organizers knew what Howard Schultz both loves and fears: use the Starbucks name, and the media come running; trash the Starbucks name, and press coverage is assured.

Daniel Gross possesses kinetic energy, a wiry frame, and an endearingly lopsided smile; and sitting across from him at a greasy spoon in the East Village in 2004, it was hard not to shout, "Amen!" He reminded me of myself when I was young. Furthermore, in an era of complacency and ambitious self-involvement, I tend to prefer any kind of social justice activism to none. Regarding Starbucks, he told me, "They're very successful at perpetuating an image of having a decent workplace. But it quickly became apparent that wasn't the case. We were living in grinding poverty. Furthermore, the workplace is unsafe. . . . The shop is designed with no ergonomics in mind, so it's no surprise that repetitive stress injuries are endemic." He pointed out that stores really have no full-time baristas: "You might work twenty hours one week, eighteen the next, thirty-two the next—there's no guarantee." If you earn under eight dollars an hour, he wondered, how can you afford health care that costs forty-eight dollars a month?

At the time of our interview, unionized home health care workers in New York had only recently succeeded in raising their wages past seven dollars an hour, and Alec and I were paying 640 dollars a month for health care. Perhaps, I ventured, Starbucks wasn't doing so badly by its workers. "The health care issue is not the biggest griev-ance," he countered. "The biggest grievance is a company where the CEO is pulling down 17 million dollars a year, the store manager is making fifty grand, our store makes a million a year, and we're taking home 180 dollars a week, less than eight hundred dollars a month."

This clearly wasn't a living wage, and Gross contended the job was grueling. "When there's half a second where you're not serving drinks, you're lifting heavy boxes," he said. "They really developed a system where they suck out your energy. You walk out of there from your shift, and you're drained. It turns out there's widespread discon-tent. We hope it will spread like wildfire."

To check out his claims, I decided to spend another day at my local Starbucks, this time on the other side of the counter, working a shift. Peak times were indeed busy, with drink orders flying, the pressure palpable. And the job is harder than you'd think. My hearing is pretty good, but I still had trouble catching all the orders. Then I had to grab the right-sized cup for the drink (paper for hot, plastic for cold) and mark down in shorthand the kind of milk ordered (whole, 2 percent, nonfat, soy, no hormones) as well as the syrup (a huge variety) and the drink type (macchiato, cappuccino, latte, Americano, tea, and, most often in summer, Frappuccino). If the order is a Frappuccino, there's shorthand for the drink's various combinations. Moreover, it's a time-consuming, pain-in-the-butt drink to make. And then there's the custom check box for various options: sugar syrup or not, whipped cream or not, and on and on. All that lovely customer choice is trouble behind the counter. It took me most of the day to get most of my orders more or less correct. And on the ergonomic end, the counter setup is not kind to short people. The stretches—to serve customers their drinks, to reach lids or Sharpie pens on top of the espresso machines—were just beyond comfortable. I couldn't really see the top shelf of the pastry case, and my effort to remove a piece of lemon pound cake with tongs resulted in a mangled mess.

Like all the baristas, in between serving drinks, I hauled ice from the back to refill the trough at the drink station, replaced the toilet paper in the restroom, emptied trash in the sidewalk seating area, wiped down tables, and checked supplies at the condiment station. After close to six hours on the job, I felt like I'd done some serious work. As Gross told me, a shift at Starbucks can be fast-paced and demanding. But is it worse than a job at McDonald's or KFC? It certainly doesn't seem any more arduous than checking groceries or waiting tables or cleaning hotel rooms or taking care of children—all of them jobs that require more skill and stamina than many people think and all compensated at far less than a living wage.

The IWW made much of the fact that only 40 percent of Starbucks workers are actually covered by the company health plan, claiming that many are not permitted to work the 240 hours per quarter (the equivalent of twenty hours per week) required for eligibility or to afford the premiums. But the young woman who served me a Starbucks drink a few months later thought otherwise. She giggled when I asked about the mission statement and confessed she didn't really remember what it said. But she did know that in just a few more days she'd be eligible for health care, and she was thrilled to be getting good coverage at roughly thirty-six dollars a month. "It's part of the reason I'm here," she said. And most of the partners at the largely Ethiopian- and Somali-staffed Starbucks in Baileys Crossroads, Virginia, had also signed on, prodded by their manager, and were glad to have a way to cover themselves and their families.

The question of scheduling and hours was perhaps the most serious concern raised by the union. It wasn't clear to me how many people worked fewer hours by personal rather than company choice; but at some stores, at least, workers seemed to have problems getting reliable schedules. Yet I met many other employees who wanted to work sufficient hours for health care and were able to do so, occasionally by picking up hours at other stores; and those costs, in the real world, are modest for decent coverage.

The union's underlying question about Starbucks is endemic to the service sector as a whole: is it actually possible to choose to work full time as a barista, and does the job provide a living wage? The answer isn't promising. Starbucks considers all its baristas to be part-time, hourly employees, even if they work thirty-five hours a week or more. A barista who works the equivalent of full time, earning eight dollars an hour plus tips (about another 1,500 dollars a year), makes roughly 17,000 dollars a year. And wage increases tend to be pretty skimpy, sometimes as little as five cents an hour after six months. Unlike a waiter in a traditional Viennese or Italian café, a Starbucks barista would find it difficult to see the job as a long-term career, unless she moved up to management.

Furthermore, the model of respect promoted by the company doesn't work for everyone. Manager quality seems by far the greatest determinant in whether a store is well run and its employees relatively content. Where a good manager builds a successful team and keeps a relatively stable workforce, Starbucks employees tend to be satisfied; where a manager is seriously flawed or faces extraordinary challenges, the system can break down. In her 2006 book, *Chutes and Ladders: Navigating the Low-Wage Labor Market*, Katherine S. Newman describes one woman's experience. After spending years working in a fast-food burger joint, the woman moved to Starbucks, only to have her substantial knowledge and expertise dismissed by a much younger and inexperienced manager. I spoke with a fair number of baristas who had suffered under bad managers.

Despite these real issues, however, IWW campaign leaders seemed far more cavalier about the benefits of the job and far more hostile to the company than the average Starbucks worker. Yes, many baristas agreed that the work is demanding; and many were indifferent to the job, seeing it as a temporary way station. But others, like Tawana and Denoris at my local store, found the training useful, valued the company's promotion opportunities, acquired mentors, and picked up new skills and new confidence.

The truth is that Daniel Gross may have worked at Starbucks, but neither his livelihood nor his future depended on it. He was a law student at Fordham, with many life options available to him. Not so for other Starbucks workers I met, for whom the job was the best opportunity available. Those real class differences were vividly illustrated in the summer of 2004, when my husband Alec and I joined the demonstrators outside the Republican National Convention in New York City. Taking advantage of this influx of protesters, the IWW had staged a campaign support action, focusing in part on Gross's Thirty-Sixth Street store. The staff inside included many workers of color. The demonstrators outside, perhaps 150 or so by generous count, were almost entirely white, many sporting the characteristic demo gear of the Black Bloc anarchists who had captured so much media play in Seattle.

Gross and a colleague confronted the police and were arrested. A young woman held forth for the media. She told the reporters that she worked at an independent coffee shop in Portland, where they compensated and treated her fairly. Surely, she said, a big rich company like Starbucks could be expected to do the same. After the cameras left, I asked her where she worked. It turned out that the coffeehouse was run by the IWW; she worked there sometimes as a volunteer, sometimes for pay of roughly one hundred dollars a month. Yes, she thought the store employed "one Mexican American girl, but the rest are Anglo."

Along with company resistance, this class disjunction may account for why Gross's unionizing vision hasn't caught on among Starbucks workers across the nation. Plenty of college-aged people temporarily make a few bucks at Starbucks; and they might find the Wobblies an entertaining diversion, particularly in cities with an active IWW cell. But for many workers on Eighth Street in Washington, D.C., and in less urban areas, Starbucks, whatever its flaws, remains a cut above most other retail options. At the airy store at the Bangor Shopping Mall in Maine, the young woman who served me had first started working for Starbucks while attending college in the midwest. After the Bangor store opened, she transferred there to be closer to home. She was grateful that the company provided health care coverage for part-time workers and thought unions should be reserved for companies that treated their workers badly. At Starbucks, she said, "They treat us as though we're golden."

The Wobblies may be big on rank-and-file democracy, but many of the baristas I encountered had heard little *about* the union and even less *from* them. This isn't to say that the New York campaign was necessarily a bad thing. As Alec pointed out, at least the IWW cadre was young and cool-looking and perhaps more likely to appeal to a young Starbucks worker than might a more conventional union campaign. In other words, the IWW has become something other than a union. It's an exclusive, carefully marketed, counterculture niche brand. And it has proved to be "sticky," in the Malcolm Gladwell sense, to the fad-conscious political left, if not to most of the workers.

Yet even though the Wobbly message is mixed and in some ways misguided, nothing excuses Starbucks' response. During the New York campaign, there was ample indication that the company was doing everything it could to deter employees from joining the union—in ways that violated at least the spirit of the law and probably the letter as well. When my brother tried to talk with store workers and customers about the IWW effort, two Starbucks regional manager types politely but firmly stopped him. In New York and D.C., employees I tried to interview about the matter frequently exhibited anxiety, even fear, about losing their jobs. They had reason to worry: Starbucks had fired several organizers under dubious circumstances. I can't swear that the activists didn't provoke their own firings (good for the brand); but even if they did, Starbucks fell into the trap and behaved as anti-union companies are expected to behave. Its actions prompted a slew of unfair labor practice charges, requiring both monetary settlements and damage control.

The organizing efforts at Starbucks exposed not just the flaws of the company but those of the labor movement as well. Unions haven't made much headway in organizing at either punitive companies like Wal-Mart or nominally more enlightened companies like Starbucks. Thea Lee at the AFL-CIO told me, "I don't know how much it's culture, how much it's bad labor law, how much it's attitudes that make it challenging to organize in sectors where we are not strong." In any case, the challenges aren't going away. As of 2006, union membership was down to just 12 percent overall and only 7.4 percent in the private sector.

Whatever organized labor is doing, it either isn't enough or it just isn't working, and Andy Stern, president of the Service Employees International Union (SEIU), is determined to change that. You might say he wants to do for labor what Howard Schultz has done for coffee—turn it into a respected brand, market it, and popularize it throughout the country to change the status quo in his field of influence.

Like Schultz, Stern is physically fit and tightly wound. His hair was a lot longer back in the early 1970s, when we were both starting out at SEIU Local 668, which represented the newly organized Pennsylvania state social service workers. But he already had the charisma, tactical savvy, and streak of get-out-of-the-way determination that would mark his progress; and he was already building the cadre of colleagues with whom he would forge the path to union leadership. In recent years, he tempers the warmth of his welcome with a sense of watchfulness; and he often looks as if it takes an effort to smile.

In 1983, the same year that Howard Schultz went to Milan and discovered café culture, Stern became SEIU national organizing director; and he was elected international union president in the mid-nineties. Over the next decade, he elevated SEIU's performance and profile as the premier growth and innovation center in the labor movement; he also became increasingly frustrated with the AFL-CIO's resistance to significant change in the face of defeat and decimation. In 2005, SEIU, representing 1.8 million workers in health care, building service, and public employment, bolted from the AFL-CIO, joining with six other unions to form Change to Win, a new labor federation determined to organize members in the growing service sector in order to staunch the hemorrhaging of labor power. "We are walking down a road, and the mileposts are clear," Stern told reporters. "Our world has changed. Our economy has changed. Employers have changed . . . but the AFL-CIO is not willing to make fundamental change. When you're heading down a road and you know where it ends . . . you have to get off that road and go in a different direction where there is hope."

Eager to counter labor's steep decline and intellectual torpor, Stern and his team had rounded up all of labor's sacred cows, including collective bargaining and employer-based benefits, and examined them for hoof-and-mouth disease. "We have a model that doesn't match up very well to the economy," he told me. "Unions developed these very complicated sets of agreements with very complicated rules. I don't think workers at Starbucks or other places are looking to be as rule-driven. We need to deal, not so much with the minutia, but with the big issues: people who want opportunities, who need health care, who are more mobile, whether they want to be or not."

Stern advocated an experimental approach toward employer collaboration to tackle the realities of the global economy and the changing expectations of workers who "now see job switching as the best way for them to learn new skills and get promotions and raises." His nine principles for effective twenty-first century unions, detailed in his promotional book, *A Country That Works*, emphasized that both employers and employees (and their organizations) have to focus on resolving problems, based on the assumption that "all parties want a mutually beneficial relationship based on teamwork."

That line of reasoning, combined with Stern's perceived arrogance and strategic knack for media attention, has angered other unionists and more than a few leftists. Organizer and author Steve Early, who recently retired from the staff of Communications Workers of America, has complained that Stern's "conservative pronouncements—usually made in front of business audiences and dressed up as creative new thinking—don't improve with repetition or further elaboration. . . . Worker activity, community engagement, and political action that might actually change the balance of power between labor and management—all get short shrift." Central to Early's critique is that "Stern distances himself from the 'class struggle mentality' that persists in some unions today."

Stern's approach flies in the face of labor orthodoxy, which continues to frame workplace relationships in 1930s sepia, when left-leaning artists created a rich culture and industrial union organizing helped make the New Deal's social programs a reality. But seventy years later, the culture's patina masks a more conservative and traditional approach to union organizing, one that describes the globalized economy as an evil mutant yet barely nods to the modern ethos of most U.S. workers. The Wobblies offer a far-left spin on the same blunt class analysis; they just wrap it in a savvier cultural package. According to Early, Stern betrays a progressive labor legacy by avering that "rank-and-file wariness about labor-management cooperation is a counterproductive 'vestige of an earlier, rough era of industrial unions.'"

These grievances exasperate Stern. "I love the 1930s," he protests. "What's not to love? But like it or not, this isn't the 1930s. The circumstances are different, and they demand a different response." His views are reinforced by Richard B. Freeman's and Joel Rogers's 1999 survey of worker-union-management relationships, which found that most workers want greater voice and influence on the job "through a more cooperative relationship with management, as well as a more equal one." While they want joint decision making and shared power, "Employees [also] want a positive relation with management, not war."

Many unionists feel that transnational corporations have, in fact, declared war on workers, rather than vice versa, cushioning bottom lines by compacting employee compensation to the lowest global denominator. While Stern acknowledges that phenomenon, he takes a more nuanced approach to eking out a viable, mutually beneficial truce. He has, for example, asserted that health and pension benefits are no longer sustainable on an employer-by-employer basis, a system that de facto makes good U.S. employers less competitive than bad ones and U.S. corporations less competitive than those in countries with national health care systems. It's a point that Howard Schultz, whose employee health care costs rival the company's coffee costs, could easily appreciate.

While critics almost uniformly focus on Stern's suggestion that unions have an obligation to help employers remain competitive, flexible, and competent, they generally ignore his assertion that employers, in turn, have an obligation to allow their workers "a meaningful and independent voice" in their workplaces on issues of quality, training, efficiency, and fairness. Stern believes this has become ever more important in an economy dominated by equity funds that threaten both unions and companies. He explained,

> You look at a guy like Howard Schultz and you say, "Okay, you're a really good employer, but you're a corporation. When does somebody come into Starbucks and say, "Schultz was a good guy, but these 50,000 dollars for manager salaries are too high; we could do it for 45,000; and these health care costs are really getting out of control. . . ." That's what worries me: when everything is personal and not institutional. There are very few publicly owned corporations that have maintained that positive outlook on their employees over extended periods of time. What is it that institutionalizes the good practices so it's not noblesse oblige?

What complicates the problem is that workplace democracy—the most important value that unions add—is not a money-making proposition. Yet it is perhaps the foremost reason for unions to exist. For authentic worker issues to be incorporated into the debates over the global economy, not to mention the outcome, workers must have a collective presence of their own, one that transcends the individual workplace and has the potential to encompass the global marketplace. No matter how benevolent Starbucks might be, it's not going to explicitly argue on behalf of worker concerns. Some of what's good for General Motors or Starbucks, Stern might argue, also benefits employees; but some of what makes life sustainable for workers, be it living wages, or health and safety regulations, can easily be sacrificed to corporate bottom lines unless there is a countervailing demand.

Actually organizing democratic, worker-based participation is always a challenge, both structurally and culturally. Given the changes in the culture, the longstanding conventions of the labor-management relationship appear ill-suited to many of today's workers and workplaces. The average age of unionized employees is rising, and younger workers aren't rushing to expand the ranks. Frances Kunreuther, director of the Building Movement Project, has been studying generational transitions in nonprofits. She notes that younger workers are coming into the workplace with different attitudes and expectations: "They don't like strict hierarchies. They want to work in teams, and the participatory part is important. They prefer a less formal, less structured work environment, where you work with others." Furthermore, the Gen X and Gen Y cohorts are characterized by their mobility. "They expect to have many, many more jobs," Kunreuther said. "Unionizing is 'I'm going to be here a long time.' People don't expect job security; young people expect to have seven careers, not one." In addition, they abhor boredom on the job and frequently harbor dreams of self-employment or entrepreneurship.

Yet economic data suggest that employer-paid health coverage, pension contributions, and safety standards are deteriorating in direct proportion to the diminution of the labor movement and that the consequences of insecurity, like so much in our current economy, are unequally distributed. According to Swarthmore psychology professor Barry Schwartz and his colleagues, "While the upper and middle classes define freedom as choice, working-class Americans emphasize freedom from instability." Freedom of choice, then, is not an equal opportunity option. The greater your assets and education, the more you see workplace uncertainty as positive or typical rather than as a cause for anxiety. Although sociologist Richard Sennett suggests that this constant anxiety can be difficult for people at every level, those likely to be hit hardest are the people who most depend on their day-to-day employment for basic survival. Likewise, burdens fall heavier on older workers who have not grown up with the technological sensibilities of speed, mobility, and electronic relationships. For workers at the Starbucks roasting plant, for whom the job meant long-term economic sustenance, issues of stability were more critical than they were for many young baristas, who used the job as a way station to schooling or other advancement.

Despite all its deficits and deceits, the IWW has pinned two issues correctly. In a Starbucks world where both employer and employee view their relationship as temporary, union membership needs to migrate with the individual from one job to the next. Moreover, building a lively shared culture, both personal and political, is integral to forging a vision that transcends the norms of nationalism and individual self-interest.

While the IWW lacks the organization to rise above its imagined grandeur, there are some precedents in existing unions, and some experiments underway, for creating union membership even when the employer isn't organized and there is no contract in force. In the entertainment industry, as in the building trades, for example, individuals join a union based on their occupational skills and work for a range of employers who have signed a union contract. Unionized actors, musicians, and ironworkers remain members of the union, no matter whom they're working for; and employers who have signed the contract contribute to a coordinated benefits fund whenever these employees work. Building trades also have hiring halls to match union workers with union employers.

In *What Workers Want*, Rogers and Freeman lay out what they call "open source unionism," a concept that's acquired both its name and, in some ways, its ethos from the world of computers. Rogers and Freeman suggest a union open to all who want to improve working conditions and job opportunities. Rather than relying on a common employer as a worker bond and on a contract as a union bond, they envision a community of workers united by shared concerns and cyberspace, augmented by in-person gatherings and work-related services (such as grievance handling and job counseling). The Communications Workers of America has experimented with variations of this model to organize workers in the high-tech sector and has a company-wide model for IBM employees; and the National Writers Union, which represents freelance writers (and to which I belong), operates in a similar manner.

One of the most interesting efforts, Working America, was initiated in 2003 by the normally staid AFL-CIO to create a collective presence for workers who do not have union representation on the job. Door-to-door neighborhood canvasses were wildly successful. By 2007, the effort had drawn more than 1.5 million members by offering information and advice on workplace issues and providing opportunities to weigh in on health care and other concerns.

Karen Nussbaum, Working America's executive director, explained: "We found that workers wanted good jobs and a just economy and figured out a way they could unite to fight for it in their communities, with an emphasis on communications rather than servicing. Two out of three people we talk to—working-class moderates and conservatives—join. They take action and support progressive economic populism. Unions in the future need to build what works, not just what is."

Developing a culture that encourages collective action and expands progressive values beyond Lou Dobbs nationalism may prove the greater challenge. Paul Garver, a colleague who spent more than fifteen years in Geneva with the international union federation that includes food and hospitality workers, thinks Americans are generally inept in this regard. "We tend to have a view of the world that is typified by the old New Yorker map of how Manhattanites see the world," he noted. Garver sees greater promise in a broader view, citing a German trade union colleague who claimed great success in recruiting young industrial workers at a Mars confectionery plant by appealing to their solidarity with the developing world rather than addressing their immediate interests as German workers. According to Garver

> Mars has long been an innovator in treating its employees as associates, paying relatively high wages and benefits, and insisting that its managers forego all obvious signs of privilege, like separate dining rooms or assigned parking spaces. American and British unions have never come close to organizing Mars factories with traditional approaches, while the German and Dutch unions using a socially conscious approach were able to make some headway. I have long wondered if merely "bread-and-butter" unionism has any chance of survival in workplaces where the employer presents even the facade of taking workers seriously and provides better than average conditions.

National Labor College president Sue Schurman suggests that union culture tends to be a byproduct of other aspects of organizational behavior rather than a discrete effort. "In the area of corporate human resources, there's often an attempt to build a 'culture of commitment,' to create shared values, beliefs, norms, and rules that promote both effective performance and satisfaction," she said. "There is an argument that satisfaction derives from high performance rather than the reverse, which is the more traditional argument."

Unions, Schurman thinks, have been slow to understand the "roses" part of "bread and roses." "Labor was very slow to recognize that the quality of work life movement, and the striving for quality itself, really appeal to workers' desires for direct individual and group influence in the day-to-day life of the workplace." Starbucks, she observes, "seems to have built a culture of performance and personal responsibility. A union that wishes to organize them will have to demonstrate that they can add some value without destroying the existing values. I know of few unions, at present, equipped to meet the challenge."

Paul Garver envisions a culture where the personal and interpersonal values that Starbucks espouses meet the collective demand for human dignity that is the best of unionism. "We need to look at the global population in some balanced way," he reflected. "What we have is a situation where a disgracefully large number of people live in abject poverty and deprivation, suffering violations of their essential rights and dignity. Unions tend to organize people who are already a little bit better off, but what do we organize them around?" The key, he thinks, is to fight violations of human rights wherever they occur.

> It's not whether someone in the U.S. makes twenty dollars an hour while someone in a developing country makes two. If a child doesn't learn to read, or dies because of lack of clean water, or is denied health care because they can't afford it, that should be absolutely unacceptable. We need to work toward a culture where you are as sensitive to those far away whom you do not know as you are to the person working next to you. It's the job of people who know something abut these issues to reach others with the message in a way that makes sense and moves people. Unions that matter in the global economy have to be in the forefront of that struggle.

This is a new way for unions to talk with each other and with their members and a new way to challenge both corporations and government regulators. It means everyone has to do something different based on an intentionally redefined shared interest.

What do workers want? "What any of us want," thinks Joel Rogers. "A picture of the world and where we fit into it, to make some

sort of contribution, and a tiny bit of love, forgiveness, solidarity."
Again, I consider the Starbucks appreciation cards—their thoughtful
design, their appeal not to outrage but to interpersonal values, their
acknowledgment of the psychic need for recognition and approval.
But neither the AFL-CIO nor Change to Win seems quite ready to
address these gentler needs and the values they imply. They don't
even have education departments to help develop or popularize a
shared global vision among the membership. And in the secret macho
core lurking under their more savvy exteriors, they still believe that
culture is merely auxiliary to the task rather than part of the task
itself. Starbucks, it seems, knows better.

But there's at least one part of the new culture that labor has
already adopted. Walk into the new wing of the National Labor
College in Maryland and you'll find it, the quintessential coffee
bar . . . with one important difference. Workers have a union contract.
You might call it the marriage of Starbucks culture and union
consciousness. They call the shop Union Perks.

8 | At the Global Crossroads

Tadesse Meskela, general manager of the Oromia Coffee Farmers Cooperative Union in Ethiopia, an organization of 115 cooperatives representing more than 102,000 coffee growers, apparently had mixed feelings about Starbucks. In an interview transcript from a June 2006 Starbucks meeting on African coffees, he spoke warmly about the company's role in advancing the well-being of Ethiopian coffee farmers: "This year we sold more coffee to Starbucks and they paid us a very good price, which is better than Fair Trade price. So we want this type of pricing for our coffees to improve the lives of coffee growers."

Yet there he was in *Black Gold*, a documentary released that year to wide acclaim. Filmed between 2003 and 2005, it followed Tadesse's valiant struggle to increase the income that Ethiopian coffee farmers realize from their crops. It also featured Starbucks as villain, implying that the company made its millions off the backs of poor farmers.

For a while, Dub Hay, Starbucks' senior vice president for coffee purchasing, wondered if Tadesse had been unaware that the film was going to portray Starbucks as a bad guy. After all, the company had been involved with Ethiopia for more than thirty years, even before the arrival of Howard Schultz, and had been buying coffee from the Oromia Farmers Union since 2003. But Dub hoped in vain. Tadesse was in fact a man on a mission; and in the fall of 2006, he emerged as a key spokesperson for the Ethiopian government and for the international anti-poverty NGO Oxfam. Their prime demand was that Starbucks recognize Ethiopia's right to trademark the names of its gourmet coffee regions. "Coffee shops can sell Sidamo and Harar coffees for up to $26 a pound because of the beans' specialty status," Tadesse said in an Oxfam press release. "But Ethiopian coffee farmers only earn between sixty cents to $1.10 for their crop, barely enough to cover the cost of production. I think most people would see that as an injustice."

If Starbucks felt betrayed by the two faces of Tadesse, Tadesse felt betrayed by the two faces of Starbucks. Yes, it pays better than fair trade prices and is arguably the most ethical major coffee company in the world. But it also uses its reputation to avoid sharing real power.

The conflict over Ethiopia's right to trademark its coffee lasted for roughly two years and involved three continents, a slew of public demonstrations, and a steady stream of media reports. The themes echoed those that had ignited the 1999 Battle of Seattle: economic relations between the global south and the global north and the role of corporations in translating capitalism for performance on the world stage. While flat-worlders like *New York Times* columnist and author Thomas Friedman enthused over the opportunities, not to mention the inevitabilities, of globalization, detractors saw it as a new version of imperialism, a way for the north to munch up both material and cultural assets. "Do we really need a Starbucks on every corner of every city in the world?" asked political theorist Benjamin Barber in the *Philanthropy News Digest*. "That's not economic competition; that's cultural monopoly, and it ends up destroying local cultures." Even Friedman acknowledged that, without some push back, the "electronic herd" of global finance will turn indigenous culture "into a global mush, and their environment into a global mash."

By 2006 Starbucks was certainly a global player. Though Schultz originally conceived of the company as a vehicle to import coffeehouse culture to the United States, he soon discovered he could export his own version back to Europe and to anywhere else in the world that seemed ready for the Starbucks coffee experience. As he told his shareholders at the 2006 annual meeting, "In 1996, we began to dream we could be an international business"; and that same year the company opened its first overseas store, in Tokyo. By 1999 Starbucks was solidifying its presence in Britain and aiming to have five hundred European stores by the end of 2003. By early 2006,

Starbucks had more than 3,000 company-owned and licensed stores outside the United States in thirty-seven countries. Its feet were firmly planted in China, its toes testing the market in Brazil, its eyes turned toward India. To Starbucks, this behavior was in no way predatory. The company was merely sharing the delight of Starbucks at an international level and, of course, increasing the bottom line.

There were difficulties, of course. In China, state news anchor Rui Cheggang took aim at a Starbucks store lodged in a corner of the imperial palace of the Forbidden City, calling it "a symbol of low-end U.S. food culture" and "an insult to Chinese civilization" and generating a torrent of response that pitted cultural nationalism against imperialism in round after round of heated blogging. And sometimes the war of words concerned real wars. One set of bloggers castigated Schultz as a Zionist and accused Starbucks of anti-Arab bias, while others condemned Starbucks for closing its Israeli outlets. In fact, Starbucks had closed its stores in Israel because of poor management and performance, while maintaining numerous stores in Arab countries; and Schultz, in real life, appeared to favor a two-state solution. In 2006, when fighting in Lebanon temporarily shut down the Beirut Starbucks, the company continued to pay staff wages and benefits throughout the conflict.

Starbucks' global expansion generated its share of satire as well as ire. "Starbucks to occupy Lebanon," proclaimed humorist Andy Borowitz on his popular website. "Frustrated in her attempts to assemble an international peacekeeping force to serve as a buffer between Israel and Lebanon, Secretary of State Condoleezza Rice said today that she had received a firm commitment from the coffee chain Starbucks to serve as peacekeepers in the war-torn border region. . . . 'We believe that Starbucks will bring peace, and failing that, lattes, to the fledgling democratic state of Lebanon,' Dr. Rice said."

The issue wasn't just about the politics and culture of real estate. Lara Wyss, one of my first guides from the Starbucks public relations department, had become public relations manager for Global CPG. (The abbreviation stands for "Consumer Packaged Goods.") Her job was to help translate Starbucks products into other cultures. In China, she told me, there are red bean Frappuccinos, which aren't sold here. On the other hand, the green tea Frappuccinos that originated in Taiwan and China have migrated back to the United States, as has the very popular strawberries and cream Frap that got its start in the U.K. Catering to the Asian passion for canned coffee beverages,

Starbucks has marketed the "chilled cup" in Taiwan and Japan; Lara described it to me as "a little milky and not as sweet as for the U.S. market." And she was bemused by the complications of translating the qualities of *qandi* (caramel) for the Japanese market: "We wanted to convey the taste of buttery, but there's no word for it. The word that was in the Japanese copy translated literally as flowery, which didn't seem right, but a Japanese-speaking staffer said the word did indeed convey a sense of richness, so we went with it." The process was an intriguing cross-cultural puzzle with the goal of bringing a world of tastes into harmony.

"What we have created is not American, and not Western," Schultz reported in 2006. "It has universal appeal." He described his visit to a store in Amman, Jordan, which he was convinced would be empty. But it was as packed as a Seattle store. "It's so busy, kinetic, I hear different languages, people are dressed differently, different religion, different politics; but the human condition is the same," he said. "The Starbucks experience cuts through all of that. We all want the same thing."

Eighteen months later, my friend Cathy Howell, on a trade union trip to Jordan, checked out several Starbucks stores in Amman, sending back photos and sugar packets with the mermaid logo printed above elegant Arabic script. Starbucks was indeed popular, she reported, and the jobs there were considered desirable, a place where young locals could mingle with international visitors and practice their English.

Starbucks stores often bridge American and host country cultures. For instance, take the bustling store in the Ebisu section of Tokyo. The staff, while not exactly bilingual, easily understands "tall cappuccino, two shots of espresso" stated in American English. The store is neat to a fault, the foam perfect, and the help deferentially polite. The vast majority of customers are Japanese, despite the fact that espresso is cheaper at the omnipresent, locally owned Doutor chain. Starbucks has more than 650 stores in Japan but trails Doutor, which has more than 1,400 directly owned and franchised stores—including its Starbucks look-alike spin-offs known as Excelsior. Both locals and foreigners are drawn to Starbucks, not just for the coffee but because it is one of the rare non-smoking oases in this nation of smokers.

Halfway around the world, there's a two-story Starbucks in the gentrified Hackesche Höfe complex in the former East Berlin. The store draws a young crowd even though it's non-smoking. "They let us sit here as long as we want," said one young woman studying with a group of friends, "and the furniture is very comfortable. I wish we could smoke, though." It's hard to say whether a thriving Starbucks at the former Marx-Engels-Platz is a poke in the eye of prostrate socialism; but the baristas I spoke with seemed to find it an acceptable form of capitalism, one that pays a little better than the locally owned coffee shops. A manager said that many young people want to work at Starbucks precisely because it's a multinational corporation: "A lot of them work here because they want to travel and think they might be able to get jobs at Starbucks in other countries."

Despite some huffing in the French press about the sanctity of domestic café culture, Starbucks quickly found a clientele, even in preservationist and Francophile Paris. The capital is strewn with multinational retail and food outlets, and Starbucks is hardly the most intrusive. The small store near Montparnasse station is usually jammed and frenetic, but people still choose to come. As Stéphanie, a local customer, told me in flawless English, "French people come here because it's international, and unlike a French café, you don't have some waiter asking you to buy another coffee or get out." How's that for switching stereotypes?

This new internationalism animates Starbucks and surrounds it. In an ordinary *kaffeehaus* on Berlin's Kurfürstendamm, Alec and I met Christina. She was blonde and lively and spoke English with a southern accent, but she wasn't American. "I'm Polish," she told us, "but I've been working in Berlin for years." And the accent? "Oh," she said, "my boyfriend's from North Carolina. He owns a sports bar down the street. I've driven all over America, and we'll move there some day."

Christina is part of a growing, mobile, multinational class of people—mostly, but by no means solely, young and middle-class—who can be seen in Starbucks and its competitors around the world. A visitor to Greece once commented that it seemed to be a country where half the people waited table on the other half. Among this new young class, half the people drink coffee in Starbucks and the other half work there, trading roles as needed or desired. Takeshi Natsuno, a young Japanese telecommunications entrepreneur, told a reporter for the *International Herald Tribune*, "Cultural differences are smaller than the generation difference. In Japan, young people are crazy about sending e-mails . . . downloading ring tones and music, or enjoying a game—same as young French people. The generation gap is much, much bigger than the country gap." What Starbucks has recognized, and is fostering, is a worldwide class of people with a lingua franca that could be called Commercio-American but might also be called Starbuckian.

Few people today have even heard of the hybrid language Esperanto, invented in the late nineteenth century by Russian Jew Ludvic Zamenhof, who saw a common language as a means to reduce ethnic conflicts in Eastern Europe. Forced to use a pseudonym to avoid the czar's censors, he called himself Doktor Esperanto, or Doctor Hopeful. The language was adopted by adventurous souls on the political left as a means of internationalizing their struggle. After all, Marx had told the workers of the world to unite, and a few generations of intellectuals actually believed that they could, envisioning cross-border solidarity, an amalgamation of cultures, and a shared language of communication.

Yet nowadays, the engines of these transformations are far more likely to be corporate than communal; and the left is as likely to oppose the smudging of economic and cultural borders as to welcome it. In his recent work on cosmopolitanism, philosopher Kwame Anthony Appiah argues against purity, tribalism, and cultural protectionism, suggesting that "cultures are made of continuities and changes, and the identity of a society can survive through these changes. Societies without change aren't authentic; they're just dead." He observes that if poor people can't afford to live in traditional ways that they treasure, that's a problem. "But if they get richer, and they still run around in T-shirts, that's their choice." In this case, talk of authenticity "just amounts to telling other people what they ought to value in their own traditions."

Among my own colleagues, though, even the treasured American notion of the melting pot had become an object of disparagement; there was a near-paranoid desire to preserve and defend each distinctive ethnicity from subjugation to the dominant society, although the permeability of culture continued to assert itself jubilantly in language, food, and family arrangements. "Is it globalization or internationalism?" queried a colleague, cutting cleanly through the paradox. But how could we tell them apart?

Internationalism, like Esperanto or the best of the melting pot, can be defined as a blend to create a new hybrid. Globalization, on the other hand, is a powerful entity subordinating less powerful ones.

By 2006, the world's lingua franca had become not inclusive Esperanto, a new language born out of many, to be equally learned by all, but American English. For many the language symbolized domination based on power; it implied winners and losers, arrogance versus indignity. Starbucks may have aspired to be an internationalist, but it had the footprint of a global giant. This is why the Ethiopian trademark issue metamorphosed from a strategic disagreement into an ideological confrontation.

Ethiopia is blisteringly poor country, ranked at 170 out of 177 countries in the 2005 United Nations Development Program Human Development Report. More than 25 percent of its people survive on less than a dollar a day; the average per-capita gross domestic product is less than 1,000 dollars. Although the country produces barely 6 percent of the world's coffee, more than 1.5 million smallholders grow the crop, which sustains 15 million people and accounts for 40 to 60 percent of the country's total exports. A significant percentage of the crop (estimates vary widely, depending on whom you ask, from a low of 15 percent to a high of 45 percent) is specialty coffee from the Harar, Sidamo, and Yirgacheffe regions, all prized for their quality and unique flavor.

In 2006 Starbucks purchased fewer than 10 million pounds of coffee from those regions, the equivalent of 2 to 3 percent of the company's worldwide coffee purchases and a relatively small percentage of Ethiopia's total coffee exports. Most of the nation's coffee ends up on the arabica commodities market, where world overproduction has kept prices low. Moreover, because the country has no port, coffee must travel 1,000 miles to be shipped from Djibouti on the Gulf of Aden. In short, low prices and high marketing costs, combined with an outdated coffee auction system and a weak infrastructure, mean that most small coffee farmers stay poor.

To combat this destitution, the Ethiopian government decided in early 2005 to pursue an innovative strategy: it wanted to trademark, or brand, the names *Harar/Harrar*, *Sidamo*, and *Yirgacheffe* to command a greater share of the prices that its best coffees fetched at the retail end in the global north. With trademarks, the country could charge distributors a licensing fee for their use. The European Union, Japan, and Canada all approved this trademark scheme. But when the Ethiopian Intellectual Property Office approached the U.S. Patent and Trademark Office to register Sidamo, they were surprised to discover that something called Shirkina Sun-Dried Sidamo was already in the pipeline. Starbucks had gotten there ahead of Ethiopia, and the patent office refused to consider another trademark that included Sidamo.

Trouble began when the Ethiopian government tried to contact Starbucks to resolve the matter. Yet the origins of the conflict were innocent enough. In 2002, Starbucks had approached the Fero Farmers Cooperative in Ethiopia and asked members to experiment with a different way of processing their coffee. Dub Hay explained, "We took the cherry, did not ferment or process it, just put it on drying beds and let it dry in the sun. There's mucilage around the seeds, and when you don't wash that off and allow it to sit, some of that flavor and the sugars are absorbed in the bean. It's more bold, more up front—not as crisp, clean, or lemony, but you get all these wild flavors."

It wasn't an instant success. "We had to convince the farmer co-op it would be a good experiment, and the first year we did it, it was a complete disaster," Hay recalled. "The coffee was undrinkable. We didn't have all perfectly ripe berries, so some of the flavors were bad. We paid them for the 40,000 pounds of coffee and threw it away. But we convinced them to try again using only perfectly ripe beans, and we got this unique flavor; I'd never tasted anything like it. We asked the co-op to help us name it and called it Shirkina Sun-dried Sidamo, *Shirkina* meaning 'partnership' in the local language. It became a Black Apron special and was a huge partner and customer favorite." At this point Starbucks applied to the U.S. Patent Office for the right to trademark Shirkina Sun-Dried Sidamo.

Most of us are generally familiar with the notion of copyrighting original literary and artistic work, patenting inventions, and trademarking brand names and logos. According to the Patent Office, "A trademark includes any word, name, symbol, or device, or any combination, used, or intended to be used, in commerce to identify and distinguish the goods of one manufacturer or seller from goods manufactured or sold by others, and to indicate the source of the goods. In short, a trademark is a brand name." But as a new era of global trade has developed under the jurisdiction of the World Trade Organization, a new raft of intellectual property laws has also emerged. Known as Trade Related Aspects of International Property (TRIPs), they were passed in 1995 to prevent entities (mostly in developing nations) from stealing or misusing corporations' intellectual property. TRIPs place the burdens and costs of enforcement on the poorer countries. Yet its proponents argued that strict adherence would encourage affluent nations to lavish their poor cousins with new business ventures and inventions to address problems of hunger and health.

Not surprisingly, however, the results are hardly salubrious. In addition to normal corporate battles to protect brand and lucre, there have also been breathtakingly venal moves to assert dominion over various kinds of property. Most notorious have been the efforts of big pharmaceutical companies to protect drug patents against the development of cheaper generics to treat HIV/AIDS and cancer. Although the TRIPs had originally included a few safeguards so that developing nations could produce generics, companies such as Novartis and Pfizer have lobbied to weaken even these modest protections. They argue that the monetary rewards promised by intellectual property are necessary to encourage scientific innovation. India, which rejected the patent for a cancer drug because a similar generic was available at one-tenth the cost, has been sued by Novartis to capitulate.

The story is similar in agriculture, where Monsanto has become a monster, harvesting seeds for subsistence crops such as maize, rice, and cotton from developing countries and then subjecting those seeds to genetic engineering. The new seeds, ostensibly engineered to withstand disease and produce higher yields, are then resold to the very same countries. The genetically engineered strains supplant heritage varieties and are often bred to germinate for one year only, forcing farmers to buy new seeds every year rather than save part of the crop for replanting. In other cases, farmers in the origin countries are prohibited by law from creating their own supply. Thus, Monsanto both wipes out native species and forces poorer nations into greater dependence and poverty.

Starbucks' invocation of intellectual property laws has been less disastrous, but it's often been silly. A number of conflicts have arisen over store names deemed too similar to Starbucks' own. Targets have included tiny Sambucks in Astoria, Oregon; HaidaBucks on Queen Charlotte Island in Canada; and Starstrucks in India. This seems rather like the lord of the manor pursuing poachers: both predatory and petty. But Starbucks also protects particular blends or products. You would, for example, be unwise to market Gazebo blend coffee or a Frappuccino. Thus, the Ethiopian situation was a notable reversal in the pattern. When the company tried to brand its new method of processing Sidamo beans, it was accused not of overzealous trademark enforcement but of stealing Ethiopia's birthright.

Ron Layton, an attorney from New Zealand, has developed and promoted intriguing ideas on the use of intellectual property as a tool for development in the global south and started a company called Light Years IP to advance the work. In a 2004 World Bank publication titled *Poor People's Knowledge*, he argues that intellectual property provides more profit than manufacturing and agriculture do: "The IP laws, although somewhat disadvantageous to developing countries, are available for enforcement in the developed markets. Fair trade interventions offer the needed model for market access and delivery systems that ensure that revenues from IP exports do alleviate poverty."

In *The Coffee Paradox*, authors Daviron and Ponte note that specialty coffee commands high retail prices not because of its tangible qualities but because of the symbolic qualities of the brand or experience. Ironically, they find, the higher the quality of the coffee, the lower the percentage of its retail price that goes to farmers. So long as farmers in producing countries sell commodities and distributors in consuming countries sell brands, the suppliers at the beginning of the chain will suffer increasing income disparity; they can only change the equation by capturing some of that intangible value for the countries of origin.

"It's not really value-added," Ron Layton corrected me when I used the term. "I call it 'value inherent.' We are shifting away from competing as a commodity to the inherent value of the coffee. If you have a shirt by a major designer and an identical one from an unknown, what makes you pay two hundred dollars for one and not the other? It's the brand, the nonphysical enhancement. . . . So we realized there's a big intangible value to this coffee that they're not getting a share of, and how do we get hold of that?"

Ethiopian coffee was a test of the intellectual property approach: the names of the indigenous coffees were already somewhat familiar in the developed world, and fair trade models were already in play. Layton and his firm assisted the newly formed Ethiopian Intellectual Property Office and its director Getachew Mengistie to formulate a plan that led them to the U.S. Patent Office, to Starbucks' Shirkina Sun-Dried Sidamo, and to the company's wall of silence.

No one at Starbucks is willing to say how this happened, but unfortunately for all concerned the original correspondence from the Ethiopian embassy was routed to an intellectual property attorney in the Starbucks legal department and was ignored by anyone whose viewpoint might have transcended legal considerations. Beginning in March 2005, K. E. Kassahum Ayele, a former Ethiopian ambassador to the United States, tried to meet with Howard Schultz to resolve the issue of the Shirkina application. He received only a curt response from a company attorney and an invitation to a dinner honoring Schultz. A press release from the Ethiopian embassy quoted Ayele as saying, "I asked to engage in substantive discussion with Mr. Schultz on the issues, not to have a debate with a lawyer and attend award ceremonies. I expected reasonable consideration and friendly dialogue, but was shocked at Starbucks' refusal to meet and to discuss the situation."

Then Oxfam stepped onto the scene. The U.K.-based nonprofit describes itself as a "development, relief, and campaigning organization that works with others to find lasting solutions to poverty and suffering around the world." With the millennium coffee crisis, Oxfam's "Make Trade Fair" campaign focused on the plight of coffee growers.

In the past, Starbucks and Oxfam had been wary partners in several small projects. For instance, they had collaborated to help a small Mexican farmers' cooperative improve the quality of its fair trade coffee; and in 2004 Starbucks U.K. had contributed 179,000 dollars to a jointly sponsored rural development effort that included irrigation and women's literacy programs in Ethiopia's East Hararge region. To avoid the appearance and prevent the reality of selling out, each party reserved the right to criticize the other. At the time of the East Hararge effort, Phil Bloomer of Oxfam U.K. told the *Financial Times*, "We want to maintain a constructive and critical relationship with Starbucks. We hope they'll challenge us, and we know we'll continue to challenge them."

When the Ethiopian trademark became an issue, the moment of challenge arrived. Seth Petchers, head of Oxfam America's coffee campaign, knew one of Ron Layton's Light Years staff members and had been following the new strategy with interest. "In the spring of 2005," he told me, "I got a call from Light Years and the Ethiopian government, expressing frustration about not being able to get in touch with Starbucks. Since we knew about coffee and had a relationship with the company, we got involved."

Oxfam and Starbucks tell somewhat conflicting stories about communications during the eighteen months between Ethiopia's first effort to talk with the company and Oxfam's public campaign to change the company's mind. It rapidly became apparent, however, that the issue involved more than miscommunication. Starbucks did not want to sign a licensing agreement. "It's not a good solution, and the details are unacceptable," Dub Hay protested to me early in the conflict. "We'd have to consult with them about how we package and market our coffee. It's just not tenable. And there's no guarantee that the fees would ever reach the farmers. It's not good for them either."

The company expressed agreement with the underlying goal of getting more money to the Ethiopian farmers but advocated instead a geographic certification, or appellation—something comparable to the name protections granted to Wisconsin cheddar and French champagne. Certification would allow Ethiopia to protect the product's good name and authenticity. Yet as its advocates pointed out, the appellation approach relies on market demand to set higher prices rather than paying direct fees for use of a name.

According to Oxfam, both the farmers' welfare and Starbucks' own reputation were indisputable arguments for signing the licensing agreement. By obstructing the trademark filing, the company was depriving Ethiopia of critical additional revenues, a figure that advocates estimated at 88 million dollars—roughly eighty cents more per pound of coffee. There were also behind-the-scenes discussions at the Specialty Coffee Association of America (SCAA) and the National Coffee Association (NCA); and reports of those discussions slipped into advocates' hands and into cyberspace, alleging that Starbucks was obstructing the trademark filings while publicly denying any such role.

Yet there's ample evidence that many association members agreed that licensing was a bad idea. "Ethiopia got some very poor advice from both the marketing and legal standpoint" was the personal assessment of Ted Lingle, former director of SCAA. "No one wants to beat up on the Ethiopian farmer; there's no PR value that comes out of that. But the specialty market doesn't really need Ethiopian coffees." He noted that, out of 3 or 4 million bags of coffee from Ethiopia, perhaps half a million are high-end coffees. "The world has otherwise thought of them as a Brazil substitute, a commercial supply. Their market reputation really isn't much, and now they feel they can inflate what little they have. The market is not going to support it. The effort is misguided and doomed to fail."

Progressive roaster Paul Katzeff was equally blunt. "I think it is a good discussion to have but a bad idea to move forward," he said.

"The market forces will overwhelm this idea, or the idea will destroy the Ethiopian coffee industry. The Ethiopians get some of the highest prices for their coffee. I pay two dollars a pound and have for a decade. The problem," he added, "is that the farmers don't see the money. It gets stolen before it gets to them. They should clean up their corruption. That would be putting the blame where it belongs."

Nonetheless, in 2006, Oxfam and Light Years convened a cadre of progressive advocates, including Co-op America and Catholic Relief Services; they envisioned a "big noise" strategy waged with street demonstrations, letter-writing campaigns, and a heated Internet presence to pressure Starbucks into an agreement. These factors alone would have been enough to create a collision course. But Starbucks was about to be hit from another quarter as well. In 2003, two young British filmmakers, Marc and Nick Francis, decided to make a documentary on how the poverty crisis in Ethiopia was intersecting with the coffee industry. Nick Francis told me:

> I first went to Ethiopia in 1997, and when I was there, I was thinking, "I'm in the birthplace of coffee, yet this is one of the poorest countries. How can that be?" Then in 2003, we learned that Ethiopia was facing another famine, like the one in '84 that led to the Live Aid concert. But unlike '84, even the richest coffee-growing areas were caught up in the crisis. At the same time, we were seeing more and more coffee shops everywhere, in Britain, in the U.S. There was this mushrooming coffee industry, but the people who grew it were in this absolute humanitarian emergency. We wanted to make the connection between the two, between the coffee-consuming public and the growers.

The result of their two-year odyssey was *Black Gold*, which premiered at the Sundance Film Festival on January 24, 2006, generating a buzz of its own. The documentary follows Tadesse Meskela from the Ethiopian coffee fields and the Oromia offices in Addis Ababa to the trade shows of Europe and the United States to seek a market for the beans. "We wanted to feature a protagonist from Africa who is out there doing something rather than waiting for charity and goodwill," Nick explained. For the filmmakers, Tadesse's work challenged our western notion that Africa survives solely on aid from the developed world.

By way of the farmers in the cooperative and Tadesse's efforts on their behalf, the film exposes the web of trade regulations that keep farmers in developing countries poor, even while transnational corporations in the global north prosper. Women painstakingly sort millions of beans; and viewers observe the hunger and substandard housing that accompany poverty. Juxtaposed with these images are the cosmopolitan cafés of Europe and America, the comfort of conspicuous consumption, the places of commerce where deprivation in one part of the globe is turned into the wealth of another.

And like most recent efforts to hold the coffee industry accountable for the plight of the farmers, the film can't resist featuring Starbucks as a predatory Goliath. In a scene praised by *Washington Post* film reviewer Ann Hornaday, the camera pays a call on the original Starbucks store at Seattle's Pike Place Market, where two ever-so-bubbly baristas welcome the crew. Hornaday comments, "During the film's most painful sequence, his [Tadesse's] efforts and Ethiopia's persistent, crushing famine are juxtaposed with the vapidly cheerful corp-speak of two Starbucks baristas."

Yes, the baristas are excessively perky as they purvey coffee and the Starbucks experience; yet they are also model employees, supportive of each other, efficient, and proud of their company. At the time of the filming, the young women were entertaining a tour from the Specialty Coffee Association, to which the filmmakers had attached themselves to avoid asking Starbucks or its employees for permission to film. How could these young women know that they would be featured as unwitting symbols of the harm that transnational coffee giants inflict on poor Ethiopian farmers? At the progressive screening I attended, they were also the objects of disparaging audience laughter. Great, I thought. Because these Brit filmmakers couldn't, or wouldn't, interview Howard Schultz, they're making two low-wage workers the target of their comparison.

Nick assured me this wasn't his intention: "People are laughing at what they're saying, like 'Starbucks touches people's lives all over the world,' not at who's saying it. The intention is not to mistreat them but to illuminate the issues, because they are the foot soldiers." He said that the filmmakers had spent six months trying to interview someone from Starbucks for the film, to no avail. Audrey Lincoff recalled meeting the filmmakers after a conference presentation and told me they had once asked to interview Schultz on very short notice, which he was unable to accommodate. The filmmakers claim that subsequent calls went unanswered. The final frames of the film say that the big-four coffee transnationals and Starbucks refused to comment.

When I noted that Starbucks, which buys just a small percentage of Ethiopian coffee, had been made the villain of the piece rather than Nestlé, Proctor & Gamble, Kraft, and Sara Lee, which buy exponentially more coffee, Nick suggested that my cultural bias was influencing my viewpoint. "The film isn't about Starbucks," he insisted. "They're a very tiny part. It's just that in the U.S. people look for Starbucks; it's the cultural reference point that gets illuminated. It's very much a lifestyle, and people may see it as a critique of their own lifestyle choice." Nevertheless, the film sent a far sharper message about Starbucks than it did about the companies more accountable for Ethiopia's plight. And with the conflict about trademarks mushrooming, *Black Gold* itself had struck gold: the filmmakers had received the perfect media hook for their film, and they lost no time in making it part of their publicity campaign.

Starbucks' response to the film was curiously flat-footed. At the beginning of June 2006, the company held an African Coffee Celebration, touting the continent's gourmet coffees and implicitly Starbucks' good works. Although the producers of *Black Gold* suggest this was purely an effort to counter the bad publicity generated by their film, the event had actually been planned many months earlier, and Tadesse Meskela had been invited to participate. As it turns out, Tadesse did speak at the Starbucks event, praising the company's prices and projects in Ethiopia. Then he attended the Seattle screening of *Black Gold*, where he condemned the company's perfidy. Meanwhile, although the Starbucks staff had seen the film, no one seems to have approached Tadesse to acknowledge or discuss his concerns or explore ways to blunt the mounting crisis.

There were other missed opportunities. Not only had the coffee purchasing department been working with Tadesse and his cooperative for a number of years, but Seth Petchers of Oxfam and Starbucks vice president Sue Mecklenburg had developed a working relationship during prior collaborations. Both Petchers and Mecklenburg sidestepped questions on these matters, but sources suggest that Mecklenburg had advocated a course of engagement different from the one the company actually followed and that she met internal opposition from hardliners. As a result, chances to engage the parties went begging, apparently overcome by distrust and organizational tensions about how to respond.

Faced with growing criticism and the threat of a public confrontation, Starbucks decided to back off. When the trademark for

Shirkina Sun-Dried Sidamo was approved on June 25, 2006, the company walked away from the application. "We dropped it," Dub Hay told me. "All we had wanted was to protect this coffee, the shirkina sun-dried process that we had worked on." He was aggrieved and angry. "Hurting farmers was the farthest thing from what we were trying to do. Our purchases in Ethiopia over the last four years are up 400 percent, our prices are up 40 percent. We're buying more Ethiopian coffee than we've ever bought before and paying premiums no one else has paid. So here we are, thinking we're doing absolutely the right thing helping the farmers and the co-ops, and someone's thinking that we're hurting them. It wasn't worth it. We gave it up."

But despite Starbucks' withdrawal, criticism continued. To make matters worse, Ethiopia's advocates again accused the company of pressuring the National Coffee Association to oppose the trademark filings in its stead. Starbucks and the NCA both vigorously denied this assertion, but none of the advocating groups believed them. "From my own experience of Starbucks in 2005 and nearly all of 2006," wrote Ambassador Ayele, ". . . this looks to me like a clear attempt of the company to hide behind an industry association, while Starbucks continued in its determination to prevent Ethiopia from carrying out its trademark program."

When I saw Dub Hay in mid-October 2006, he was still convinced that trademarking was a poor strategy. "Oxfam wants us to sign, and they won't listen to why we don't think it's a good idea," he lamented. At the end of that month, the story broke in the foreign press, with Oxfam in particularly strident form. "Starbucks' behavior is indefensible," Petchers inveighed to a reporter. "Starbucks works to protect and promote its own name and brand vigorously throughout the world, so how can it justify denying Ethiopia the right to do the same?" Another Oxfam spokesperson told the BBC that the company's behavior "stinks of corporate bullying."

To stave off the escalating controversy, Starbucks again offered to help Ethiopia develop and implement a geographic coffee certification, but the offer did nothing to diffuse the conflict. Oxfam New Zealand staffer Linda Broom told a reporter, "We've been lobbying from behind the scenes, but Starbucks has turned a blind eye, so now we're hoping for a public backlash."

By November, the Ethiopian government, Oxfam, and Light Years effectively mounted a coordinated effort to compel Starbucks to sign the licensing agreement. Over a period of a few months, more than

90,000 activists and consumers contacted the company to demand a change in its position. On December 16, 2006, Oxfam coordinated a day of action in the United States and abroad. Activists leafleted stores, picketed with posters picturing Ethiopian farmers, and enlisted the support of local Ethiopian communities. On a YouTube video, newly educated customers urged Starbucks to pay Ethiopian farmers more for their coffee and recognize the trademarks.

Dub Hay responded for the company with a YouTube offering of his own, sincere and low-key but wrongly impugning the legality of the trademark strategy. And according to reports, Starbucks CEO Jim Donald, meeting with Ethiopia's prime minister, Meles Zenawi, didn't seem to know the difference between a trademark and a certification. "I can't talk about the details because I don't understand them," he told a *London Times* reporter. "I'm not a trademark lawyer."

While all this may seem like nattering and ground thumping between a corporate do-gooder and a nonprofit do-gooder, the fortunes of an impoverished country were hanging in the balance. The dispute was another chapter in the centuries-old narrative between the global north and south, a tale that imbues even minor conflicts with the themes of racism and inequality. Except for a brief and brutal Italian occupation from 1936 to 1941, Ethiopia was the only country in Africa to avoid colonial rule; and its history of independence is a national source of pride and resistance. When Starbucks applied for the Shirkina Sun-Dried Sidamo trademark, many saw the move as just one more attempt to rape Africa of its resources. As Tilahun Garsamo of the Fero Farmers Cooperative told the *Wall Street Journal*, "If anyone should have the trademark, it should be us. . . . It is rude and selfish of a company to take the name of its partner."

In Ron Layton's opinion, Starbucks' behavior was reminiscent of British, French, and Israeli attempts to retake the Suez Canal after it was nationalized by Egypt. He saw it as an act of economic imperialism, although he and Oxfam conceded that the Sidamo trademark dispute was probably a misstep rather than a manifestation of evil. But Starbucks' certainty about its position, combined with its laggardly response, certainly fed the undercurrent of anti-imperial sentiment.

The Ethiopian conflict at the intersection of economics, ethics, and global culture touched questions about what constitutes free or fair trade. The WTO intellectual property rules currently protect products from the global north while ignoring those of developing nations. When commodities, whether agricultural or factory-produced, are in surplus and a sustainable return is increasingly a matter of value added through distinctive brand marketing, then it makes sense for developing nations to claim whatever brands they can. As tariffs and subsidies fall short, licensing might provide poorer countries with some control over market prices.

Moreover, it has become necessary for countries to trademark their property before entrepreneurs in other countries claim them. In 2006, for instance, a Japanese company trademarked the traditional *kiondo* dyed sisal basket design, popular as women's handbags in the United States but native to the Kikuyu and Kamba women of Kenya. At the same time, a British company tried to trademark *kikoi*, a traditional Kenyan cotton fabric. As Joyce Mulama reported for the Inter Press Service news agency, "Granting the trademark to the U.K. firm would mean that Kenyans have to request permission from the U.K. firm to market *kikoi* items despite it being a traditional cloth in Kenya. . . . This would result in losses in income and jobs. . . . The arts and crafts sector is Kenya's second-highest foreign exchange earner after agriculture and the informal sector contributes around 18 percent of the country's gross domestic product."

This is a major concern, according to Getachew Megistie of Ethiopia's Intellectual Property Office. Soft-spoken and intense, he described the dire economic circumstances that had led his country to seek new avenues for development. "We want to get to the point where we can guarantee the children of our coffee farmers one meal a day every day of the year," he told me. "The trademarking alone won't do it; we also need to improve the quality and the marketing. But if we didn't do it, we ran the risk of other countries trademarking our names. We already had a foreign company trademarking Harar in Japan."

In the end, the conflict juxtaposed two different measures of economic fairness. In Ethiopia, Starbucks paid prices substantially in excess of the New York C market commodity price. No one disputed that they were overall the best mega coffee corporation on the ground. However, the trademarking and licensing argument was based not on the commodity price but on the profits reaped on the consuming end. It was rooted not in the economics of supply and demand but in the ethics of poverty and plenty. If Starbucks paid $1.42 per pound to cooperatives and then sold it for twenty-six dollars a pound, farmers were receiving only 5 percent of the final price. If Starbucks turned that pound into fifty cups of brewed coffee sold for $1.50 each in retail stores, then the farmers' percentage dropped to less than 2 percent.

Speaking for himself, however, Ted Lingle, who now heads the Coffee Quality Institute, scoffed at that reasoning. "Roasting doesn't add value; it transforms the product," he told me. "The value the industry added was by investing in cafés that can now sell the coffee in differentiationed form. It's hard to calculate, but the 23,000 specialty coffee outlets, of which a third are Starbucks, has invested perhaps some 9.6 billion dollars. They're recapturing that investment through their pricing."

Lingle didn't see why Ethiopia was entitled to more from Starbucks, given that the company was already paying above-market prices. "The disconnect is that they pinpoint the market price in the U.S., not in Ethiopia," he said. "A third of Ethiopian coffee is actually sold for domestic consumption at whatever that real market price is." Lingle also noted, as did others I spoke to, that Ethiopia's governmentally controlled coffee system returns only a small percentage of the per-pound price to the farmers. He estimated the figure at barely 25 percent, as opposed to 95 percent in Brazil.

To trademark advocates, though, Starbucks' large profit margin versus the low return to Ethiopian farmers was like CEO compensation versus the stumbling wages of workers. Rather than merely evaluating whether the paycheck is greater than the one provided by similar corporations, progressive companies need a higher standard of equity. And by that measure, they insisted, Starbucks was not living up to its claim of virtue.

That attitude has made Starbucks feel unfairly targeted. Despite some new premium brands, the big four coffee giants have little reason to care whether or not the word *Sidamo* or *Harar* appears on a can of Folgers or a jar of Nescafé. Worldwide, Starbucks is the biggest single buyer of gourmet coffees that touts the country of origin on the bag. As Schultz told stockholders in March 2007, "The largest U.S. signer to the trademark license, so far, buys one shipping container of their coffee a year. We buy three hundred containers." But that very dominance meant that Ethiopia and Oxfam had to pursue a successful outcome with Starbucks if they wanted to implement the trademark strategy at all.

So how does Starbucks determine what it can afford, or is willing to pay, for coffee? "By talking to the growers and asking, 'What do you need to be sustainable?'" Dub Hay told me. "What do you need to give inputs to your farm, to prune, and pay pickers, in other words, keep your farm at levels where it can produce our quality and make a little profit? That's what we want them to do."

Yes, he said, there were outside influences like C market prices and general market conditions. "We put it all in the wash and say, 'What do I think is right, and does the farmer agree with that?' Remember, we spend four hundred person-days a year on coffee farms, so this isn't a phone call that happens to someone on the other end you don't know. The reason we pay substantial premiums is that we have customers who enjoy what we buy so much that they allow us the flexibility to pay better than market prices because we're selling it by the cup. It becomes a negotiation, except we're a company that doesn't try to negotiate the final penny."

Starbucks could presumably choose to pay more than it's paying, but it's not the home of "always low prices" either. Rather, the company walks a fine line between being profitable enough to please Wall Street and principled enough to please social justice advocates. Although one could argue that it's done well at achieving a viable balance, it runs the risk of satisfying neither and must constantly justify itself to both, which can be a thankless task.

Its more aggressive opponents remain convinced that Starbucks, like all corporations, is incapable of making an honest mistake. All errors are attributed to bad faith; the company's motives are berated, its missteps celebrated, and all its actions viewed through a prism of cynicism. The supercynical argue that the accuracy or inaccuracy of the particulars doesn't really matter because the company is surely bad enough to deserve the negative blast. Hence, Reverend Billy of the Church of No Shopping had no problem with saying, "You're stealing trademarks from Ethiopian coffee farmers. Starbucks is the devil."

But some progressives take a more nuanced approach. The National Labor Committee, run by Barbara Briggs and Charlie Kernaghan, was established to help protect worker and human rights in the global economy. Since 1991, the committee has focused U.S. consumers' attention on offshore clothing sweatshops, most notably exposing the Honduran sweatshops that sewed the Kathie Lee Gifford line for Wal-Mart. Briggs and Kernaghan are masters at holding corporations accountable, often through the canny use of publicity to magnify their organizing. Over the years, they've developed a sophisticated view of corporations and tactics.

Briggs acknowledges that, in choosing a public target, "the calculus includes how well-known the brand is, and how much the brand will want to protect its image. It's not so much how good or bad the company is on a theoretical level, but what we actually see on the ground." She suggests that the difference in how to proceed depends a lot on what happens once a human or workers' rights issue has been flagged. "We've found that even the best companies have some pretty lousy places," she told me. "The difference is, the good companies called us and told us what they were doing to correct the problem. We didn't hear that from Wal-Mart."

Here again was the all-important factor of responsiveness. In the Ethiopian situation, Starbucks took more than a year to engage, a delay that cost them dearly. But even consistently responsive companies are not off the hook unless their response helps rectify the problem. And as Briggs points out, the desire to address issues with openness, alacrity, and effectiveness is sometimes prompted by knowledge of the consequences of inaction. She told me:

> I see value in doing both things—negotiation and direct action—because even executives from some of the most progressive companies out there, who really do have solid departments that are doing certification and worker rights, have said to us, "We wouldn't be doing any of this if it weren't for the Kathie Lee Gifford scandals." That doesn't mean that the people working on these issues aren't very committed to human rights, and it doesn't mean the company hasn't developed a code of ethics and a responsive corporate culture. But that development came out of scandal, pressure, and there's a context of "if you don't do the right thing, then something bad can happen."

"But," she was quick to add, "I think the reverse is also true. If we were simply raising the evils of one company after another, with no flexibility and no nuanced approach about being willing to work with the company, then I think the companies wouldn't take things seriously either. I think it takes both things to be effective."

A key criterion for a confrontation and the way in which it is waged is whether it benefits the people in whose name the effort has been undertaken. Not all struggles for greater justice can be won, certainly not in the short term, but it helps to have a meaningful and achievable outcome in mind. For some radical campaigners, like the IWW, the publicity sometimes seems more important than the outcome. Ethiopia, on the other hand, needed real solutions and an agreement. "Starbucks is a valuable partner," Getachew told me. "We just want to make the relationship more meaningful. Both they and we want to stop the loss of farmers and small traders. And we want to resolve our differences amicably."

It looks like Getachew will get his wish. At the fourth African Fine Coffee Conference in Addis Ababa in February 2007, Dub Hay announced that Starbucks would not oppose Ethiopia's trademarking initiative: "It is Ethiopia's absolute right to take the course they think is best for Ethiopia and we will not oppose that." He sweetened the Starbucks response with commitments to double the amount of coffee the company buys from Africa, jumping from 6 to 12 percent of its total by 2009. He also promised a 1-million-dollar revolving microloan fund for Ethiopia and 500,000 dollars to CARE International for a literacy program in the country. And the company committed to opening a farmer support center in East Africa.

"We made a mistake," Jim Donald told me, echoing, or maybe leading, others in the company to the well. "We treated it as though it was a legal issue. But it wasn't. It was a relationship issue." Bingo. Starbucks took a bit too long to reach this conclusion, but it finally did. Although company experts still seemed to think the licensing idea was misguided, they had decided to suspend judgment and help Ethiopia's experiment move forward.

When I did my last interviews at Starbucks on April 3, 2007, Howard Schultz and Jim Donald were meeting with representatives of the Ethiopian government. A month later Starbucks agreed to negotiate a licensing agreement, and the deal was inked in late June. As has so often been the case, the conflict drew massive attention. By comparison, the resolution received little notice.

Given the trademarking scheme's experimental nature, there is no way to know if the strategy will be successful. The greatest boon to farmers might be Starbucks' commitment to buy more coffee, make more loans, and offer greater technical expertise. But at least the campaign had moved Africa's plight to the head of queue.

For a company that likes to portray itself as artfully balancing the demands of profit and principle, the Ethiopian crisis was a hard test. Starbucks didn't do a very good job of handling it, but the company survived and learned something more about its role in the world, although what and how much would have to await the next crisis. "When you sign a copy of the book for me, I'll tell you whether I think the resistance was worth all the aggravation," one Starbucks player ruefully told me. I thought I knew the answer.

But Getachew was thrilled with the outcome, and hopeful. "Once we were actually able to talk with them, we were able to start resolving the problems," he told me. "It's like me sitting here with you. We haven't met before, but we get to know each other. And next time we know each other a little better, and we grow to understand each other."

9

The View from Headquarters

Howard Schultz has a signature riff—"growing big while staying small," shorthand for expanding Starbucks' reach and brand while retaining a sense of intimacy. Easier said than done.

The tension burst into public view in February 2007, when www.starbucksgossip.com scooped a Valentine's Day memo from Schultz to his top staffers. The memo vividly expressed his fears about "the watering down of the Starbucks experience, and, what some might call the commoditization of our brand. . . . Some people even call our stores sterile, cookie cutter, no longer reflecting the passion our partners feel about our coffee."

Gasping, Wall Street and the media proceeded to parse every word. But in truth Schultz was only saying what most of his employees and many of his customers already knew: today's Starbucks is more like a chain store than a neighborhood café. Witness the Starbucks that my husband Alec frequented near his work: the staff changed constantly, the macchiato was often dreadful, and no one acknowledged that they'd ever seen him before.

On levels from the personal to the institutional, Starbucks is trying to adapt its original values and culture while expanding at warp speed. As I talked with officers and staff, both old-timers and new hires, many were struggling with both sides of the Schultz equation. At headquarters there seemed to be an accelerated reshuffling of staff as the older generation began to retire and departments were reorganized and expanded to meet the demands of a larger global enterprise. New management styles disquieted veterans; production efficiencies robbed older roasting-plant workers of their artisanship. And now Howard Schultz had publicly worried that the stores' new automated espresso machines diminished both theater and intimacy. Yet those same machines significantly sped service while reducing repetitive-motion stress injuries, and the plants' computerized roasting equipment processed millions of pounds of coffee into reliable blends to quench a thirsty empire.

In 1997, when Schultz wrote *Pour Your Heart into It*, he was already preoccupied with the conundrum of growing the company but not outgrowing its values: "The danger is that the bigger the company gets, the less personal it feels, to both partners and customers. If our competitive advantage has always been the relationship of trust we have with our partners, how can we maintain that as we grow from a company of 25,000 people to one of 50,000?" Try 150,000 in 2007, and climbing.

In the decade since Schultz published his book, there have been innumerable articles, business school case studies, and books about the Starbucks way of doing business. Many describe the principles of "surprise and delight," "make it your own," and other poetic homilies, all of which have their uses in building a culture or, depending on your level of cynicism, a cult. But when it comes to practice, the leadership tries to follow more prosaic but critical steps. They take risks on new ideas and innovations; they learn what works and what doesn't; they take care of their people; they protect the company; they reflect on their practice. And they take the long view.

These precepts led, in 1994, to the hiring of Sue Mecklenburg as Starbucks' first director of environmental affairs. Now vice president for sustainable procurement practices/supply chain operations, she's had a front-row opportunity to watch the company grow. Mecklenburg reminded me of a decorous yet stylish librarian, every hair in place and a twinkle in her eyes. Once she was the only staffer officially engaged in what is now called corporate social responsibility; now the CSR department employed twenty-five people. "The whole company was on the eighth floor," she told me. "Now we're on six or seven floors of this building. On a day-to-day basis, how you get the work done and whom you interact with is very different. But growth has been a very organic process. I liken it to the growth of a family: you increase numbers, grow older, get new experiences, but it's still a family. That connection, that culture of values, that's the reason we came here, and the reason we stay."

My research associate Stephen Wood has expertise in development and trade issues, and he assures me that all corporations are inanimate and soulless, geared to seek profit no matter how caring its founder or employees might be. Elizabethan jurist Sir Edward Coke concurred: "Corporations cannot commit treason, or be outlawed or excommunicated, for they have no souls." Nevertheless, U.S. law gives corporations the same rights as persons, although the persons who run them often escape liability for the sins of the corporations. And there's plenty of evidence that people can influence a corporation, just as they do the body politic or any other organization. By law, a public company must in certain respects prioritize the profit of its stockholders over humanitarian reform. But individuals have plenty to say about how that's done and how the balances are calibrated. In some rare cases, individuals even lead a rebellion against the norm.

Howard Schultz has frequently been portrayed as a maverick in corporate America, and Starbucks would probably be different if he were not at the helm. "He's an amazing corporate leader," said Sam Salkin, former CEO of Peet's Coffee. "He's done something very few others have done. He had a nascent idea, and built it with principles and values. And he's basically stayed true to them. For a public company it's hard to imagine it getting much better in terms of a notion of human-centered values." Still, the landscape is constantly shifting, and it's difficult to balance the needs of different constituencies. Take the Starbucks child-care center. "It was the number-one thing requested by the parents in the Starbucks employee base," Schultz related, "and we built this fantastic facility. Well, six months later, it was overrun, and there were people angry with me because we didn't build it big enough."

He was clearly frustrated as he told the story. "If I showed you an e-mail from somebody who's so angry with me because she can't get her child in, well, what can I do? We built something that's world-class, and unfortunately the population's growing. We have the same thing with people waiting for parking spots. We built a second garage. . . . I mean, it's never going to be enough."

The child-care double-bind is a complication of growing big while trying to stay small. And there are times when even Starbucks' core values are at odds, caught between growth on the one hand and cultural integrity on the other. Consider the licensed stores in airports, along the turnpike, or in myriad other venues. To the average consumer, those kiosks look like Starbucks; but in fact they are operated by third parties whose employees may or may not be treated as well as Starbucks treats its own workers. "It's not fair," declared a young worker in a store along the Pennsylvania Turnpike. "We have to do all the things that Starbucks workers have to do, but we don't get what they get."

The Pennsylvania Turnpike rest-stop concessions are run by HMS Host, now a subsidiary of the Italian company Autogrill, Benetton, which operates Italy's toll roads and roadside restaurants. Described by Leslie K. Cappetta, its executive vice president for North American business development, as a "consolidator of brands," the company employs unionized workers in some U.S. locations, including the Miami and Chicago airports. But those along the Pennsylvania Turnpike are not unionized, and pay and benefits tend to be skimpy. Pay starts at under seven dollars an hour, although workers who staff the Starbucks concession get paid more than their colleagues at Nathan's Hotdogs or TCBY. Employees have to work for several years before they get benefits, and there are no benefits for part-timers. "I have a little speech for the person who manages several of these plazas," Shari Donaldson, a composed and smiling worker, told me. "It would say, 'You need to take care of your employees so they will sell for you. At HMS you are good to customers but not to the employees, even those who've been here five, six, seven years.' "

The percentage of licensed stores has crept steadily upward—from 27 percent of U.S. stores in 2003 to 36 percent in 2006. (Including international stores, the percentage in 2006 was almost 43 percent.) With the licensed stores forming a larger part of the mix and employing workers who are treated less well than their counterparts at regular Starbucks stores, Schultz acknowledged that keeping the company values intact has become more challenging: "We can't hide behind that. If it has Starbucks' name on it, it's Starbucks." But as he explained to me, if Starbucks decides it wants to open in places with a master concessionaire (supermarkets, hospitals, some college campuses, turnpikes, airports), it really doesn't have much choice. "If we don't go there, a competitor's going to. The right decision from a commerce perspective is, we need to be in these places. So we go, and we begin a process of working with the licensee on these issues, and it is swimming upstream a lot of times. Am I happy that these people don't feel like they're being paid properly? No, I think it's wrong. But I can't control it at this point. It requires time; we need more leverage in the process. We've been successful on a number of issues, but it's not perfect."

Then CEO Jim Donald, too, was aware of the potential problem. "It's a concern," he told me. "The experience and quality of beverage sometimes won't be the same as in a company-operated store. We're trying to have much more interaction at the top. The head of their operations will come in once or twice a year for immersion. We talk about our guiding principles and the way we treat our partners and try to square it up with them. We've also increased the amount of supervision; where district managers once had twenty venues to oversee, they now they have fifteen. And we also have access to the workers through voice mail, and we treat them as partners when we can." But communication without health care still means no health care. As Dave Olsen, a Starbucks old-timer and senior vice president for culture and leadership development, rightly noted, "My view of culture is 'the way we do things around here.' Aspirations are important, but action is defining."

Growth strained company-owned stores as well. New stores require more training capacity and new managers, and sometimes the company seemed to have trouble keeping up. Headquarters, however, denied this: "We don't foresee problems with recruiting and training for growth. We are constantly recruiting ahead of the curve. We rely a lot on our current partners to bring us talent and help us find the right people for the team." Nonetheless, during visits to local stores, I often sensed that managers were under considerable pressure to find and keep good teams.

Systemic growth and culture change also overlap with the personal. For many employees, especially those who are newer and younger, expansion means opportunity for advancement. For others, size and even promotions come with a cost. Brantley Browning was part of the more recent crop of employees, hired to manage the consequences of growth and growing right along with the company. He's blond and lanky with a small gold earring and a persona that's both edgy and wholesome. "I know it's a mouthful," he joked as he handed me his business card. "It's a very balanced name, two Bs, eight letters in each, and, yes, I know it sounds incredibly Waspy." A social programs manager in the corporate social responsibility department, Browning described himself as "an internal consultant on international development" to develop "social value-added" programs in producer countries. "As we got more sophisticated," he said, "and grew in size, and wanted to make more significant investments, the company decided to hire someone full time to take a look at that."

Browning became interested in international development while teaching in the indigenous coffee regions of Panama. "Before that, I was going to be a lawyer, working for an NGO on environmental issues or some such," he explained, "but that experience in Panama left an indelible impression on me. I ended up going to D.C., looking for development work at an NGO and doing temp work." One of those temp jobs took him to the World Bank. "No way I'm going to work for the Antichrist, I thought, but I had to work somewhere. I justified it by saying it was the temp agency paying me. . . . I went from heavy skepticism and reticence to thinking, this is complicated. There are a lot of things I can't stand about the bank but also some good; if you take too much of a black-white position, you miss some of the fine print."

Meanwhile, he'd gravitated back to coffee, completing his graduate field work on the coffee crisis in Central America and writing a paper for Oxfam; and when he saw an ad for the Starbucks job, he was intrigued. "It was a leap of faith for me," he said. I'd never worked in the private sector, and I needed to know the company was serious in order to commit. The first question I had was, where is the corporate responsibility department located? If they had reported to communications, marketing, or brand, that would have been an instant *no* for me. I decided I was willing to put it next to my name and help take it to next level."

Today Starbucks is one of a global galaxy of companies involved in foreign direct investment (FDI), defined by the United Nations Conference on Trade and Development as "investment made to acquire lasting interest in enterprises operating outside of the economy of the investor." Coffee was and is a prime area of FDI, and Browning noted that FDI exceeds direct aid in developing countries and is a significant way to transfer wealth from rich to poor countries—or so the theory goes. In practice, the line between facilitating development and rapacity is not always so clear-cut.

CSR wasn't the only Starbucks department to undergo changes. In 2005, Lori Otto became the company's government affairs director. In plainer terms, she's a lobbyist. Her predecessor had worked for the Clinton White House and, like that administration, had embraced both unrestricted trade and human rights. Otto, however, had been a Republican operative (although she does lay claim to a Clintonite husband). Her hiring may have been a pragmatic company move, given the biases of the Bush administration. Yet her former employer, the now infamous U.S. Senator Larry Craig of Idaho, was not merely a Republican but a staunchly conservative one: his voting record earned him a zero rating from both the Human Rights Campaign and the League of Conservation Voters. She seemed an odd choice for a company that had been an early adopter of domestic partner health benefits and a proponent of environmental sustainability.

Otto was well spoken and likable, and her views reinforced my researcher's perspective of the neutral corporation. "I don't see Starbucks as liberal or conservative," she said. "Starbucks has a philosophy about how it deals with its people, and how it wants to treat its people and customers, and that doesn't belong to any political party. I don't find it a conflict at all. It's exciting to have differences of opinion and good debates within the company."

But how one treats one's employees and customers *is* inherently political as well as social, and certainly a company that lobbies in favor of free trade and health care or refuses to lobby against the minimum wage is taking a political position. If Otto's view were consonant with those of the Starbucks leadership, why had she worked for Larry Craig; and if her views meshed with those of Larry Craig, why had Starbucks chosen her? Whatever the case, it seemed at odds with Starbucks' rhetoric about its hiring.

"We're pretty careful about the people we bring in," Sue Mecklenburg told me. "We're trying to get that cultural fit. If you look at our performance reviews, 50 percent is job responsibilities and 50 percent core competencies—our values. You need to make that cultural commitment. It's not a blind search for people who can just run the business, but people who can keep the values going." Yet apparently growth-precipitated change required different compromises. It also meant rewiring ideas and relationships.

In 2005, Starbucks senior vice president Wanda Herndon retired. She had, most recently, headed the global communications department, which included the media group headed by my key contact, Audrey Lincoff. Herndon, one of the first people I'd interviewed at the company, was flamboyant and direct with a caring management style: she knew the names of her employees' children and never failed to check in on how her staff and their families were doing. Her department was organized along traditional lines: that is, by target audience—media relations, internal communications, consumer relations, other external audiences, and miscellaneous projects.

After her retirement, the job description was expanded to include brand strategy; and her successor reorganized the department to meet the new demands of company mega-stardom. She created a trendier model: a corporate group, dealing with finance and business media; an innovation group, concentrating on rollouts of new music, beverages, food, and consumer-packaged beverages; an international group, focusing on company growth and partnerships abroad. The production end was turned over to a communications resources group. Audrey's area, now known as "good coffee, good company," was created to mirror the work of the CSR department.

Ever the consummate professional, Audrey voiced only enthusiasm for her new role and support for the re-visioning process. But as we traveled together in Costa Rica in the fall of 2006, I sensed that she was wistful for those former nurturing work relationships, now replaced by efficient business transactions. And although I continued to meet many staff people who exceeded my expectations, I noticed that a certain sameness was creeping in. Headquarters staffers were often charming, always professional, but occasionally hard to tell apart.

I'd seen similar changes in larger nonprofits and unions, a realignment of vision and personnel to manage growth and address the realities of global economic life. The resulting structure was sometimes more effective and more accountable, but change had a cost. Becoming a lean, mean, fighting machine can attract leaner, meaner employees. Eccentricities, both dysfunctional and poetic, that often characterized early innovators began to vanish. This wasn't necessarily bad, but it was a shift, rather like what happens to a neighborhood when chains replace independently owned stores: you may gain efficiency and reliability, but the consistency robs you of uniqueness, that flash of the unexpected that can challenge and excite.

"You would expect that," Mecklenburg observed, restating common business wisdom. "There are very few companies where entrepreneurs have the same skills as managers. We can't have people who're just making it up. It's too big for that; there's too much that needs to be well managed, so we need excellent managers."

In 2005, Jim Donald became the company's third CEO, taking over from Orin Smith, who had taken over from Schultz. Unlike Smith, Donald had come from the outside. His résumé included a stint at Wal-Mart, the anti-Starbucks—another odd cultural fit. During that year's annual meeting, Schultz followed up on all of

Donald's remarks, somehow overshadowing him. But in person, sitting across from me at a small round table in his office, Donald was engaging, like a pixie on speed. He leaped into our discussion with a frankness that contrasted with Schultz's growing caution. This didn't erase my doubts about bad habits he might have picked up at Wal-Mart, but it did pique my interest.

Donald was primarily raised by his mom, a checker at a Publix supermarket in Tampa, Florida. By age twelve, he was already working after school to help out with the family finances, and he got an early start in the grocery business. Over the course of his career, he's worked directly under numerous corporate founders, including Sam Walton at Wal-Mart and Joe Albertson at Albertson's, and also had stints at Safeway and Pathmark before arriving to work with Schultz. "We're like an old married couple," he said, when I asked about his relationship with Howard. "We're very tight. We butt heads, but to have him to bounce things off of is a blessing. People, strategies, innovation—Howard is the visionary still. I'm the keeper of the beans. I say, 'great idea, but . . . 'and we go from there, put our priorities in order, and we move forward from that point. Howard is much more the creative sort than I am. It leads to very candid discussion."

Though he admits to having once been mostly a tea drinker, Donald said he learned to love good coffee and to embrace the big-small challenge. He was known in the company for sending personal notes and making phone calls to store managers and for his endless rounds of store visits. During a staff meeting in a huge auditorium, Donald asked how many people there had gotten an e-mail or a message from him. As Mecklenburg recalled, "Thousands of people stood up. He has an unbelievable commitment to front line, and it sets an example."

When I suggested that many people now yoked Starbucks with Dunkin' Donuts and McDonald's rather than with local coffeehouses, Donald bridled. "I'll never forget an article by the head of Dunkin' Donuts," he told me. "He was talking about team members, as they call them, in a way that it was clear they were the franchisees' employees. I actually think it's good for our little part of the overall coffee category that super-premium coffee is getting to be everywhere; but I say our secret of success is through our partners and making sure that we take care of them in every way we can. That's the differentiating factor between us and Dunkin' and McDonald's."

For Donald, partner commitment extended from headquarters, not just to the stores but back along the supply chain to the source:

Regardless of where I sit and where I'm doing business in the global economy, I'm learning there's investments that have to be made to get to the growth. And what those investments are—social investments, or actual trade, or loaning money, or agronomy centers. It all counts to make sure they're with you every step of the way. It's not just showing up one day a year; it's going back in and talking with them, seeing what works and what doesn't work. It's no different than partners in the store. Are they going to be around? Are you paying enough to sustain their lifestyle and help them sustain the environment?

But sometimes the social investments that make work sustainable for people are not easily compatible with the investments in efficiency required for growth. In 2004, I took my first tour of the Kent roasting plant outside Seattle. It's the oldest of Starbucks' four (soon to be five) roasting plants, those places where the green coffee from origin countries becomes the roast we buy in the store. The Kent plant is easy to miss if you don't have specific directions, and the company carefully restricts plant visitors and guards its proprietary roasting secrets. It sits inconspicuously in the back of a small industrial park, one of those low, anonymous, seemingly windowless structures distinguished only by a discreet sign sporting the mermaid logo. There's nothing stereotypically "Starbucks" about the plant. It's a factory, dominated by machinery, where workers shovel beans into large industrial roasters just as previous generations of blue-collar workers once shoveled coal.

On the wall behind the security desk hangs a large photo of the company's previous roasting facility. Most of the guys in the photo look like hippies. The picture shows four roasting machines, the kind that need human supervision, packed into a space that resembles a giant garage with a loading dock at the back. Almost the entire operation is visible in this single shot.

In the back of the photo stands a young, slender, long-haired employee named Tom Walters. At the time he hosted my 2004 tour, he'd been with Starbucks for twenty-two years, one of two plant employees left from the old days, before the little specialty coffee company met Howard Schultz. Tom had filled out a bit, but he still had plenty of hair, a bear of a guy in jeans and a T-shirt, whose role as official guide failed to obscure his quirky individualism or sharp tongue.

Tom learned the roasting trade from Jerry Baldwin, who learned from Alfred Peet himself; but the plant where he'd mastered his trade bore only a faint resemblance to one we now toured. Built in 1993, the 350,000-square-foot facility is about twice the size of a SuperTarget. It employs three hundred full-time workers and close to one hundred contingent or temporary workers, and it operates 24/7. Sacks of coffee arrive via the port at Long Beach, California, and are shipped by truck or rail to a green coffee warehouse near the plant. More than 1.5 million pounds a week are processed in Kent, the equivalent of more than 10,000 sacks, mostly burlap, stamped with country of origin and shipment number, which wait on rows of pallets in a cavernous part of the facility.

Workers on platforms slit open the sacks and subject the green beans to a cleaning process to remove foreign objects. Over the years, they've shaken numerous knives, bullets, money clips, and other strange memorabilia out of these sacks of coffee. From there, the beans, sorted by type, travel through snaky black tubing into one of eight green coffee silos. Then they're measured out according to roasting recipe and sent off to the roasting drums, where air and heat combine to roast the beans to the correct level of darkness for each blend. The plant has six large automated coffee roasters, and every batch is analyzed electronically to make sure it meets the profile. The scent of roasting coffee permeates the air.

Tom's tour, with its barbed humor and lively personal commentary, was unique among my Starbucks experiences. Schultz had frequently referred to him as an example of what Starbucks was about: an embodiment of its coffee traditions and enduring familial spirit. And Tom was clearly grateful to the company for bringing security to his life and awed by its stupendous success. Yet as we walked past rows of coffee sacks and along production lines, he spoke with longing about the old days, when roasting coffee was an artisan craft rather than a mechanized task. He clearly had no use for the syrup-based products and Frappuccino mixes that, in his opinion, were a sacrilege to the religion of fine coffee. There was a time when Starbucks was all about coffee. But it had outgrown its roots.

These contradictions between growing big and staying small made 2006 a tough year. The Starbucks stock price bounced up and down, from a high of more than forty dollars a share to a low of less than twenty-nine dollars; and commentators described its same-store sales as "lackluster." The company seemed to lack its usual élan in dealing with complaints ranging from the serious to the ridiculous, creating skittishness on the profit side of the equation. There was the Frappuccino meltdown, for instance, when extreme demand for the icy blends was blamed for slowing down baristas and midsummer sales. Mishaps involving free drink coupons aggravated customers. And Dunkin' Donuts and McDonald's announced new forays into the specialty coffee market, aggressively challenging Starbucks' dominance.

Simultaneously, there were the IWW accusations of union busting, Oxfam accusations about Ethiopian trademarks, and the fracas over the store in the Forbidden City, not to mention protesters in cow suits demanding hormone-free milk and articles linking caloric overdoses in Starbucks beverages to obesity. Plus the usual scalding-coffee lawsuits, and at least one plaintiff alleging predatory real estate practices to stifle competition. It wasn't serene, and it often wasn't pretty.

Then early in 2007, two more tidbits spiced up the busy Starbucks news and gossip mill. *Consumer Reports* declared McDonald's the winner in its coffee taste test, pronouncing Starbucks coffee burnt and bitter. This was followed by Schultz's infamous Valentine's Day memo. One could imagine that Starbucks execs were fairly apprehensive as the date for the company's annual meeting rolled around.

By 6 A.M. on March 21, 2007, people were already lining up at Seattle's McCaw Hall, and by the time the doors opened at 8 A.M., the line was snaking along the plaza. Several thousand stockholders cheerfully warded off the chill with samples of the company's latest offering, dulce de leche latte, each little cup swirled with a hat of whipped cream. They knew that, despite a scheduled start time of 10 A.M., McCaw's 2,900 seats would be filled in the first rush, with latecomers banished to Siberia in the auxiliary hall next door, to follow the proceedings on the big screen far away from the live-action drama.

Starbucks' annual meetings have a history of drawing small clusters of protesters, but this year there was an extra frisson of tension on the plaza. As a small combo of musicians entertained the waiting ticket holders, Starbucks staff, augmented by extra security and a few city cops, kept a sharp eye on the crowd and the streets. Shayna Harris from Oxfam and her video crew were threading their way through the line, trying to interview stockholders about the Ethiopian conflict, although most people appeared reluctant to speak. Her colleague Seth Petchers was among the first attendees inside the hall, preparing his presentation for the Q&A session that always concluded the meeting. Outside, a lone protester, an elderly woman, carried a small sign supporting the Ethiopian cause.

An IWW sentry lingered near the curb, apparently awaiting reinforcements. Eventually, two dozen anarcho-demonstrators showed up with signs excoriating Starbucks for anti-union and anti-farmer behavior, although very few actually seemed to be baristas. While the crowd inside nibbled pastries, the IWW demonstrators drummed on the white plastic tubs that have become de rigueur for such events and preened for the TV cameras in front of a gigantic inflatable rat, the current prop of choice on blue-collar union picket lines.

It was an underwhelming display of opposition, but on stage the impact of a year's worth of turmoil was evident. The upbeat razzle-dazzle and exuberance that characterized my first annual meeting in 2004 were gone. While a clever performance number opened the event and there was an amusing sequence of amateur YouTube postings starring Starbucks, the production was pared down, the mood less giddy. Even the live performance that usually culminates the meeting was scrapped; apparently *Dreamgirls* star Jennifer Hudson had thrown a diva tantrum and was bounced off the program.

For most of the meeting, Howard Schultz, Jim Donald, and Martin Coles, the president of Starbucks International, vouched for the company's long-term financial performance, its full-steam-ahead expansion plans, and its abiding values of quality and goodness. The news wasn't all bad, not by a long shot. Even in a rough year, Starbucks had a record that other companies might envy. Despite its uneven financials, revenues had climbed by 22 percent. The number of stores had grown by 2,199 to a total of 12,440. Brazil and Egypt had joined the roster of countries hosting Starbucks stores. The company had forged a relationship with iTunes and expanded its line of CDs, and its second book selection was on the bestseller list. To buoy the faithful, Schultz announced that Sir Paul McCartney would be the first artist featured on Starbucks' very own record label. And yes, here was Sir Paul himself, via satellite, talking with Howard. "Talking to a Beatle. It's wild. Who would have ever thought?" Schultz marveled to the audience. Who could have predicted that a little coffee company could come so far?

And yet.

Shultz and his team outdid themselves to prove themselves worthy of continued "loyalty and trust." Their spirited offense now had a new and urgent streak of defensiveness. The officers displayed charts

showing the company's remarkable growth and upward financial tra-
jectory: the 10,000 dollars invested in 1992 now worth 467,000 dollars; the 250 million dollars in capitalization now at 24 billion
dollars. Meanwhile, they reiterated again and again Starbucks' commitment to be a "different kind of company," one that values a social
conscience as much as shareholder earnings. Schultz's memo of corporate self-reflection, he told the crowd, was no eschatology but a
single example of hundreds of similar memos he'd sent over the years
to challenge partners to do better, reach higher, and continue "the
entrepreneurial push for excellence" that had made the company
an icon.

Its iconic status, he continued, had brought rich rewards but had
also turned the company into a symbol of globalization and capitalism, making it the target of fringe unions and intemperate NGOs. He
assured stockholders that the company remained principled and
praiseworthy in its relationships with its own employees and, contrary to Oxfam's claims, its coffee suppliers. As if to emphasize the
stellar benefits that Starbucks provides to coffee-growing countries
(and present a narrative to counter the Ethiopian controversy),
Rwanda's president, Paul Kalama, was on hand to address the assem-
bly. "My country is linked to Starbucks in friendship and partnership
through coffee." he assured the audience.

"We welcome debate and criticism," Schultz said, "we are not
perfect. . . . But we will continue to build, grow, and give back to people. . . . We're a coffee company, but we have the license and ability
to extend the brand beyond our core business to enhance the experience. . . . And we will continue to be a company you can trust and
admire, not only for the profit that it makes, but for the good that
it does."

The shareholders applauded. But to detractors, the speech was just
more hollow rhetoric. Over the past year, the company had, in their
opinion, shown its true colors. It had revealed its corporate muscle and
greed by bullying farmers and workers. It was threatening to destroy
local culture with its relentless global expansion. Now, adding insult to
injury, it was papering over its sins with disingenuous spin. In 1999's
Battle of Seattle, demonstrators had raised these issues against the
WTO, and they were raising the same issues against Starbucks today.

But in its transformation from hometown hero to global giant,
Starbucks' biggest challenge was probably more personal. After the
annual meeting, I asked to go back out to the roasting plant. I was

hoping to reconnect with Tom Walters, maybe ask him how he felt about the Schultz memo and the impact of growth. But Tom was no longer there. Instead, my guide was Gregg Clark, director of plant operations, who had worked at Kraft and the Starbucks roasting facility in York, Pennsylvania, before coming to Kent. Whereas Tom was a coffee guy, a roaster, who wrapped his tongue lovingly around coffee words, Gregg lingered over the machinery.

Together we admired the clever Willie Wonka—style contraption that pours the beans and ground coffee into packaging. There are sixteen packaging lines, half for whole beans, half for ground coffee, that produce bags of different sizes and weights. The packaging material looks like a wide reel of film with a design printed on it. A little pressure valve is planted like a bull's-eye in the packaging logo to release the gases generated by the roasting process without letting in oxygen. This invention, which keeps roasted coffee from going stale, has helped make the Starbucks empire possible. Then the film is formed into a sleeve and filled with coffee. The machine creates a seal at the back and bottom of the sleeve, and fan belts alongside help the coffee flow evenly. Then the bags are vacuum-sealed: oxygen out, nitrogen in. A "pick and place" machine lifts up the packages and spins them around to a place where the tops are snipped down, and they proceed along a belt to a spot where the plastic flaps are glued on and finally to where a gizmo folds them in. Then workers in teams of two box the coffee bags for shipment. At the end of my visit, I didn't quite know how Clark felt about coffee, but I knew he loved the machines that produced it.

I was finally able to track down Tom Walters. He wasn't able to discuss the circumstances surrounding his departure, although he didn't seem happy about them. I suspect that his candor had become too much for a company that was tightening its control over its image. "I'm forty-eight," he told me, "and I worked there twenty-four years of my life. It used to be that we were in the forefront. It was all about quality." Now it seemed about money, and exponentially more conservative.

The best years, he said, were before the stock went public in 1992, when workers were carefully hand-roasting coffee to develop a loyal following. Then it seemed, almost overnight, they pulled the rug out from under the experts and brought in executives and MBAs. Soon all the people who taught Tom to roast were gone. In 1995 the plant switched to computerized roasters, and from then on the pride that used to accompany the craft seemed to diminish.

Although Tom still respected Schultz and the original goals of the company, he seemed to feel an ever-widening gap between the company's rhetoric and its values. Similarly, one of my interviewees had suggested that the headquarters was full of wonderful people but was rapidly "hemorrhaging at the heart." That person told me, "I think Howard accomplishes what he sets out to accomplish, but he's let the company fall into the hands of people who don't share his world view. Now the end justifies the means."

Even though Tom no longer worked at the plant, he cared enough about Starbucks to worry about its future. "I hope," he said wistfully, "that Howard's memo is in time to retain the passionate people they will need to make the changes that can save its soul."

Adding to the disquiet was the sense that Starbucks had become too enamored of itself to maintain either perspective or collegial relationships. When I asked workers at the Eighth Street store near my house whether they'd received any advice from Starbucks head-quarters about dealing with the new Dunkin' Donuts, one of them shrugged. "They have an arrogance about it," the worker told me. "They've weathered all the big guys and succeeded, and now they don't think they have any competition."

A staffer at a smaller roaster commented, "There's a significant arrogance. But within the wholesale ranks, they're really no better than anyone else: we're all roasting, grinding, brewing. But you'll never get a Starbucks person to tell you you're doing a good job. They do a nice job, but they beat the competition up. For them, it's all the brand; it's like they want to win the battle." Indeed, as the company has grown larger, the urge to protect often seems to collide with the need to reflect. That instinct to fight and defend from a place of power has made it harder to address assaults on the company's motives and brand. It has sharpened the hostility of the company's critics and has dulled the sensitivity of the company's response.

Late in 2006, I walked into Audrey Lincoff's office, where she was pondering a memo from Howard. He was on a tear about people smoking at the tables and chairs in the area abutting the parking lot in front of the building. He wanted it to stop. Audrey was okay with dis-couraging tobacco use but uncomfortable with a dictatorial fiat to keep employees from smoking outside on their breaks. As was too often the case these days, no one wanted to raise the concerns with Howard; and Audrey was trying to figure out how to accommodate him without infringing on other people's rights in public spaces.

The next time I visited, four or five months later, tasteful signs had been posted around the outdoor seating area: "We are committed to maintaining a healthy environment for our partners and our guests. Please join us in that commitment, and please do not smoke in this area."

But Audrey had thrown in the towel. She was gone.

10 Capitalism Is Like Fire . . .

John Sage, president of Pura Vida Coffee, sat with me in his decidedly un-Starbucks-like Seattle office, located in a low warehouse-style building redolent of counter-culture, dimly lit, with bright posters and mismatched furniture, catty-corner from Mermaid Central across the street. "I'm always arguing with my lefty friends, but capitalism as a system is value neutral," Sage insisted. "It all depends how you make your money and what you do with the profits."

He was explaining the unique Pura Vida structure, which pairs Pura Vida Coffee, a for-profit, fair trade coffee importer and roaster, with Pura Vida Partners, a charity that holds the coffee company's voting shares and uses company profits for projects in coffee-growing countries. "Capitalism is like fire," he told me. "You can use it to cook a great meal, or it can burn down the house."

"Sure, it's like fire," said Alec, when I reported the conversation. "If you don't regulate it, it burns down the house."

My friend Beatrice Edwards countered, "It's an intelligent fire; it finds its way around the regulations meant to contain it."

"No," Alec reconsidered, "capitalism is more like molasses. It coats everything and leaves it sticky."

At its core, the Battle of Seattle was about the competing cultures and consequences of capitalism, which in its pure form relies on private enterprise rather than government control to regulate the marketplace. It pitted the WTO framework of free trade and privatization against the global justice vision of fair trade, in which corporate profits took a back seat to human rights, environmental sustainability, and a fairer distribution of wealth. Free-market pedants hold that "no rules is good rules" and that regulation of the marketplace should be avoided at all costs. Opponents argue that free trade has plenty of rules—nine hundred or so pages of them in the North American Free Trade Agreement alone. It's just that those rules favor the corporations, governments, and individuals who are already rich and powerful. The global monetary establishment holds that the path to all good outcomes is spurred by free-market expansion and that profits trickle down from the top to benefit the masses. The global justice forces claim this approach isn't working and have catalogued increases in income inequality and environmental destruction to prove their point.

Sage straddles the divide, laying claim to the structure of capitalism and the purpose of global justice. Call his approach culinary rather than slash-and-burn capitalism. I, however, have always agreed with that other fence-straddler, the economist John Maynard Keynes, who believed that government regulation was necessary to ameliorate the harms of a totally free market. In his words, "Capitalism is the astounding belief that the most wickedest of men will do the most wickedest of things for the greatest good of everyone." My sentiments exactly.

How do we get these notions? A colleague who's been to school more recently than I says that, these days, *economics* is defined as "the science of how individuals make choices and trade-offs in the face of scarcity." But for me economics—the way we organize our resources and our labor to meet our needs and enrich our lives—has always been less science and more sociology. Fundamentally, economics is not merely about finance but about ideas, people, and values. Economist Duncan K. Foley has even gone so far as to equate economics with theology. Ever since Adam Smith made his case for free markets, Foley says, economists have adopted the fallacy that "it is possible to separate an economic sphere of life, in which the pursuit of self-interest is guided by objective laws to a socially beneficent outcome, from the rest of social life, in which the pursuit of self-interest is morally problematic and has to be weighed against other ends."

Although I've spent most of my life dealing with the consequences of market forces on working people, I'm far from being an economist. But just as we each have personal politics, we each have an economic story to tell, one that gives meaning to our money and that we use to interpret the world and our place in it. And it's worth delving into these stories because, as Foley observes, "the economic way of thinking is just as value-laden as any other way of thinking about society."

My personal economic biases began in a first floor apartment on Ninety-first Street and Amsterdam Avenue in the heart of New York City's Upper West Side. My parents, refugees from Nazi Europe, had come to this country with little beyond their smarts and their trades—my mom as a seamstress, my dad as an opera conductor. To help pay the rent (150 dollars a month in 1952), they boarded a succession of young singers in the back room.

My parents were both working freelancers, their businesses overtaking our family furniture in a wild profusion of fabric and paper. They slept on a couch in the living room, which also housed my father's piano and doubled as my mother's fitting room. The dining room, anchored by a large table that served as family central, also contained a sewing machine, a dressmaker's dummy, a rhinestone press, and a wall of shelves dangerously laden with sewing supplies. In addition to their children and our friends, an endless stream of visitors cycled through the apartment: singers for voice lessons with my father, showgirls for fittings with my mother. We may not have had much money, but we were no poorer than most of our neighbors.

In only two instances do I recall feeling deprived, and both involved attire. When I was lucky, my mother sewed my clothes; but her time was money, and she couldn't spend it all on me. As the smallest person in the supply chain, I received an endless string of hand-me-downs from neighbors, all the items at least a season or two out of vogue. My mother, though not unkind, was seldom swayed by my protests. When I pestered her for saddle shoes, she informed me that just because everyone else had them was no reason that I needed them, especially when I had two perfectly good pairs of shoes in the closet. And when we finally exhausted the supply of hand-me-down coats, my mother insisted on buying the last parka on sale, a hideous red and green plaid that I despised every day I wore it and still think of with loathing, decades after its demise. Nonetheless, there was always a little money for theater tickets, those most coveted of birthday gifts, and always room at the table for a friend.

Thus are our lives studded with lessons about money and values—the guts of economics. If you can't afford the rent, take in a boarder. Acquire a skill. Time is money. You don't have to keep up with the Joneses. Work hard. Search out the bargains. Self-worth isn't about possessions. Choose your priorities. Enjoy the small luxuries. Share what you have. Moms rule. And don't go into debt for a pair of saddle shoes.

That was only the beginning.

Like so many others in New York in the fifties, our household was shadowed by the unspoken lessons of the Holocaust. My mother's parents were death camp victims; my paternal grandfather had died in an internment camp; and my surviving grandmother, who lived with us, was a gray shell lamenting her losses. Although my parents never dwelled on these tragedies, they instilled the moral lessons they'd gained from their experiences: that we were accountable for our own behavior and responsible for the general well-being of the larger community—values, as it turned out, that were frequently incompatible with the free-market economy.

They led by example. One year, we accompanied my father to Cincinnati, where he was spending the summer season working as a prompter at the Cincinnati Opera. He sat in a subterranean booth at the front of the stage where only the singers could see him; his job was to give them their lines if they forgot their cues. We were watching a dress rehearsal for *Rigoletto*, and the soprano had just missed a high note. The visiting Metropolitan Opera conductor erupted with a stream of invective, silencing the other singers and musicians midnote. Suddenly I saw my father hoist himself out of his booth, rise onto center stage, and shout back at the conductor in a mix of English and Italian, "You cannot do this, performers are not to be treated this way, they are entitled to respect!" I knew, even then, that I had witnessed something important. I also learned that principles have a price. My father's chances of a coveted position at the Met were gone for good.

My mother wasn't exactly pleased about this affair, but she also practiced her own forms of resistance. She had grown up in a little German village near Munich and was ten years old when the Nazi regime first prohibited Jewish children from attending school. "You can't just sit around the house and worry," her bright and subversive mother told her. She sent her daughter off to apprentice with a seamstress, thus giving my mom a fail-safe livelihood that served her for the next seven decades. When it became clear that the Nazis were out for blood, my mother's parents organized the collection of money, visas, and affidavits to send the village children on a transport to safety in Britain—an early lesson in the importance of collective action.

In truth, my mother could never quite make up her mind about money. She didn't like worrying about it and, for many years, had longed for a set of matching dishes that didn't come from the dime store. But when our temple decided to move from across the street to across town, she threw a fit. "They're only moving to the East Side to get a richer congregation," she snapped. "They're supposed to stay here where they're needed." She refused to have anything more to do with it. She also maintained a Robin Hood approach to her dressmaking business, charging wealthy women handsomely for her work so that she could make concert gowns at a discount for starving young singers. She may not have finished primary school, but she understood the principles of income redistribution. So, eventually, would I, thanks to college, Karl Marx, and the sixties.

My family moved to Pittsburgh in the summer of 1965, when my father took a teaching job in the fine arts department at Carnegie Tech (now Carnegie Mellon University). Although we kids were indignant at being wrenched away from New York, my mother mollified us with promises of a house with a garden and a room for each of us. There's no question that the move gave us another view of reality. In New York, we'd lived in a neighborhood where economic status didn't feel very important and where immigrants of all kinds and colors seemed to outnumber the native-born citizens. But in Pittsburgh there were no integrated neighborhoods, and you could get a panoramic view of the city's class structure as you rode the downtown bus. Along the riverfront, the Jones and Laughlin steel mills spewed flames that lit up the night, while the little old houses of the Slavic, Irish, and Italian mill workers wound up and around the hills. To the right was the Hill District, the old black neighborhood gouged out by urban renewal and eminent domain to build highways and the Civic Arena. Straight ahead were the U.S. Steel and Mellon Bank headquarters, all glass and glint. Our country's economic history and destiny were all laid out on that landscape—rags to riches, rolled iron to robber barons.

Today the mills are gone, replaced by computer labs; and the little houses are variously gentrified or decayed, the mill workers gone. The Hill continues to struggle, now older and shabbier, while gentrification laps at its downtown and university borders. New residents work at thriving college and hospital complexes, all within easy access of a Starbucks; the glass and steel headquarters still rise over the rivers. Countless public buildings carry the names of the plutocrat-philanthropists—Carnegie, Mellon, Hillman, Frick, Scaife—who extracted fortunes from their underpaid factory workers and in return paid for libraries, museums, and parks for the edification of the masses.

Pittsburgh turned out to be a great laboratory for economics, and the classes I took at the University of Pittsburgh illuminated the lessons of the landscape. Crusty old Dr. Johnston showed only contempt for the antiwar protests surrounding the campus, but he knew his economic theory and demanded that we learn it too. It went something like this:

Adam Smith first put forth the idea of free-market capitalism in 1776, the year America declared its independence; and the two notions have grown up in tandem. Capitalism starts with people's needs, which beget ideas to meet those needs. Some people then hire others to help implement the ideas, a process that begets industries small and large, which spit out products and services. The exchange that ensues constitutes trade, which begets competition for the greatest number of buyers, which results in the growth of the most competitive industries and the disappearance of the rest. This yields profits for the owners of the surviving enterprises, which then trickle down through wages and investments, generating a cycle of economic activity organically calibrated by Smith's poetic and slightly creepy "invisible hand." This leads to the ever-popular "rising of all boats," which begets general prosperity, well-being, and happiness.

Karl Marx, however, saw things differently. Roughly at the point where some people hire others and form competitive industries, yielding profits for successful owners and wages for the rest of us, his version takes a turn, rather like a genealogy that follows the children of the mistress rather than the wife. Marx suggests that, while the owners get rich, the rest of us get screwed. Our work adds surplus value to the goods and services, which the bosses appropriate for themselves, which begets the growth of a small affluent owning class and a large struggling working class, with ever-larger disparity between the two. This breeds discontent in the workers, which begets revolution, which leads to the redistribution of wealth among all and to communal ownership, which begets general prosperity, well-being, and happiness.

For a large new generation of middle- and working-class students, with more females and minorities in the mix, the Marx version was much more enticing. Rather than stolidly procreating profits, Marx's explanation brought power, greed, lust, and redemption into the marketplace, turning Smith's notion of competition into armies of winners and losers on a battlefield that favored the controlling rich and was strewn with the bodies of the fallen.

And we knew who those fallen were: black people, women, the poor, the displaced, the exploited—the unsung strivers and strugglers on the short end of history's stick, both here and around the world. In other words, the actual and metaphorical "us." Suddenly, the issue wasn't limited to Marx's class analysis. Race and gender had entered the picture. As the civil rights movement and the new women's movement were proving, suffrage was not sufficient; true equality required a reconfiguration of democratic relationships. Vote or no vote, blacks could not fully join American society while still hounded by the cultural and economic legacy of slavery. Women likewise were burdened by wage inequality and public and private oppression, often backed with violence. New scholarship and victims of the status quo were questioning the notion that white men and western culture were superior. But the guys at the top weren't (and often still aren't) ready to yield their position without a fight.

The Vietnam War conveniently linked all these philosophical strands. If you saw the conflict as part of the cold war, you might have called it the Battle of the C's—capitalism and communism—represented by their all-too-earthly surrogates, the United States and the Soviet Union. Or you might have seen it as one more example of colonialism grounded in racism. Why did governments think they could take over someone else's country just because they wanted its bananas, gold, oil, land, ports, or cheap labor? Also we couldn't help noticing that most of the takers were white guys from the First World, as they so snottily called the developed west. And how was it that a disproportionate number of soldiers drafted to fight the Vietnam War were black and poor?

Fired by these questions, we put our socioeconomic theories to immediate use, protesting the war, racism, poverty, and innumerable lesser injustices. From then on, I was hooked. The idea of using collective action to improve life for individuals and the larger community, be it a neighborhood, a workplace, the nation, or the world, nourished me through thirty years working in progressive unions and nonprofits. I would remain suspicious of the consequences of capitalism—all the way to the streets of Seattle and into John Sage's office.

Sage grew up a decade later, and a continent away. He was raised in progressive Berkeley, California, son of a park service landscape architect and a public school teacher. But he was fascinated with business from a young age. "I'm not sure where the biz gene comes from," he told me. "It was there as early as I can remember." Although he defines himself as progressive, he disagrees with the left's tendency to make capitalism the culprit for the world's ills; and he's got reason to appreciate its efficacy. He went to Stanford University and Harvard Business School, graduating into high tech when it was booming. His Microsoft marketing gig left him financially comfortable, and the buyout of his subsequent high-tech startup left him a multimillionaire.

Sage found an opportunity to put his money to good use in 1997, when he reconnected with Christopher Dearnley, a friend from business school. Dearnley was a pastor working with poor children in Costa Rica but was low on funding for his projects. Together, he and Sage hatched an idea to sell Costa Rican coffee in the States to fund Dearnley's work in Costa Rica. Sage kicked in 1 million dollars, becoming one of about thirty private shareholders, and began creating the company's double-breasted structure of profits in the service of charity. "We were founded with charitable intent and have maintained charitable control through the way we structured ownership of our shares," he explained. "It ensures long-term preservation of the mission."

It generally takes six to eight years for a business venture to gain its footing; thus, even with indulgent private shareholders, Pura Vida had no fast track to profitability. Sage initially compensated by underwriting both the business and the charitable entities. But "even if you're rich, that's not really a viable solution. I remember that a professor at Harvard said, 'If you can't meet the demands of the capital marketplace, all you have is an expensive hobby. You might as well take up flying.'" By 2007, however, the company was supporting itself and approaching annual sales of close to 1 million pounds of coffee. Sage had also committed to allocating five cents from each pound sold to support the foundation's work, with a goal of reaching fifty cents per pound sold in the next five years.

Economists contend that continued growth is necessary for a successful business. David Harvey, a leading social theorist on global capitalism, puts it simply: "A capitalist has money, puts it into circulation, and comes out with more money at the end. . . . The dynamic of our society, a capitalist society, is powered by the push always to accumulate capital, to make a profit. Profit means the system has to expand, because there has to be more at the end of the year than there was at the beginning. . . . A capitalist system must grow or bust."

Sage agrees. When I suggested that Pura Vida might not want to be as large as Starbucks, he laughed and said, "If I could, I would." Sage believes the growth imperative is hardwired into the genes of entrepreneurs. "Apart from the financial imperative, if you're really proud of your product, you have a zealous missionary desire for everyone to know yours is the best. You're almost genetically predisposed to open in a new location or get it onto another campus. You gotta do it."

Paul Katzeff, the pioneer independent coffee roaster from California, isn't as interested in growth. "Quality of life was the leading edge of our decision to do this," he said. "We just grew one town at a time, radiating out from the center until our reach was a two-hundred-mile arc." But he shares Sage's enthusiasm for capitalism. "I love capitalism," he told me. "There is nothing wrong with it when in the hands of honest, sensitive people who want to enjoy life, share the rewards of hard work fairly, and have an intimate relationship with their employees, customers, and suppliers. I have built a small giant of a business that shows how to make money, live an honorable life, and support suppliers and employees while also taking care to support the planet."

So here are these cool guys practicing capitalism with gusto, in a way that satisfies themselves and arguably does good in the world. Clearly, they are relatively small boats on the broad sea of capitalism—more artisanal than industrial. Yet Howard Schultz would probably make similar arguments about his larger vessel. He would contend that, by doing well and increasing success while practicing social responsibility, Starbucks enriches not just itself but its suppliers, employees, and satisfied customers. He would mirror Sage's assertion that capitalism is merely a tool, a value-neutral instrument that can be used for positive or negative ends.

Not so, says Vijay Prashad, director of international studies at Trinity College in Connecticut and a prolific writer on economic issues. "The statement that capital is value-neutral is an individualist statement—that it takes ingenuity and hard work for success, that the game is not rigged, that the umpire doesn't favor corporations."

"There can be good firms, but not good capitalism," he told me. "It's two different levels of analysis. On one level, your capitalist firm makes decisions on market position and ability to attract investment and such. But on another level, there's an enormous amount of literature on how a global system of capitalist accumulation generates inequality." And that, he contends, is far from value-neutral. "Everything has a certain value; there are just differing frameworks for those values."

This lively discussion is a current preoccupation of academics, including economists, who spend much time considering the interrelationships of capital accumulation, development, democracy, and societal benefit while the ghosts of Adam Smith and Karl Marx hover fretfully in the background. At issue are the competing concepts of free and fair. If the marketplace is free from regulation, does that automatically mean it's not fair? If it's fair, is it automatically not free? Some economists insist that free is about process while fair is about consequences; but these days, both concepts imply process and results and co-exist on a tangled continuum of impurity, never wholly free, never wholly fair—and usually far from either ideal. Moreover, these ambiguities exist in the context of a world gone global, awash in capital that has loosened itself from its geographic and physical moorings.

For anyone with a computer, the global context has become markedly more intelligible, so much so that we—and especially the young among us—take for granted the fact that we can send and receive information from around the world in real time. It's harder, however, to comprehend the consequences of transnational capital on national governments. In an undated, unclassified CIA study titled *Intelligence and the Market*, Gregory Treverton, then of the RAND Corporation, described a world in which, as we move from "territorial state" defined by geographic borders to "market state" defined by the absence of borders, "The role of government will be transformed. The government of the territorial state was a doer; 'make, buy, or regulate.'

For tomorrow's public managers, the choice will be 'cajole, incentivize, or facilitate'—'carrots, sticks, and sermons.'"

Implicit in this analysis is the migration of power from governments to corporations, with a society's priorities determined by market forces and profit margins rather than human needs and social planning: in other words, we get more brands of toothpaste and designer jeans but no affordable hearing aids. This is the nightmare scenario that the left envisions, the inevitable consequence of capitalism that panders to the lucrative desires of the affluent rather than the less profitable needs of the world's disadvantaged. In such a world, says Leslie Sklair, a sociologist at the London School of Economics and Political Science, "The transnational corporation is the major locus of transnational economic practices; the transnational capitalist class is the major locus of transnational political practices; and the major locus of transnational culture-ideology practices is to be found in the culture-ideology of consumerism." Implicitly, the three are tightly meshed; and in a nutshell, this is the reasoning behind the 1999 Seattle protest—a strike against the way in which all aspects of global society have converged in the hands of a transnational plutocracy.

In the years since the Battle of Seattle, the ascendancy of the transnational corporation has been outstripped by pure financial speculation as practiced by large hedge funds and private equity funds. These funds exist, say experts, because of an overaccumulation of wealth, the result of unbridled free-market capitalism. "There was a massive wave of transnational investment in the 1980s and 1990s, leading to overcapacity and overproduction," explained William Robinson, professor of sociology at the University of California at Santa Barbara, in an interview with the Greek newspaper *Eleftherotypia.* "Capital began increasingly to seek an investment outlet through financial speculation—the notorious 'casino capitalism.'"

This free-floating speculation has serious consequences for those whose fortunes are tied to real assets, be they factories or commodities such as coffee. "Finance capital is the most mobile and transnationalized fraction of capital," said Robinson. "Money capital exists in cyberspace, where it recognizes no borders and faces few, if any, state controls. Money capital subordinates fixed capital. Those who control money capital can appropriate values anywhere in the world by financial manipulation and relocate them on an ongoing basis to anywhere else in the world."

For this reason the price of coffee on the C market can fluctuate many times a week, or even over a day, no matter what the actual value of the beans might be, creating huge insecurity for the farmers and small traders whose lives are tied to the actual commodity. This speculative process also permits, as Marx suggested long ago, the value of the product to become ever more detached from the people who produce it. Their poverty is no longer discernibly connected to our consumption. As Vijay Prashad puts it, "Finance capital has collapsed time and space. It comes and leaves in a flash. It's a tsunami that has washed away the beach of human rights."

This capitalism is not merely a fire but a flood. It sweeps the value away from the product, tears workers from their work, rips floors from ceilings, and lays waste to the lives of the countless poor. So where are the floodgates and levies to secure the coastal plains? How can we reclaim and rebuild the connections that give meaning to our economic lives—individually, as a nation, as a world?

Rigid free marketers assert that the market itself is the only protection anyone needs, but my progressive colleagues and I question both the premise of a free market and its ability to protect any interests beyond its own. Like Ueli Gurtner at Fedecocagua, who passionately believes that what passes for free trade in the coffee sector is really the protection of a small coffee plutocracy, my friend Beatrice Edwards, director of international programs for the Government Accountability Project and a specialist on the Latin America economy, is indignant about the free market assertion. "The entire job of an Alan Greenspan or a Ben Bernanke, as chair of the Federal Reserve system, is to manipulate capital to secure business interests," she told me, citing both the savings-and-loan scandal of the 1980s and the ongoing subprime mortgage crisis. In both cases the government has bailed out unscrupulous loan institutions while consumers are losing their homes.

Bea scoffed, "They're always yelling, 'Let the market do it, let the market do it!' But capitalism can't exist without state security. It creates organizations to protect business from the macro-consequences of its micro-decisions." Yet when poor countries or poor people seek the same cover, different rules apply: that's the time to invoke the free market.

Bea, among many others, singles out the health care system as the locus of greatest tension between market needs and national needs. "Here's where the technology is the most aggregated, but you're only entitled to it if you can pay for it out of your wages, and more and more people can't," she said, pointing to President George W. Bush's move to eliminate state-supported health care for children from working families of modest means. "Here's where we're facing the severest ideological contradictions, when the profits of insurance companies are given priority over children's health."

I suggested to her that, at the point where ideological contradictions begin to exert negative consequences and threaten profits (or so some free marketers argue), the system readjusts. When global warming threatens the future of the coffee crop or chills coastal real estate investments, the market begins to look for answers. Yet as we both agreed, by then it's usually too late to save either the coral reef or the poor. "It only changes when it hurts the rich," Bea said. "By the time the market corrects—whether it's about the environment or about medicine—the poor are dead."

Still, despite its intellectual thrill, the argument wasn't as neat as we wanted it to be. Our bellyaching about capitalism always seemed to butt up against the lack of robust alternatives, and older experiments were biting the dust. "China Confronts Contradictions between Marxism and Markets," reported the *Washington Post* in 2005, citing an eighteen-month campaign "to modernize Chinese Marxism . . . [and] reconcile increasingly obvious contradictions between the government's founding ideology and its broad free-market reforms." The article described the ongoing dialogue among Chinese academics and government officials as they struggled to justify free-market economics in the nuances of Marxist studies. Reporter Edward Cody described an internal debate "pitting those who advocate pressing ahead with liberalizing reforms against those who say the country must hark back to its socialist roots because too many people are being hurt by the transformation."

Writing in the *Guardian* in 2005, James McGregor described China as a society in which communism remains the official ideology while the practice is anything but. "The 'Yan'an Spirit' of self-sacrifice and simple living is still the professed ideal for Chinese officials," he wrote. "Officials still endure endless speeches and propaganda study sessions where the words of Marx and Lenin are swirled into ever more creative combinations. They then climb into their Audi or Mercedes saloons and check stock prices on their mobile phones as they head home to apartment buildings named Beverly Hills, Park Avenue or Palm Springs. . . . For most party officials, life is guided by the proverb zhi lu wei ma (point at a deer and call it a horse)."

Furthermore, democratization in China is progressing at a slower pace than capitalism, while inequality is on the rise. There are those in China, and in the former Soviet Union, who don't necessarily see the changing cost-benefit equation as an improvement. As McGregor notes, while the safety net under the poor has not yet completely frayed, "A country that was until recently poor but safe has become one that is unsettled and insecure. There is nothing to believe in but making money."

Although adamant free marketers refer to it pejoratively as "populist," a consensus is developing around the idea that human rights and the environment need some global protection from the fiscal flood. But protecting these rights and resources requires us to exempt certain components of our relationships, be they interpersonal exchanges or actions on the world stage, from the sole criterion of profitability. In a book review for the journal *Foreign Affairs*, Nobel Prize–winning economist Joseph Stiglitz suggested:

> The debate should not be centered on whether one is in favor of growth or against it. The question should be, are there policies that can promote what might be called moral growth—growth that is sustainable, that increases living standards not just today but for future generations as well, and that leads to a more tolerant, open society? Also, what can be done to ensure that the benefits of growth are shared equitably, creating a society with more social justice and solidarity rather than one with deep rifts and cleavages of the kind that became so apparent in New Orleans in the aftermath of Hurricane Katrina?

The Tomales Bay Institute, now part of Common Assets in Minneapolis, has proposed the concept of "the commons" to define things we should communally own and protect for the collective good. These things are as varied as air and water, sidewalks and libraries, nursery rhymes and the Internet; but all are components of public physical, political, and cultural space. Yet Peter Barnes, a progressive entrepreneur and author who helped found the institute, notes that Walt Disney has claimed ownership of fairy tales and that energy companies pollute air and water as though they own them— although cleaning up the mess is very costly and frequently subsidized by public money. Freedom from regulation, assert proponents

of the commons, is not cost-free; it just shifts the gain to the corporation and the cost to the public. "Think of it as an operating system,"
said Barnes. "We want to upgrade capitalism to protect nature and
reduce inequality. The right says no to government, yes to markets.
The left says yes to government, no to markets. We need to get out of
that box."

When Barnes proposes the idea of the commons and Sage raises
the proposition of value-neutral capitalism, both imply that the practice of capitalism can be either good or bad, depending on the outcomes. If the relationships advance human rights, the process is
environmentally sustainable, the product is not inherently harmful,
and the profits increase global equity, their reasoning suggests it's
good. If the relationships diminish human rights, the process is environmentally damaging, the product is inherently harmful, and the
distribution of profit increases global inequality, then it's bad.

But how does accomplishing good translate into real-world
terms? Many of my colleagues thought the European Union's method-
ical redistribution of collective resources to raise living standards in
poorer member countries represents the progressive politics of the
possible. But even the EU economies constantly battle free-market
pressures, and the outlines of a countervailing imperative remained
blurry.

If capitalism is like a fire or a flood, what is socialism? "It's the
fire department," said one friend, while another cynically consigned
it to "ashes." Younger colleagues without a personal cold war history
find the capitalism-socialism dichotomy useless. "We hardly talk about
it any more," said Stephen, my twenty-three-year-old researcher. "I
believe in capitalism, lightly regulated for greater equity. It's obvious
that nothing else seems to work better."

"I'd like something other than the current capitalism," said the
young emergency-room doctor who lives across the street from me.
"But for socialism, we need people to be good, better than we are, less
greedy."

And there it was, the heart of my parents' lessons. I had been
taught that one should work hard for sufficiency but that surfeit was
akin to gluttony, a kind of sin. Free-market capitalism though, was
based on individual and systemic accumulation, often to excess, on a
theoretically level playing field without collective responsibility for
collective well-being. I recalled a longtime progressive strategist's
conversation about the gains of the women's movement. "The insight

of our generation was that the personal is also political," she said. "My fear is that we are in an era where the political could become purely personal." She worried that prevailing politics would dictate that being poor or rich is solely a personal matter, dependent on personal attributes, with no systemic analysis or accountability. So, indeed, it has become; so, at least, our privately oriented public rule making has become. Likewise, the remedies for inequality have moved away from the collective to the personal, away from policy to charity.

Howard Schultz grew up in economic circumstances fairly similar to my own, but he perceived his childhood as deprivation and vowed to leave it behind. According to his plan, once he'd achieved his goal, he would leverage his success to help others achieve economic and professional gains. But he believed that a change in his own actions, rather than a change in the system, would create transformation. And one could argue that he has succeeded beyond all expectations in changing his circumstances, and those of others.

Yet every morning when I get into the shower, I think about Darfur. Hot water on demand, taken for granted, is a sign of my privilege in a world where others have no drinking water. It would take more than charity, more than individual wealth, to change that equation. It's good to have some roses as well as bread, my parents taught me, but one is not entitled to have too much cake in a starving world.

Vijay Prashad acknowledges that "Our context is an unfortunate one," with few extant alternatives to capitalism beyond small cooperative experiments. "We tend to be more forgiving to 'good capitalists'; even left-wing regimes have accommodated themselves to a greater or lesser extent. But that shouldn't blind us to the broad basic problems that exist. There is an alternative. But what does it look like? We have very few answers for that, and that hems us in. But the solutions will come."

In the interim, he advises, we should follow the tao of a thousand flowers blooming. "We should be very generous to those around us. We need to experiment ideologically and strategically. In India there's a tradition of cooperative industry, but not so much elsewhere. Still, if you have a cooperative bookstore that works, maybe someone will say, 'Why can't we run the hospital the way we run the bookstore?' We can all criticize somebody else's attempt, be it a collective or micro-finance. But remember, Gandhi called his book *Stories of My Experiments with Truth*, not *My Truth*."

"It is the greedy bastards that think only about themselves that ruin the capitalistic system," thinks Paul Katzeff. "I never was sophisticated enough to be against capitalism. I was against 'capitalist pigs.' That's different. Now instead of being against, I am doing what I preach: being or creating a model that others might learn from. Perhaps learn that you can do business in many different ways, and that your business can and should reflect your highest values, and of course the values of sustainability in a world that needs help."

At what point does it cease to become capitalism and become socialism? Or vice versa? Perhaps it matters less than we think. The world, it seems, is one economic ecosystem with a host of economic macro- and microclimates. We're either on the grid or off the grid or hanging out in the system's many nooks and crannies. As one of my colleagues once said, "We don't have a party line, but we do have a bottom line." It makes little sense to hold Starbucks accountable for the systemic malfeasances of capitalism or transnational finance; for that we have to find a different venue, a larger frame. But if we begin with the values by which we make decisions about the balance of profit and principle, we have a baseline by which to measure both Starbucks and ourselves.

11 Goodness As Battleground

What's good? And who gets to decide? Can capitalism ever be good? How about globalization? A transnational corporation? An employer? How about us?

These were the questions that growled and rumbled beneath the Seattle protests, and my colleagues were not of one mind about the answers. "People who go into corporate management didn't sign up to be civil servants," notes Liz Butler, who works at ForestEthics. "But increasingly, the crucial decisions are being made in boardrooms, and we need them to take on that role." In her opinion, because Starbucks claims to be a good citizen, we progressives have to hold the company to its promise. Marshall Ganz, a veteran organizer who teaches at Harvard's Kennedy School, emphasizes the importance of developing alternate power structures to keep business interests in check. "Corporations do what they do," he said, "which is to make money. If they do it responsibly, so much the better. But the real problem is that we don't have strong enough governments or other public institutions to constrain them or provide countervailing power."

Marshall's answer is to build other strong institutions, including unions, to keep corporations from operating freely at the citizens' expense. It's our duty as moral human beings to demand a better balance and organize it into being. Furthermore, he's skeptical of business classes that focus on ethics. "Those are the *rules* of behavior," he told me. "Morality, that's about what you actually *do*, how you behave. It's like St. Augustine's difference between knowing good and loving good"—you can know what's good and still behave badly.

On one level, each of us gets to know or love good by whatever combination of faith, need, experience, voracity, and empathy guides our lives. But when a transnational corporation arbitrarily decides what's good for us, that judgment can be invasive and global, affecting as many people, and sometimes as much money, as a small government. Furthermore, unlike a government that we ostensibly select, business allows hardly any of us a role in choosing its leaders or decision makers.

Corporate social responsibility is the catchphrase for the point at which companies decide how much or little good they must attempt to be successful and profitable in the marketplace. Writing in the *New York Times Magazine* in 2004, journalist Michael Lewis interviewed a Berkeley professor named Kellie McElhaney, who told him, "I get very nervous when I hear people say, 'We do it because it's the right thing to do.' I don't think unprofitable corporate goodness is sustainable."

Of course, a company can still be profitable while indulging in a few selected morality-driven projects. It's a way to adhere to Milton Friedman's "the business of business is business" while satisfying critics and their own sense of goodness. Despite his counterculture roots, Bo Burlingham, editor-at-large for the magazine *Inc.*, thinks that's probably an appropriate balance for publicly traded companies. "When you go public, you basically are taking people's money," he said. "Along with it come certain obligations, both legal and moral, to provide what you promised, which is to do everything you can to maximize investment. If you don't want to do that, don't take their money." This is why Burlingham prefers privately held companies that don't have the same obligations and constraints. But he added, "I don't think there's anything in capitalism that forces people to be polluters, treat their employees badly, be harmful to community. It's a total cop-out. You have to do what's in interest of shareholders; well, yeah, but you don't have to do illegal or unethical things in their name." He pointed me toward a debate in the magazine *Reason*, a libertarian publication dedicated to "free minds and free markets." The debate pits Friedman against Whole Foods' founder John Mackey, who unlike Schultz is positively boastful about his anti-unionism while embracing organic produce and New Age management-speak. Mackey asserts:

The most successful businesses put the customer first, ahead of the investors. In the profit-centered business, customer happiness is merely a means to an end: maximizing profits. In the customer-centered business, customer happiness is an end in itself, and will be pursued with greater interest, passion, and empathy than the profit-centered business is capable of. . . . To extend our love and care beyond our narrow self-interest is antithetical to neither our human nature nor our financial success. Rather, it leads to the further fulfillment of both.

Friedman, whom Mackey considers a "personal hero," responds that the differences between the two viewpoints are rhetorical. Quoting from his 1970 article in the *New York Times*, he says:

In practice the doctrine of social responsibility is frequently a cloak for actions that are justified on other grounds rather than a reason for those actions.

To illustrate, it may well be in the long run interest of a corporation that is a major employer in a small community to devote resources to providing amenities to that community or to improving its government. . . .

In each of these . . . cases, there is a strong temptation to rationalize these actions as an exercise of "social responsibility." In the present climate of opinion, with its widespread aversion to "capitalism," "profits," the "soulless corporation" and so on, this is one way for a corporation to generate goodwill as a by-product of expenditures that are entirely justified in its own self-interest. . . . If our institutions and the attitudes of the public make it in their self-interest to cloak their actions in this way, I cannot summon much indignation to denounce them.

Progressives might share Friedman's belief that CSR cloaks hide daggers, but a whole business of goodness has evolved to encourage the goodness of business. More than 1,000 participants attended the 2006 Business for Social Responsibility (BSR) meeting in New York, which was accompanied by an eight-page *New York Times* advertising supplement packed with the lingo of *collaboration, sustainability*, and *stakeholders*. Aron Cramer, president and CEO of BSR, confirms that "attention to CSR is mushrooming. In 1995, when I started here, there were very few codes of conduct to guide dealings with suppliers. Now there are thousands, and more than a thousand corporate CSR reports." Founded in 1992, BSR was originally grounded in the ethos of Ben & Jerry and Tom's of Maine: smallish, successful enterprises infused with sixties sensibilities. Now its participant companies include the likes of Coca-Cola and Wal-Mart, companies not primarily known for beneficence or good citizenship. BSR has a good reputation for sparking dialogue that encourages companies to move ahead with CSR initiatives. But Cramer acknowledges that no company will be expelled from BSR for failing to live up to its word. "Our philosophy is that we're ready to work with any company that's serious," said Cramer. "No company is irredeemably bad. We do not set standards or give seals of approval. We leave that to others."

These contradictions also dog the U.N.'s Global Compact, a voluntary network of corporations, NGOs, and trade unions subscribing to ten principles that address human rights, labor standards, environmental responsibility, and opposition to corruption. The compact replaced the U.N.'s Center on Transnational Corporations, whose mandate had been to monitor and curb the abuses of global corporations. But opposition of large member states ultimately led to the center's dissolution, and the subsequent Global Compact is self-regulated by its corporate participants with no outside verification or oversight. Even so, as of mid-2007, only 106 of the roughly 3,191 participating companies were based in the United States, and only six of those were in the food and drink category. Three were coffee companies: Starbucks, Dean's Beans, and Green Mountain Coffee, the latter two leaders in fair trade beans. A fourth was the Omanhene Cocoa Bean Company. The remaining two, however, were the Coca-Cola Company and Coca-Cola Enterprises (Nestlé is a Swiss signatory), both of them companies with ethical baggage. As with Business for Social Responsibility, corporations could sign on to the ten mildly noble principles and then go about their business. And a number of the signatories, according to participating NGOs, had done just that: they'd joined but then continued to violate basic human rights provisions.

Kathryn Mulvey is director of Corporate Accountability International (CAI), formerly known as INFACT, and she sees the Global Compact as a very big problem. CAI, one of those "others" that Cramer referred to, gained recognition for its groundbreaking campaign against Nestlé, which had been marketing infant formula to poor countries that lacked clean drinking water; mothers mixed the formula with contaminated water, and infants sickened and sometimes died. After the successful Nestlé campaign, CAI took aim against big tobacco; the result was the International Framework for Tobacco Control under the U.N.'s World Health Organization, which prohibited tobacco advertising and promotion.

"NGOs around the world are highly critical of the Global Compact because it includes notoriously abusive corporations like Nestlé, Royal Dutch Shell, and Coca-Cola," said Mulvey. She believes these companies are hiding behind the U.N. logo to enhance their images, knowing that they can violate the principles with impunity. "By confusing rhetoric with reality," she said, "corporate-driven voluntary codes and initiatives can also undermine the case for binding, independently enforced international policies to hold global corporations accountable to the interests of society." The issues raised by the Global Compact are not dissimilar to those attached to the Common Code for the Coffee Community, which gives members of the "mainstream coffee community" (including Nestlé, Sara Lee, Kraft, and the big trading houses) an opportunity to ascribe goodness to themselves without necessarily having to change how they do business.

No wonder so many progressives take a jaundiced view of CSR. They're inclined to see efforts at environmentalism as "greenwashing" and avowals of employee friendliness and other socially responsible claims as "bluewashing"—token amounts of good that mask greater evil. In an opinion piece for *commondreams.org*, Phillip Mattera, who heads the Corporate Research Project at the nonprofit Good Jobs First, cautions against trusting this sudden coziness between large corporations claiming environmental epiphanies and the environmental movement. He notes that many previous avowals of environmental enlightenment have been largely bogus, as when Mobil Chemical claimed that its Hefty trash bags were biodegradable and BP touted its investments in renewable energy. "It would behoove enviros to be more skeptical of corporate green claims and less eager to jump into bed with business," he wrote. "After all, the real purpose of the environmental movement is not simply to make technical adjustments to the way business operates but rather to push for fundamental and systemic changes."

These concerns were evident among colleagues who talked with me about Starbucks. Many were absolutely convinced that whatever good the company did was only for appearance rather than for true decency. But while there were problems in how Starbucks has interpreted its mandate to expand into every available corner of the globe,

I couldn't shake my sense that most company managers desperately wanted the company's goodness to be real. Yet the question remains: what is Starbucks willing to give up to earn its virtue?

In 2007, Sandra Taylor, Starbucks' senior vice president for CSR, looked both less corporate and more confident than when I first met her. Her windowless office glowed with mementos. Her hair was in fabulous braids, her presence both imposing and warm. When I first interviewed her in late 2003, she had recently moved to Starbucks from Kodak and was feeling her way into her position. In her job as senior vice president, she guided decisions at the intersection between Starbucks the corporation and Starbucks the world citizen, and reported directly to CEO Jim Donald. Her tasks included overseeing farmer codes, governmental relations, diversity initiatives, and environmental integrity—a big job and often a dicey one, as the Ethiopian trademark conflict illustrated.

Like most other corporations, Starbucks has a charitable foundation, a basic, nonrisky way of meeting its citizenship goals. The foundation has traditionally supported community literacy and parks programs for children, mixing in disaster assistance because, as Taylor noted, disasters "often happen where we have stores or buy products. But when we deal with something like the tsunami in Indonesia or Hurricane Katrina, we try and think not just about the immediate but how can we be involved over the long term? How many people are talking about the tsunami today?" In response to those two disasters, the company budgeted 1 million dollars a year for each, with money docketed for a five-year period.

Taylor's portfolio also reflected the company's priorities and her own passionate concern about the fate of African women. In recent years, Starbucks had been buying coffee from Rwanda, which is trying to rescue its coffee farms from the ravages of a protracted war. "As a result of the genocide, women now own many of the farms and run the milling stations, trying to re-create and rebuild," Taylor told me. "That got me excited, so immediately we found a way to provide training for these women."

One of her tasks had been to reevaluate the company's approach to philanthropy and increase its overall impact. "What we learn over time is that the larger we grow, the clearer we need to be about what we stand for, and we have to be responsible for what we pick," she said. Her review process resulted in a new focus on the issue of clean drinking water, which dovetailed nicely with Starbucks' recent acquisition of Ethos, a small, socially conscious, bottled water company that donates some profits from each sale to support clean-water projects in Africa.

Why did Starbucks decide to focus on water rather than HIV/AIDS or hunger or any of the many other worthy causes that attract companies and celebrities who want to do good—or at least be seen as doing good? Bono, lead singer of the rock band U2, had, for example, launched Product Red to support HIV/AIDS programs in the global south, primarily in Africa; and numbers of corporations had signed on. On a recent walk past the windows of a Gap store, I'd noticed a stylish display of T-shirts, each bearing the word *RED*, posed alongside posters of stars decked out in the same shirts. Apple, Converse, and a number of other fashionable brands had committed to offer modish red-hued merchandise and allocate a percentage of profits to Bono's campaign.

Yet although the effort seemed consonant with Starbucks' style and substance, Starbucks wasn't on the list of sponsors. Taylor explained:

> Before we acquired Ethos water, we thought our focus should be about education and literacy. But we realized there was an expectation that a global company should take on a global issue. So my team sat down with a copy of the U.N. Millennium Development Goals, and we went through each of them and asked, "What seems to resonate with Starbucks?"
>
> I thought, "Where is there not enough activity from the corporate sector?" We decided that where we could make a difference was on access to clean drinking water and not HIV/AIDS. So that's why Product Red didn't really fit.

Also, without access to water, there is no coffee. "We looked at where our product comes from—coffee, tea, and cocoa. Water is so much a part of the processing of those crops," she told me. "And so much of what we sell in our stores is water as well, in every cup of coffee. That resonated with us. We thought there was an opportunity for us to take an integrated approach."

The U.N. Millennium Goals seek, among other things, to halve world poverty by 2015; and focusing on those goals by hiring staff with commitment and expertise speaks to the corporation's seriousness. On the other hand, water concerns are hardly new: NGOs have been dealing with water access and scarcity for decades. Moreover, the issue of bottled water is fraught with political implications. The spring water business is an extractive industry, which can damage existing ecosystems. It also involves the use of plastic bottles that are inherently antithetical to environmental sustainability. But in consultation with its advisors, Starbucks determined that its financial commitment to water projects in the developing world and its capacity to advance U.S. education projects about the issue were worth the trade-off on bottles, although Taylor and the company acknowledged the inherent contradiction.

Are goodness programs that slice a little money off the profit margin of a *RED* T-shirt or an Ethos bottle primarily created for the good they do the beneficiaries or to burnish a company's image? "It's a typical approach these days," observed Rob Walker, who writes the "Consumed" column for the *New York Times Magazine*. "Sell something to First World consumers, and a little of it will go to something else. It's not particularly plausible to me, to think of buying a bottle of Ethos water as your ethical hit, 'I'm doing my part to help the poor.' It's done more to add value to the brand. And it provides a false sense that shopping can solve everything."

Furthermore, he thought that skimming five cents off the price of a bottle of water or becoming a successful entrepreneur of anti-brand T-shirts or sneakers were not sufficient to reduce poverty and promote equity. "It's probably wrong to think doing exactly what you were doing without sacrificing anything solves everything. It's often the case that fighting large significant problem involves sacrifice."

Kathryn Mulvey at CAI concurs. "Who'd have thought twenty years ago that you'd walk into a supermarket and there'd be an aisle full of bottled water?" she told me. "Water bottlers have created a market where none existed before. So we see Ethos as another one of the brands that exists there. It's really a social responsibility image brand for Starbucks, part of their social marketing. If the corporation were really looking for solutions, then donating a nickel on each bottle of plastic-encased water isn't the biggest contribution they could make."

A deeper concern is that global justice activists view bottled water as part of a massive, and venal, scheme to commodify and privatize water. As people become accustomed to bottled water at prices that exceed the per-gallon cost of gasoline, paying for a critical necessity that was once in the public domain becomes a legitimate cost. Audrey Lincoff and I briefly discussed this problem during our travels in Costa Rica. She held that, to resolve problems of inequity,

one needed to create a market model and then make change by applying the model. I countered that clean water is a human right and
should be excluded from the imperatives of the free market system.

When I broached the subject to Taylor, she said, "I would never
suggest we sell bottled water to poor people in Africa or India. I drink
tap water, but I know I have a choice. My passion is around those
places where there are no taps. I want to dig wells, and identify
sources of water for those communities. Bottled water doesn't even
enter into that conversation for me."

"I've compartmentalized my thinking," she added, recalling how,
on a visit to Ethiopia, she sat in a field talking with village elders. "We
were talking about wanting to help girls and provide them with an
education. And the elders said, 'If you want to help the girls, get us
water.' Girls spend hours every day walking to get water—three hours
there and back. They won't go to school after puberty because there are
no sanitary facilities or latrines. It's those people I think about, not
those making choices between tap water and bottled water."

For Taylor, the ability to channel more money into water projects
was a good trade-off for selling bottled water in Starbucks retail stores.
"If consumers don't buy Ethos water, they'll buy some other water
somewhere else," she said. "This way, at least they get to learn a
little about the issue, and we get to give more to water projects."

For Mulvey at CAI, however, bottled water remains extremely
problematic. "[Starbucks] makes it seem that promoting bottled water
is a solution, but if we have contaminated public tap water, we need to
commit the resources to clean up our water systems, not create a system where those with resources can buy bottled water and the rest are
out of luck." She pointed to a South African initiative to put in prepaid, privatized water meters. "People started using contaminated
water, and they had the worst cholera outbreak in the nation's history.
If bottled water is presented as a solution to our water problems, we'll
have bigger and bigger social and health gaps between those who have
resources and those who don't." CAI has targeted the major players in
the 55-billion-dollar bottled water industry—namely, those recurring
bad actors Nestlé, Coke, and Pepsi, which together account for close to
half of the bottled water consumed in the United States. But Mulvey
warns that if current water trends continue, close to two-thirds of the
world's population will be without sufficient water.

In Starbucks' case, donating a percentage of each bottle of Ethos
to fund access to clean water is much better than not doing so, but

coming out against bottled water might be the visionary position for the long haul. As global NGOs increasingly campaign against bottled water, the company might want to reconsider its approach. Not long after my conversation with Taylor, a number of other companies leaped onto the 2007 U.N. World Water Day bandwagon. Notably, Procter & Gamble rolled out a Children's Safe Drinking Water effort. It remained to be seen how Starbucks would position its own efforts and if they would ultimately be significant.

Corporations always point to their charitable ventures to reinforce their claims of virtue. Of far greater significance, though, is how a company handles its power and its relationships. On that front, the Starbucks record was mixed. By 2006, environmentalists rarely had serious concerns about the company's impact in coffee-growing countries, where Starbucks was acquiring an exemplary record as a protector of biodiversity and water. Domestic environmental watchdogs voiced only occasional gripes about paper waste and insufficient recycling. Starbucks has also accommodated complaints about the healthiness of its products, vetting grievances, checking avenues for action, and implementing satisfactory resolutions. Faced with chanting protesters in cow costumes (courtesy of a cluster of safe-food organizations), Starbucks eventually sought suppliers for hormone-free milk. With vehement encouragement from Science in the Public Interest, which threatened to bust the company for calories, the company eliminated transfats from its store offerings and introduced lower-fat Frappuccinos and more healthful salads—although as far as I could see, most customers still gravitated toward the fully loaded options.

But a few big issues remained, all of them rife with contradictions, all continuing to haunt the company in its quest for model corporate citizenship: between employee-friendly processes and anti-union practices, between humanitarian vision and global product reach, between cultural pluralism and cultural hegemony, between being a neighborhood store and the biggest coffeehouse chain in the world.

Campaigns against Starbucks have ebbed and flowed, many of them spurred by specific corporate missteps such as the Ethiopian conflict and anti-union harassment at the Kent roasting plant. But a nexus of detractors, including hardline fair traders, strident anti-corporate activists, and cultural jammers, have fought Starbucks as if its very existence were the problem. As a result, the company faces a constantly moving hurdle: the moment it leaps over one objection, another appears. And if a "good" company like Starbucks is continuously slammed for not doing better, why should other companies, including its competitors, make the effort at all? No matter what happens, the challenging organizations have a win-win situation: if the company succumbs, they've defeated it; if it doesn't, their militancy is reaffirmed as noble. Does their effort ultimately achieve more good for a greater number of people? That question is often lost in the scuffle.

As a union and community organizer, I've had ample opportunity to reflect on how targets are chosen to expose injustices to public view. Much of the theory about target selection comes from the work of Saul Alinsky, the curmudgeonly father of modern community organizing. Alinsky, who started out as a Chicago social worker, championed the right of powerless people to collectively demand change in the system and take direct action to win it. In *Rules for Radicals*, he exhorts, "Pick the target, freeze it, personalize it, and polarize it." He goes on to explain, "One of the criteria in picking your target is the target's vulnerability—where do you have the power to start? Furthermore, any target can always say, 'why do you center on me when there are others to blame as well?' When you 'freeze the target,' you disregard these arguments and, for the moment, all the others to blame."

So for decades we've been doing just that. We pick the targets, not necessarily because they most deserve confrontation (although sometimes they do) but because they are most visible, most newsworthy, most vulnerable, most concerned about protecting their good name or brand—and even sometimes most anxious to do good. In other words, Starbucks is the perfect fall guy.

Yet in reality Starbucks is, in many cases, far weightier than its competitors on the goodness scale. "Compared to the conventional coffee giants, Starbucks is in a totally different league, whether it's Fair Trade, C.A.F.E. Practices, lending for small farmers, or internal employee policies," said Paul Rice, head of TransFair USA, the fair trade certification and labeling organization, in whose name many of the protestors took to the streets. "You read their CSR report and compare it to the general indifference of Kraft, Sara Lee, or Nestlé, and it's obvious that Starbucks is best in its class. I've been working with this company for seven years; they do CSR because they believe in it. Alongside their business reasons, they hold genuinely progressive values. I understand that strategy of going after relatively better companies, but I can also understand why people at Starbucks feel that some of the activist pressure has been unfair."

The strategy of targeting the most sympathetic employers has been common in the labor movement as well. Historically, unions often tried to raise the bar by first negotiating with a better employer, using the new gains as a standard for subsequent negotiations. But there were indications that, when it came to companies in the global economy, placing the highest demands on those who already did the most threatened to put them at a competitive disadvantage, especially if their less decent competitors were left unchallenged.

One of my colleagues watched this dynamic at work in a labor dispute involving a major brewery. "It had one of the very best contracts in the industry," he told me. "True, they wanted some flexibility, but there was no indication they were trying to weaken the union, or cut wages or benefits. But this faction went after them, mostly as an opportunistic way to position a leader as an aggressive bargainer. They publicly whipped the company at huge public events. It was wrong; it was despicable. There were no real gains, and it took a long while to repair that relationship. For those of us who do this work, it has to be about credibility as well as progress."

Mulvey at CAI tends to share this perspective. "That's why we almost always go directly for the industry leaders," she told me. "You have to assess who's really doing the most damage and put your attention and resources there. We had this experience when we were working on tobacco issues. It was very attractive to go after the R. J. Reynolds Company and Joe Camel because the character was very popular at the time, and everybody thought, 'It's a cartoon character; it appeals to kids.' But we quickly discovered that Philip Morris was much more dangerous and the Marlboro Man was much more appealing to teens. So that's where we put our energy."

When I raised the subject of targeting with Barbara Briggs at the National Labor Committee, she said she feels it's critical to target the industry lowlifes who, by their reach and greed, push standards downward, although she acknowledged that progressives occasionally have a penchant for targeting affluent niche markets instead. "There's a lot of excitement about fair trade, and developing an enclave alternative is a nice thing," she told me. In her opinion, it gives people with disposable income a way to feel better about their purchasing choices and helped educate and engage people about the issue. "But we're not going to end child labor, sweatshops, and human rights abuses unless we also come up with a strategy that confronts the likes of Wal-Mart and Procter & Gamble, a strategy which affects the mass production and distribution network. Otherwise millions of workers around the world fall into deeper and deeper misery."

When labor seriously focused on Wal-Mart, it tackled an employer that actually was bringing down the wages and standards of others in its sector and having an enormously negative impact on U.S. policies and standards. Wal-Mart is fifty-four times larger than Starbucks—345 billion dollars in annual revenues compared to 6.4 billion dollars—and its policies have a more direct effect on living standards. A coffeehouse company, no matter how ubiquitous, is no comparison.

Despite the easy rhetoric of the left, Starbucks is a different case. Only in its dealings with unions did the company exhibit what I consider immoral behavior. Unlike many, Starbucks refrained from lobbying on labor issues and eschewed membership in the U.S. Chamber of Commerce; but it aggressively, and sometimes illegally, tried to keep its workers from supporting unions. And it was wrong.

Even with this serious caveat, however, if the most basic platform is "first, do no harm," Starbucks has done pretty well. It produces neither arms nor excessive pollution; people aren't dying because of what it makes; and given that no one is going to expire for lack of a Frappuccino, it doesn't price people out of necessities.

Challenges to its virtue have most often centered on how the company should allocate its revenues to compensate farmers and workers along the supply chain. The controversies are not based on comparisons with its competitors (where Starbucks already excels) but focus on demands that the company move even closer to an ideal of justice. This discussion is bracketed by questions of floor and ceiling. What is the minimum compensation at which a person can live in dignity? What is the maximum compensation that can be allocated to people at the top of the scale before the system becomes de facto unjust? As the presidency of George W. Bush has tottered to its close, the widening income disparity between the bottom and the top has faced greater scrutiny from the media and the public. That disparity is mirrored in the discrepancy in pay between corporate CEOs and their employees. In 2007, Congress passed the first federal minimum wage legislation in ten years, raising the paltry minimum of $5.15 an hour to the slightly less paltry sum of $7.25 by 2009. No state had a minimum exceeding $7.80. Meanwhile, according to the Institute for

Policy Studies' 2006 Executive Excess report, the average CEO made 411 times the pay of the average company worker, as opposed to only forty-two times as much in 1980. "If the minimum wage had risen at the same pace as CEO pay since 1990," the report notes, "it would be worth $22.61 today."

IWW organizers were fond of pointing out that, while a hard-working Starbucks barista working close to full time earned roughly 17,000 dollars a year, Howard Shultz's total compensation in 2006 was 4,798,745 dollars, plus 99.4 million for cashing in stock options. Even without the options, Schultz made roughly three hundred times as much as the average barista—a modest salary compared to the earnings of some top corporate executives and sports stars but still enough to give one pause.

A similar calculus was applied to the price that Starbucks paid coffee farmers for their beans. Whereas the 2006 C market fluctuated between $0.94 and $1.30 per pound and the fair trade price was $1.26, Starbucks coffee purchases for the year averaged $1.42. Opponents argued that, with Starbucks charging twenty-six dollars for a pound of Ethiopian coffee or earning roughly one hundred dollars for the drinks served from that pound in the stores, farmers were getting less than 5 percent of the value, an immorally small share.

In truth, there is little concrete proof that a reduction in CEO compensation would automatically result in higher pay for the workforce. With the size and scale of global corporations, we do not yet know what the impact would be. Nor do we know whether Ethiopia's licensing agreement will ultimately yield the desired result. Rather, excessive CEO compensation and exorbitant corporate profits have an entirely different significance. In a society where status and power, not to mention housing and health care, are integrally tied to income and so inequitably distributed, those figures are a graphic representation of who has it and who doesn't. The conspicuous wealth of the cake eaters accentuates the plight of those without sufficient bread, and the latte drinkers are juxtaposed against those who have no water.

One noted global justice activist is indignant that Starbucks executives are able to send their children to private school while the children of coffee farmers have to walk to school barefoot through snake-infested country. According to such an equation, Starbucks can never do enough. But not every global justice activist makes such impossible demands. "We're not going to be able to go backward," said a leader at CAI. "We're not asking people to suffer comprehensively, but to behave wisely. . . . To put in place the controls, accountability, and rules that make equity and sustainability possible."

The difference in these definitions of goodness—between being better than the rest and being good in a larger moral economic context—seems to be where the rub of capitalism hits the road of global economic equity, back to Marshall Ganz's distinction between the rules that guide corporate ethics and what constitutes morality in the larger scheme of things. The real challenges of protecting human life and human rights at the struggling end of the global income spectrum are formidable.

When it comes to making poor people or poor countries more affluent through well-paid labor and innovative development, as opposed to charity and aid, no organization, methodology, or ideology has been consistently successful. It's easy to take out one's frustration on Starbucks or any other big enterprise that's getting rich while the people at the bottom stay desperately poor. Yet Starbucks is not an oil company, making a profit out of a scarce resource whose extraction, transport, and use defile the earth. It's not Big Pharma withholding life-saving drugs to fatten its bottom line nor an Enron that bilks shareholders and the public. It's not a Nestlé driving down the market price of coffee whenever it can nor a Wal-Mart wresting the last cent from its supply chain. Starbucks' lobbying efforts have been very limited, it doesn't have a PAC, and it makes no political contributions to candidates.

Rather, Starbucks has taken what was previously a surplus commodity subject to unpredictable market fluctuations and carved out a niche for fine coffee that can command a higher price. It has almost single-handedly expanded the specialty coffee sector from a small enclave into a worldwide phenomenon. Its success has increased demand, sales, and prices for high-end coffee farmers, creating new opportunities for sustainable farming and sustainable lives.

Domestically, it has not undercut the coffee prices charged by the local mom-and-pop coffee shops, and it has not undercut the wages. In fact, it generally charges more, pays better, and provides more benefits. Meanwhile, the number of small coffee shops and their sales continue to rise.

Is this enough? Maybe not. Is it better than most? Absolutely.

During the Ethiopian trademark controversy, I asked Paul Rice of TransFair USA about measuring fairness by the percentage of retail value that goes to the farmers as opposed to the per pound price. He told me,

I know it sounds good, but I actually feel that's the wrong focus. In the commodities trade, lots of steps have to happen between farmers and consumers. To reduce the number of middlemen, farmer cooperatives become millers, transporters, traders, and exporters. That's a huge leap forward. But most Third World farmers don't yet have the capacity to, say, roast and package their own coffee and export the finished product to the U.S. market, much less establish their own retail outlets up here, at least in the short term. So there's a necessary role for coffee roasters and retailers, and they incur lots of costs that have to be reflected in retail pricing. So the farmer's percentage is, unfortunately, destined to remain fairly small. I think it's unfair to say farmers are getting only x percent of retail.

His different perspective, he told me, had come from his experiences in Nicaragua.

In 1990, farmers were getting ten cents per pound in the Nicaraguan market. I organized an export cooperative, and we sold to the Boston-based Fair Trade pioneer, Equal Exchange, who paid us the Fair Trade price of $1.26 per pound. That first year, after milling and export costs, we were able to pay farmers a net price of one dollar: ten times more than their neighbors down the road were getting. "Pablo un Dólar," that's what they started calling me. It was the difference between starvation wages and survival. The analysis of what it means in pure terms is an intellectually interesting exercise but, in the end, it's not the most important yardstick of success.

That doesn't mean we shouldn't encourage Starbucks to do good and to do better or that Ethiopia isn't entitled to its trademarks. But it does raise questions about where and how we expend our energies and whom we choose to pillory.

12 Bread. Roses. Coffee.

If Starbucks has forced me to reassess the dance of conscience and capital, it's also led me to reconsider the role of individual leadership. At the beginning of my research and again toward the end, I interviewed Starbucks founder Howard Schultz, SEIU president Andy Stern, and global justice activist Medea Benjamin. Howard, of course, was central to the story; Andy and Medea, both part of my extended "movement tribe," served as interpreters of data, lenses through which I could examine Starbucks' perceived flaws. Together, the three leaders embody in human and organizational form the bits of my own life that converged so vividly in Seattle: a trade unionist with a passion for global equity and a taste for strong coffee.

Each leader sits on the progressive side of the political table, but they do not necessarily view one another as allies; Medea and Howard are in fact adversaries. Yet my interviews have forced me to conclude that they have more in common than any one of them might choose to admit. All are definitely Type A personalities: tense, driven, and ambitious. All have gained reputations as iconoclasts and trendsetters. Under their leadership their organizations have expanded and flourished; and all have challenged others in their field with bold ideas and structural innovations. Former employees from each organization tell tales about the ruthless pursuit of goals, excessive demands for loyalty, and high-minded public principles belied by high-handed internal practices; other co-workers are fiercely committed to them and their respective enterprises. All three have attained a certain star status based on a combination of smarts, success, charisma, guts, and skillful public relations. None seems to need much sleep.

The leaders also hold two significant tenets in common. First, the world they separately envision is internationalist in culture and spirit, transcending geographic boundaries yet remaining accountable for human rights, basic fairness, and environmental sustainability. Second, each believes that government must play a role in assessing and counteracting the inequities that flourish in a free-market economy. If the events in Seattle pointed up their differences in world view, the grim politics of the new millennium—the discouraging 2000 election, the 9/11 World Trade Center bombings, the Iraq war, and the interminable Bush administration, with its privatizing of public assets alongside growing income disparities—accentuates the values they share.

Yet their personal backgrounds and ideologies have led them to different organizational homes and predisposed them to seek different forms of redress. Howard is a quintessential American liberal, espousing a social role for government and business; but he is content with capital market solutions and sees no need for a radical perspective. He believes in using his own success to help others achieve economic and professional gains rather than in changing the system. After all, he's already changed the way we drink coffee.

As the founder of Global Exchange and a longtime Starbucks adversary, Medea is a proudly anticorporate radical who rejects the liberal approach. She believes that both the union and the business models are top-down and ultimately unsustainable. "It's much more exciting to look at worker ownership and cooperatives," she told me. "We're about an alternative vision of how we want to spend our lives and our money, so we can step out of a corporate world with which we are not comfortable."

The labor movement, which needs both capital's material blessings and the radicals' anticorporate fervor to rectify income and power imbalances, has always kept a foot in each camp. Increasingly, Andy has found himself reaching out in both directions, sharing the stage with Wal-Mart's CEO to promote health care reform but also funding Wal-Mart Watch to call the company to public account for its damaging policies. It's a risky strategy. Unions and companies are generally depicted in head-to-head conflict. But it may well be that labor also plays a bridging role between business capital and radical conscience in the pursuit of a more equitable distribution of wealth.

These days, the Democratic party is the most inclusive road to a nominally more progressive agenda. But the crumbling of labor has created a big divide in its ranks. The right, knowing that labor has traditionally made the difference between good intentions and good change, has systematically savaged it. Yet even businesses that see themselves as liberal often want nothing to do with unions, and the global justice movement and unions share little cultural glue to cohere them. As 2007 drew to a close, it seemed entirely possible that Andy's effort to reconstruct the bridge would be shunned on both shores; corporations might feel powerful enough to ignore any accommodation, and leftists were already dismissing his initiatives as collaboration with the enemy.

Both in the United States and around the world, however, progressive change generally occurs where labor and a broad swath of the intellectual community are allied. In the first half of the twentieth century, little of the legislative agenda promoted by U.S. radicals and condoned by liberal business interests came to pass until unions gained power. Only then did unemployment insurance, social security, and occupational health and safety become law. Only then did the grueling work of mine and mill become a path into the middle class and into a college education for the next generation.

Howard, along with Andy and Medea, believes in the goals of economic security and equal opportunity. But systemic democratic change, like reforming the health care system, is not a company-centered decision like substituting arabica for robusta. Public corporations don't have the mandate or the will to prioritize societal well-being over profit, and progressive organizations alone don't have the power to change the equation. Without government impetus to bind together business and civil society, social goals fall by the wayside; and without an amalgam of interests, no such government can win. "I don't think there's any question that the world economy is getting rebalanced," Andy told me. "It's not a bad thing, but there are no rules. It's a competitive race that only through supply and demand is starting to bring up wages and benefits in places like China. But it's not the intention; it's just the result. So it's not thoughtful. It's not directed toward a planned outcome of 'wouldn't it be great if in twenty years everybody in the world could eat and have health care?'"

Forging a bigger vision—and electing a government willing to pursue it—requires an intact bridge from conscience to capital with leaders and institutions to anchor it. Howard, like Andy, understands this. "I can't apologize for the fact that we're a business that has to make a profit," he said. "I can't apologize for the fact that we have a global opportunity, and I can't apologize for the fact that we are expanding. But I can meet people more than halfway and say, 'Listen, if you allow us to do the things that we have to do as a business, we believe you will see that we can be a very strong advocate for doing business the right way, and you can use us as a model, and perhaps we can learn something together.'"

Perhaps. In the early days of my research, Howard Schultz and Andy Stern were strangers to each other. Given that both were notable public advocates of revamping the health care system, one would think they should have met. After all, health care had propelled Howard to take his first lobbying trip to D.C. "I tried to frame this as not a Democratic or Republican issue," he related. "It's just un-American that 50 million people don't have health care." He acknowledged that he shared this concern with unions but was cautious about pursuing alliances. "I think they absolutely should have a seat at the table, and I've never denied a conversation with anyone who wanted to talk to me about these issues in a constructive way," he asserted. "But we don't want to be used; it's tricky, a lot of people have a lot of agendas."

In 2006, however, when Andy invited Howard to address the SEIU executive board, Howard decided to accept. The meeting went well, and both leaders seemed pleased to have made the connection. Nonetheless, when Andy and business leaders stepped out in public to jointly promote health care reform, Howard was not in the fore-front. When it came to collaborative efforts that implied powershar-ing, Starbucks, true to form, seemed unwilling to take the next move.

Goodness, one of my colleagues has suggested, should be judged on how we wield whatever agency or power we have in our sphere of influence, whether large or small. Both Howard and Andy were flex-ing and testing to determine the sizes of their spheres, their personal and organizational tolerances for risk, and the latitude their constituents would allow them.

And Medea? Just as the counterculture always reinvents the edge, so does the political left; and its existence creates a cascade of ideas and possibilities. In the United States, the left doesn't command power to control, although its influence often exceeds its numbers. Almost by definition—by brand, if you will—it prefers to remain in the opposition rather than engage in the long, frustrating process of compromise. But although "big noise" can be unpredictable, and sometimes misplaced, we need it to remind us of the bigger problems: ending the Iraq war, promoting single-payer national health care, raising the alarm over the commoditization of water, insisting on a larger share of profits for African coffee growers. Unhampered by constraints of accountability to shareholders or voting members, activists can act flamboyantly and advance controversial issues further up on our personal and political agendas. At its best, the global justice movement reminds us to dream the big dreams of justice and peace.

"So, what do you *really* think about Starbucks?" my friends ask. "Is it good or bad?"

For more than a year I equivocated. I liked many of the Starbucks people I'd met—from the workers at my local shop on Eighth Street to the managers at headquarters. I'd grown to respect its initiatives in coffee-growing countries, although I hated how the company dealt with unions. I admired the management's intelligence and its nuanced approach to problem solving, though I grew weary of its company-speak. Yet I still just couldn't fathom how a drive-through window could be referred to as a "third place." Yes, it was neither home nor work. But respite? Moment of community? Give me a break!

Finally I knew: Starbucks is the Bill Clinton of corporations.

It's endearing and exasperating. It wants to be good and do good, but the company and I don't always agree on what that is. It's very smart, and it feels my pain; but occasionally it does something dumb that damages its reputation and belies its espoused values. It's sometimes less than brave in leading the way toward greater fairness; but then again, sometimes it does better than I expect. It hedges its bets and learns from its mistakes, although it still retains one or two blind spots. Sometimes it disappoints, but often it provides the meeting place it promises, a comfy touch of class, and a decent cup of coffee.

And just when I think it's not living up to expectations, I think of the competition—not the alternative coffeehouses that have always lived on the fringes of conventional commerce (that's why they're alternative) but the McDonald's and Wal-Marts of the world. Think of Bush, and you'd rather have Clinton. Think of other transnational corporations, and you'd rather have Starbucks as a neighbor, an employer, and a global citizen.

In some ways, Starbucks has succeeded too well. Depending on your point of view, it has either infiltrated the national culture or become it. Quite possibly both. As a consequence, observers can have trouble seeing the company for what it is: a successful, aggressive, transnational chain of coffee stores. Not, however, a conspiracy.

Like many successful entities, from individuals to nations, the source of Starbucks' competitive edge is also the source of its most conspicuous flaw—a passion to secure dominance that leads to a culture of excessive control. Starbucks prefers relationships that are one to one or, more accurately, power to no-power: company to worker, company to farmer, company to consumer. The moment the workers, farmers, or consumers unite for a larger voice—be it through a union like the Operating Engineers, a large cooperative like Fedecocagua, or even the government of Ethiopia—Starbucks considers that action a threat to its corporate control and a challenge to its goodness. Then it resists. Sometimes it behaves badly. And occasionally, if opponents make enough noise to threaten its image, it backs down.

This is where the labor and global justice movements come in. They are a countervailing force to corporate power, organizing the people working at the bottom of the ladder to say, "No!" if the rules that come down are inequitable, inhumane, or simply wrong. Oxfam called its Ethiopian campaign a "big noise" for a reason. I'd like to think that Starbucks could have resolved the conflict without all the drama, but the evidence is not convincing.

On the other hand, noise should be about more than easy publicity. The campaigners at Oxfam have a record of positive advocacy on behalf of the world's poor, and they confronted Starbucks on an issue where the company wielded influence. But it makes little sense for global justice activists to hold Starbucks accountable for our excesses of consumption, the mixed consequences of gentrification, or the evils of capitalism. As Heath and Potter point out in *Nation of Rebels*, cultural politics, while fun, doesn't necessarily make meaningful change for the people who need it most.

The dream that my parents inspired, that drew me into the labor movement decades ago, is the one I still cherish today: a world where we all can live in dignity, with mutual respect and peace, equitably sharing resources and decision making; where everyone is entitled to good air, food and water, housing, and health care from birth to death; where all people can grow to their full potential through education and work;

where we are free to think, create, play, worship or not, sing what we want, and love whom we please, provided we cause the least harm possible to other people, our planet, and our universe; where we use consensus more than coercion to accomplish these goals and always stretch ourselves to ensure that others share the same rights and privileges as we do. I like to think that Howard, Andy, and Medea all share a similar vision. Our conflicts arise in how we define "sharing resources and decisions equitably"; but to have that discussion, we need to see ourselves, and each other, without the fog of our own hyperbole and the hype of others.

The left likes to say, "Another world is possible." But really, our only option is to change the one we have. We don't get to magically start over. We have to work with what's already here, imperfect and inequitable as it may be.

While profit, privatization, and class distinctions have long been fixtures in American public life, they have been unusually pronounced in recent years, and the disparities have become harder to ignore. It's no wonder, then, that so many of us want to drown our sorrows, and our differences, at Starbucks, which seems to provide a small affordable luxury in a relatively egalitarian environment that lulls the racial and class divides that lie at the heart of our fears. But coffee is supposed to be a stimulant, not a soporific; and to the extent that Starbucks obscures the hard questions that confront us, it lulls us into harmful complacency.

We can't blame Starbucks for our inattention, however, nor for the rapacity of the American economy. But as the company strives and succeeds in its quest to become a major player, it will have to take criticism as well as praise for issues that it may only inhabit, not create. And as Starbucks cranks up its rhetoric about goodness while its workers and patrons scrutinize the company's actions, it stands to be caught in a disparity between the two. As I've learned from personal experience in the labor movement, when the divide between principles and practice becomes too wide, people both inside and outside the institution lose faith. Starbucks will have to align how it actually is with how it wishes to be seen, and that task will continue to be a formidable challenge.

On my last visit to Starbucks headquarters, as the Ethiopian crisis was heading toward closure, I met with a high-ranking staff member who had been involved in the process. It had been a bruising episode for the company, which had not handled the conflict well.

Howard had publicly accused Oxfam of exploiting the issue as a fundraising ploy, and many on the Starbucks staff felt betrayed by the nonprofit in which they had risked some trust.

When I asked about longer-term collaborative consequences of the falling-out, the officer half-smiled. She was a student of history, she said, which had taught her to take the long view. "Time passes; things change," she reminded me, and possibly herself. New players and new opportunities emerge, old enemies become allies again. Another world may be beyond us, but truth and reconciliation are possible.

And a good cup of coffee wouldn't hurt.

Acknowledgments

This book is my first. It was fun, and it was hell; but without a lot of help from a lot of people, it would have been no fun at all.

The book started out as a small article, "The Starbucks Paradox," in *ColorLines*, a magazine published by the Applied Research Center. My running buddies at ARC are an inspiration. Francis Calpotura, Rinku Sen, Sonia Peña, and Gina Acebo are the best of companions at the intersection of the personal and the political. Thanks also to Tram Nguyen and to Gary Delgado, who provoked my thinking and provided space and time to write.

Without Harold Simon at the National Housing Institute, this book would be an abandoned project in my desk drawer. After I suffered early setbacks, Harold called me up and urged me on. He hooked me up with Rutgers University Press and provided some much-needed institutional support. Even though he didn't know me well, he was a true movement colleague when I needed one.

Marlie Wasserman at Rutgers University Press has been the best of editors—kind, direct, and so smart. I'm lucky my work fell into her hands. One of Marlie's many skills is assembling a great team, as she has done at the press. Christina Brianik, Alicia Nadkarni, Elizabeth Scarpelli, and Jeremy Wang-Iverson, among others, coddled me and my manuscript. I was also lucky to be assigned poet Dawn Potter as my copy editor. Her wise and ruthless scrutiny improved the book, and her empathy and humor eased the process. I also owe a ton to my intrepid volunteer researcher and reader Stephen A. Wood. Because I had neither a university affiliation nor money, Steve's participation was a true gift. His sharp eyes and sharper mind honed my thinking and my prose. And thanks to Beverly Bell, who sent him my way.

Special appreciation to Andy Stern at the Service Employees and Medea Benjamin at Global Exchange for their perspectives and analyses. The work they do makes our world a better place. They don't give up, and that gives me hope.

At Starbucks, I'm especially grateful to Audrey Lincoff, who was director of media relations when I started this project, and to Lara Wyss in the media relations department. They are superb professionals, but they also embody all the employee attributes listed in the Starbucks Green Book: they are welcoming, genuine, knowledgeable, considerate, and involved. In addition, I received help from Megan Behrbaum in the project's early phases, from Valerie O'Neil and Tara Darrow in the final phase, and from Kenny Fried in Washington, D.C. Tawana Green, former manager of my local Starbucks, was one of the first people I interviewed and remains one of my favorites. She and a succession of staff members at the Eastern Market store tolerated me and my questions with openness, generosity, and warmth. They are among the slew of Starbucks people I interviewed for this book. I appreciate them all, and many are listed in the source notes, but special thanks must go to Howard Schultz, who took time, several times over, to share his unique insights and sharpen mine. I say some tough things about Starbucks, but there's also much to admire. He has created a remarkable company. I'm also indebted to Dub Hay and Sandra Taylor, whom I pestered more than once. And a plaudit to the folks at the Starbucks Agronomy Center in Costa Rica for their hospitality and their knowledge, especially Peter Torribiarte, Jessie Cuevas, and Carlos Mario Rodriguez.

The folks at Fedecocagua in Guatemala, especially Gerardo Alberto De León, Ulrich Gurtner, Onelia Fernandez, and Adolfo Monterroso, eased my journey and facilitated my research in many ways, even though they didn't know me and had no idea what I might write. Betty Hannstein Adams, the Guzmáns, and especially Fernando Fahsen were also generous in candidly sharing their experiences and making me feel welcome. And in Costa Rica, I was lucky to meet Rodolfo Murillo Bogantes and his family, one of those connections that adds magic to a journey. Stefan Wille and Konrad Brits provided coffee trading tutorials, along with astute insights and a sense of humor. Seth Petchers, Jim Reynolds, and Paul Rice were also especially helpful.

Robert Goodier at Rainforest Alliance in Costa Rica helped me, journalist to journalist, even though I was no more than a voice at the other end of the phone line, and put me in touch with Ben Witte, who served as my colleague and translator in Costa Rica. Jeronimo Bollen provided a valuable orientation on Guatemala, as did Bob Perillo.

Blue Mountain Center gave me a place to begin the work before I knew exactly where it would take me. And the Carlsens lent me their house in

Antigua for a few days, making the trip both affordable and far more pleasurable. Phil Mattera, contract advisor for the National Writers Union, helped me through my first book contract. Thanks also to my artistic aunt, Nadia Shepard, for her spirit and support and to my sister-in-law, Julie Marino, for prowling Starbucks in China.

Randy Barber, my friend and comrade for more than three decades, helped me run the 10-K. He has encouraged me through many endeavors and provided a sounding board for my half-baked notions. So, too, has Paul Garver, with whom I've shared ideas and politics for close to forty years.

Mae Ngai gave me an important gift early on and her encouragement throughout. Judith Levine advised me on how to organize my research, and Cathy Howell has been a true *compañera* year in and year out.

My family is my good fortune. My parents, Rudolph and Anita Fellner, individually and together have filled my world with their love, critical skills, imagination, and innate passion for justice. My sister Jane Fellner in Seattle (along with the four Friedman guys) put me up, and put up with me, through numerous visits to Starbucks headquarters. Jane has a knack of asking the pointed question at a critical moment, and her engagement helped me move forward.

Above all, I'm indebted to my brother Gene Fellner and my husband Alec Dubro. Gene has been my political comrade since our teens, my trusted reader, the first person I call about everything and anything. Alec, the indispensable ingredient in the making of this book, is an original thinker, witty writer, and excellent editor who scrutinized the pages long after the *S* word made him roll his eyes. He remained patient even when I was less than pleasant company, offered love and encouragement, and joined the quest for a perfect cappuccino. He's the cream in my coffee and a joy in my life.

All the good stuff is to their credit, and the mistakes are my own.

Notes

This book relies on many sources, most notably a series of interviews I conducted over the course of nearly four years, many in person, some by phone, several augmented by the occasional e-mail. Unless otherwise credited, quotations are drawn from these interviews. Perhaps two dozen people, including many baristas and a few industry insiders, didn't want me to use their names because they feared reprisals from the company or didn't want to alienate Howard Schultz.

Among the Starbucks officers and employees I interviewed were Jim Alling, David Angel, Paula Boggs, Brantley Browning, Gregg Clark, Jessie Cuevas, Jim Donald, Tawana Green, Willard "Dub" Hay, Wanda Herndon, Denoris Hill, Vernon Jones, Taryn Krajcer, Audrey Lincoff, Ken Lombard, Martha Looney, Elaine McClelland, Scott McMartin, Sue Mecklenburg, Dave Olsen, Lori Otto, David Pace, Barbara Schmid Adamczyk, Howard Schultz, Marvin Speller, Sandra Taylor, Kokeb Teferi, Peter Torribiarte, Tom Walters, and Lara Wyss. Many are no longer with the company.

Other interviews included Betty Hannstein Adams, Jeff Alexander, Jeff Angell, Medea Benjamin, Jeronimo Bollen, Gordon Bowker, Barbara Briggs, Konrad Brits, William Bryski, John Buchanan, Bo Burlingham, Liz Butler, Leslie Capetta, John Cavanagh, Steve Coats, Scott Coil, Aron Cramer, Alix Davidson, Mike Dolan, Shari Donaldson, Kimberly Easson, Beatrice Edwards, Fernando Fahsen, Mark Flemming, Nick Francis, Kenny Fried, Marshall Ganz, Paul Garver, Robert Goodier, Daniel Gross, Peter Guiliano, Ulrich Gurtner, Felipe Guzmán, Maria Guzmán, Shayna Harris, David Heilbrunn, Ricardo Hernandez, Ted Howes, Earvin "Magic" Johnson, Keith Kaboly, Paul Katzeff, Charlie Kernaghan, Kate Knorr, Frances Kunreuther, Ron Layton, Thea Lee, Gerardo Alberto De León, Ted Lingle, Adolfo Lizano, Alyce Lomax, Kelle Louaillier, Kenneth Vincenzo McCracken, Christopher Mellgren, Getachew Mengistie, Tadesse Meskela, Adolfo Monterroso, Kirsten Muller, Kathryn Mulvey, Rodolfo Murillo Bogantes, John Mutchka, Karen Nussbaum,

Ray Oldenburg, Leif Pedersen, Bob Perillo, Seth Petchers, Vijay Prashad, Jim Reynolds, Paul Rice, Joel Rogers, Juan Gerardo Arturo Roman, John Sage, Sam Salkin, the Sanchez family, Sue Schurman, Amy Scoczkas, Andy Stern, John Talbot, and Rob Walker.

Starbucks was extremely cooperative, even though I was candid about my concerns and my political biases. Often, especially at headquarters, a public relations staff member sat in on the interviews. Starbucks discourages personnel from talking with the media without oversight or at least permission from headquarters.

I conducted three interviews with Howard Schultz and two each with Medea Benjamin of Global Exchange and Andy Stern at SEIU. All were generous with their time and insights.

Starbucks provides a great deal of written information about the company, much of it published on its website (www.starbucks.com). This includes annual reports and corporate social responsibility (CSR) reports, which are readily available. Where I mention figures about the company without specific attribution, they generally come from these sources.

I did a lot of coffee drinking and observing at Starbucks stores around the United States and in a few foreign ones as well, not to mention at independent coffeehouses and competing chains. In some, I officially interviewed people; at others, I simply chatted with staff and customers and watched the goings-on. I paid roughly six visits to Starbucks headquarters in Seattle and took two tours of the Kent roasting plant.

A few books were particularly helpful. An invaluable start was Howard Schultz's own book, written with Dori Jones Yang, *Pour Your Heart Into It: How Starbucks Built a Company One Cup at a Time* (New York: Hyperion, 1997). I relied on Mark Pendergrast's *Common Grounds: The History of Coffee and How It Transformed Our World* (New York: Basic Books, 1999), a thorough and thoroughly engaging look at coffee's complex history. *The Coffee Book*, by Nina Luttinger and Gregory Dicum (New York: New Press, 2006), was an accessible primer. Daniel Wilkinson's *Silence on the Mountain: Stories of Terror, Betrayal, and Forgetting in Guatemala* (Durham: Duke University Press, 2004) helped me interpret my Central American visits and was an unanticipated inspiration.

Finally, and inevitably, I owe a debt to the World Wide Web and Google, through which I had access to myriad sources. I am a big fan of Google Alerts, which speeded media mentions of Starbucks to my inbox, and of TimesSelect, which gave me access to all articles about Starbucks that had ever appeared in the *New York Times*. In addition, the Internet is buzzing with references to Starbucks, whether you want to see a dozen amateurs singing "Taylor the Latte Boy" on YouTube or peruse pictures of celebrities carrying Starbucks cups. There is also much to be learned at Jim Romenesko's website, www.starbucksgossip.com, and www.ihatestarbucks.com. What a hoot.

INTRODUCTION: THE GLOBAL ECONOMY COMES HOME

Figures on Starbucks growth can be found in the annual reports and 10-K filings, available at www.starbucks.com. Go to the investor page and follow the links.

Information about Starbucks locations comes from the locator on the Starbucks website and from MapQuest. Of course, these figures keep changing. By the time you read this, they'll be different. Cathy Howell scoped out Starbucks in Amman, Jordan; Julie Marino checked out Shanghai; and Mark Flemming reported on other Chinese locales.

USDA figures on coffee consumption are from Erin Allday, "Coffee's Perk—It's Healthy," *San Francisco Chronicle*, June 10, 2007, p. A1.

Figures on Starbucks' share of the world's coffee come from Starbucks. The composite numbers for the big four in coffee are harder to find because much of the information comes through traders; however, 60 percent was a fairly consistent figure among traders and coffee experts. See John M. Talbot, *Grounds for Agreement* (Lanham, Md.: Roman and Littlefield, 2004), 103.

"The romance of the coffee experience, the feeling of warmth and community people get in Starbucks stores" (Schultz with Yang 1997, 5).

Information about the increase in stock prices is from Schultz, annual meeting remarks, March 21, 2007.

Insight about globalization and international finance institutions comes from the director of the Institute for Policy Studies, John Cavanagh, whose work on the Philippines was one of the first studies on globalization. Cavanagh and Sarah Anderson, with Thea Lee, wrote *Field Guide to the Global Economy* (New York: New Press, 2000), one of the best comprehensive looks at globalization from the left's perspective.

"Challenges for the Global Trading System in the New Millennium" is from a speech by Mike Moore, director-general of the WTO, to the Council on Foreign Relations, Washington, D.C., September 28, 1999.

Information on the trade deficit and the Uruguay round are from www. wto.org/english/news_e/spmm_e/spmm08_e.htm.

See Holger Jensen, "Globalization on the Line at Seattle WTO Meeting," *Rocky Mountain News*, November 28, 1999, p. 51A.

On the AFL-CIO and the progressive sector, see Kim Fellner, "In Search of the Movement: 1960s Activists in Labor," a paper for the Center for Labor-Management Policy Studies, City University of New York, 1989. At the time, I conducted interviews with Gus Tyler, then seventy-eight years old and the former education director of the International Ladies Garment Workers Union (now UNITE HERE), and with David Livingston, president of District 65, United Auto Workers. There is a rich trove of literature on the impact of McCarthyism on the left, academia, and American labor unions.

The best introduction to the United Farm Workers and Cesar Chavez is probably Peter Matthiessen's *Sal Si Puedes* (Berkeley: University of California Press, 2000).

On labor, check out *The Cold War against Labor: An Anthology*, by Ann Fagan Ginger and David Christiano (Berkeley, Calif.: Meiklejohn Civil Liberties Institute, 1987).

For an overview of the AFL-CIO connection, see Ted Morgan's "Lovestone Joins the AFL" and "Lovestone Joins the CIA," in his *A Covert Life: Jay Lovestone* (New York: Random House, 1999), 141–55, 195–243.

See Daniel Cantor and Juliet Schor, *Tunnel Vision* (Boston: South End Press, 1987).

For a broad view of José Bové, see Florence Williams, "The Roquefort Files," *Outside* (January 2001), available at http://outside.away.com/outside/environment/200106/200106bove.html.

Much of my knowledge of the Seattle protests is firsthand and from a trove of informal material I collected at the time. There are a number of anthologies about the Seattle protests, but none are particularly illuminating. Contemporaneous news coverage and journalistic commentary are better bets.

Learn more about *ColorLines* at www.colorlines.com, where you can also link to my article "The Starbucks Paradox" (Spring 2004).

Reverend Billy has made a brand out of his Starbucks' protests, but I heard about it from my friend Judith Levine; it also appears in her book *Not Buying It* (New York: Free Press, 2006).

CHAPTER 1: THE EMPIRE STRIKES GOLD

Much of the material in chapters 1 and 2 is derived from Starbucks' annual reports, 10-K filings with the SEC as documentation of annual meetings, and the company's CSR reports.

The Starbucks annual meeting on March 30, 2004, was the first one I attended. I also attended in 2005 and 2007.

For Schultz on global opportunity, see *Associated Press*, March 30, 2004, available at http://www.msnbc.msn.com/id/463385/.

The dispute over the Starbucks store in Beijing's Forbidden City was extensively covered in 2006 and continued until the store's closure in July 2007.

The nonfat milk story appears in Janet Adamy's "Starbucks Chairman Says Trouble May Be Brewing—Brand Could Be Compromised," *Wall Street Journal*, February 24, 2007, available at http://online.wsj.com/public/article/SB117225247561617457-2aHDakD9Ci3xmYxig_PQ9BAebU4_20080224.html.

In 1994, coffee prices rose sharply. See Erik Ipsen, "Your Early Morning Jolt: Coffee Prices Are Soaring," *International Herald Tribune*, June 28, 1994, available at http://www.iht.com/articles/1994/06/28/caf.php.

Mintel, a market research firm in Chicago, is the primary source for all kinds of interesting data about coffee consumption and coffee houses (http://www.mintel.com). The other source of specialty coffee data is the Specialty Coffee Association of America in Long Beach, California (www.scaa.org).

Schultz writes about the mission statement and his childhood in Schultz with Yang (1997); the coffeehouse epiphany is on page 52. We also talked about them in our interviews.

"Kerouac opened a million coffee bars . . . " is from William Burroughs, "Remembering Jack Kerouac," in *The Adding Machine*. (New York: Seaver, 1986), widely quoted by others.

Caffe Trieste has its own website (www.caffetrieste.com); and my husband, who once lived in the Bay Area, where he drank lots of coffee and occasionally worked in coffeehouses, provided a historical tour of the area coffee dens.

The third place concept was elucidated by Ray Oldenburg in *The Great Good Place* (New York: Paragon, 1989). I used the later paperback edition (New York: Marlowe, 1999) and also interviewed Oldenburg by phone.

"We're in the business of human connection and humanity . . . " appears in "Howard Schultz: The Star of Starbucks: Scott Pelley Meets the Man behind the Coffee Empire," which aired on *60 Minutes* on April 23, 2006, and is available at http://www.cbsnews.com/stories/2006/04/21/60minutes/main1532246.shtml.

See Jon D. Markman, "Starbucks' Genius Blends Community, Caffeine," on MSN's *Money Central*, February 16, 2005, available at http://moneycentral.msn.com/content/P107679.asp.

"By 1915, 86 percent of coffee . . ." is from Pendergrast (1999, 116), where he also discusses the development of branded coffee.

For more on branding imbued with psychic qualities, see Naomi Klein, *No Logo* (New York: Picador, 2000), a new classic on the subject. In my 2002 edition, the quotation appears on page 7.

See Malcolm Gladwell, *The Tipping Point* (New York: Little, Brown, 2002), 12. For some reason, his theory of how epidemics occur seems particularly well suited for talking about Starbucks.

As of 2005, Starbucks' regular customers averaged eighteen visits a month, according to Dorian Lynskey in "Stir It Up," *Guardian*, October 6, 2005, available at http://arts.guardian.co.uk/features/story/0,11710,1585825,00.html.

The figures on the stored value cards come from http://www.starbucks.com/aboutus/Company_Factsheet.pdf.

CHAPTER 2: RUNNING THE 10-K

For this chapter I used the 2005 10-K and CSR reports, except as otherwise noted.

See Brian Lund, "Starbucks' Brand Power," *Motley Fool*, December 5, 2000, available at http://www.fool.com/portfolios/rulebreaker/2000/rulebreaker001205.htm.

"Hot customers put Starbucks on ice," quipped New York correspondent Andrew Clark as shares dropped 11 percent; see the *Age* [Melbourne, Australia], August 5, 2006, available at
http://www.theage.com.au/news/business/hot-customers-put-starbucks-on-ice/2006/08/04/1154198331746.htmltheage.com.au.

See Allison Overholt, "Thinking outside the Cup," *Fast Company* (July 2004): 50–56, available at http://www.fastcompany.com/magazine/84/starbucks_schultz.html. Her mention led me to the Theodore Levitt classic, "What Business Are You In?," *Harvard Business Review* (July–August 1960): 45–56. An excerpt is available at http://harvardbusinessonline.hbsp.harvard.edu/hbsp/hbr/articles/article.jsp?articleID=R0610J&ml_action=get-a.

Stephen A. Wood contributed research and valuable insight to the discussion of Starbucks' music ventures. Early forays are covered in Schultz with Yang (1997). Otherwise, information has been culled from media reports, annual meetings, and interviews with Schultz and Ken Lombard. Many are noted in the chapter, with some specifics following.

"Customers from Taipei to Topeka . . ." said Ken Lombard, quoted in "Starbucks to Go 'All-McCartney' on June 5," *Los Angeles Business*, May 17, 2007, available at http://losangeles.bizjournals.com/losangeles/stories/2007/05/14/daily31.html?t=printable, and widely quoted elsewhere.

"After two years of testing the machines at 15 stores in Seattle . . ." is from "Song over for Most Starbucks Music-CD Burners," an unsigned article on *TCMnet*, May 26, 2006, available at http://www.tmcnet.com/usubmit/2006/05/26/1660842.htm.

Starbucks began selling the *New York Times* in 2000; see http://www.writenews.com/2000/080300_starbucks_nytimes.htm.

You can find out about Peet's Coffee and Tea Company at www.Peets.com. I used the SEC filing from March 16, 2006, pp. 1–2, available at "Company Info: Investor Pages" on the Peet's website. Information about the Peet's passion also came from interviews with Gordon Bowker, Jim Reynolds, and Sam Salkin.

The information about COGS regarding coffee and milk was cajoled out of Starbucks insiders, who generally dislike sharing this kind of information. Figure on the amount of beans the company purchases and total and average per-pound prices are part of the CSR report.

Jon Glass's comment appeared in Brad Stone's "Grande Plans," *Newsweek*, October 4, 2004. For a smattering of news reports about the "insatiable and unchecked" suit on real estate, see Melissa Allison's "Starbucks Sued over 'Unchecked Ambition,'" *Seattle Times*, September 26, 2006, available at http://seattletimes.nwsource.com/html/businesstechnology/2003275648_starbucks26.html. Independent coffeehouse owners, in both my interviews and news stories, are divided about whether Starbucks is a bane or a boon, as I discuss in a later chapter. The coffee expert was not willing to have his name used, but his story is not unique. It's possible that real cutthroat competition involves bigger players and fancier real estate, although to most of us the competition on our neighborhood street corner is more evident.

According to the USDA (http://www.ers.usda.gov/Amberwaves/June03/pdf/awjune2003datafeature.pdf), by 2001 Americans were consuming fewer than eight gallons of whole milk per person, compared with nearly forty-one gallons in 1945 and twenty-five gallons in 1970.

The *Time* comment is from the April 16, 2004 issue, available at http://www.time.com/time/magazine/article/0,9171,993982,00.html.

TimesSelect is a wondrous search feature of the *New York Times* archive that came along with my newspaper subscription. I was fascinated to follow the pattern of Starbucks' growth as reflected in the number of articles and content of coverage. The patterns stayed roughly two years at one level and then made a substantial jump. The Marian Burros article, "De Gustibus; In Seattle, Espresso Is Raised to an Art," ran on May 3, 1989.

The titles and authors for the stories for April 22, 2007, follow this sequence: Elisabeth Malkin, "Certifying Coffee Aids Farmers and Forests in Chiapas"; Liza Featherstone, "In Brooklyn, Hipsters Sip 'Fair Trade' Brews"; Elaine Sciolino, "Paris Chic, on the Cheap"; Vincent M. Mallozzi, "Junior Achievement on a Major League Scale"; Graham Bowley, "Goal! He Spends It on Beckham"; and Mark Sarvas, "Hello, Stranger."

See Michael E. Porter and Mark R. Kramer, "Strategy & Society," *Harvard Business Review* (December 2006), available at http://harvardbusinessonline.hbsp.harvard.edu/email/pdfs/Porter_Dec_2006.pdf.

The Fleishman-Hillard/National Consumer League Study, "Rethinking Corporate Social Responsibility," was published in May 2006, based on a 2005 survey. The figures I cite are from pages 2 and 3 and are available at www.csrresults.com/CSR_ExecutiveSummary06.pdf.

The *New York Times* ads appeared on August 27, 2006, p. 14; September 14, 2006, p. A21; January 21, 2007, p. 10; and February 18, 2007, p. 20.

On the *Daily Reveille* plaint, see Emily Byers, "Witnessing Hope," *Opinion*, January 18, 2007, available at http://www.lsureveille.com/home/index.cfm?event=displayArticle&ustory_id=8e3e7a68-ccd1-49e4-896e-23919ef838ea.

The quotations from Bo Burlingham are from a phone interview. His book is *Small Giants: Companies That Choose to Be Great instead of Big* (New York: Portfolio, 2006); the book's website is http://www.smallgiantsbook. com.

CHAPTER 3: BANKING ON THE BEAN

My opinionated synthesis of coffee history and information about the coffee chain and certification come from an assemblage of sources. There are a ton of books about coffee, but several were critical resources: Benoit Daviron and Stefano Ponte, *The Coffee Paradox.* (London: Zed, 2005); Luttinger and Dicum (2006); Pendergrast (1999); and Talbot (2004). Talbot's *Grounds for Agreement* is an indispensable discussion of the coffee chain and certifications, and *The Coffee Paradox* offers a more controversial, modern political analysis. Additional material came from interviews, reports, and web sources. A phone interview with Talbot was also extremely helpful.

My research included trips to Costa Rica and Guatemala, where I was able to follow bean processing on three cooperatives and two farms and interview a wide range of coffee growers and other experts along the chain.

Stefan Wille at Coricafé, a trading house in Costa Rica, generously gave me an introductory lesson in trading, and Konrad Brits at CTCS Limited in the Great Britain gave me a second lesson via phone. Dub Hay, Starbucks' senior vice president for coffee and global procurement, was an invaluable guide at the New York Board of Trade and offered insight on the Starbucks approach to coffee, as did Sue Mecklenburg, vice president for sustainable procurement practices, and Scott McMartin, a veteran from the coffee department.

On Brazilian coffee, see the USDA's "Tropical Markets: World Products and Trade" (2004), available at www.fas.usda.gov/htp/tropical/2004/06-04/ June%202004%20Cover.pdf.

According to Worldwatch Institute (http://www.worldwatch.org/node/1486), "Farmers harvested nearly 7.4 million tons of coffee beans in 2002—an all-time high and almost double the harvest in 1960."

U.S. and European coffee consumption figures are from http://www. top100espresso.com/coffee_consumption_statistics_report.html.

The Thurber quote and the El Salvador story appear in Pendergrast (1999, 42, 182–84).

See Talbot (2004, 95).

Information about American liquid coffee consumption is from a document of the USDA's Foreign Agricultural Service (FAS), available at http://www. fas.usda.gov/htp/tropical/2002/06-02/coffusco.pdf.

See *Euromonitor International* (http://www.euromonitor.com/Hot_Drinks_ in_the_US).

On gourmet coffee drinking, see the USDA figures at http://www.fas. usda.gov/htp/tropical/2002/06-02/coffusco.pdf.

On interactive and illustrative websites about the coffee money chain, see Kelly Whalen, "Your Coffee Dollar," in "Coffee Country" on PBS's *Frontline/World*, May 2003, available at http://www.pbs.org/ frontlineworld/stories/guatemala.mexico/coffee1.html. On tracing the

value chain, see Oxfam's 2002 coffee report, "Mugged," p. 24, available at
http://www.oxfamamerica.org/newsandpublications/publications/
research_reports/mugged/mugged_coffee_report.pdf.

On hedging, see Talbot (2004, 111). The Max Havelaar book and this quotation
are well known. I transcribed it from Pramoedya Ananta Toer, "Best Story;
The Book That Killed Colonialism," *New York Times Magazine*, April 18,
1999, available at http://query.nytimes.com/gst/fullpage.html?res=
9504E4D81E39F93BA25757C0A96F958260.

Equal Exchange (www.equalexchange.com) is considered a pioneer in U.S.
fair trade efforts. The Paul Katzeff quotations are from e-mail exchanges on
June 14–15, 2007. A long-time leader in the Specialty Coffee Association of
America, he believes "there are now about 1,200 small and medium-sized
roasters in the USA. I believe that 95 percent of them have progressive politics because they have to deal with the issues of fair trade, shade and
organics, and farmers. The trade has made it so they can't escape those
issues. Even Starbucks has had to do something to show it is not a monster.
We in Specialty are the caring part of the coffee industry, and all the roasters are part of or under that umbrella."

The websites of both FLO (http://www.fairtrade.net) and TransFair (http://
transfairusa.org) have massive amounts of data. I also benefited from interviews with TransFair's president Paul Rice and Kimberly Easson, its director of strategic relations.

On the growth of the organic foods movement, see "The Origins of Organic
Agriculture in the United States," available at http://attra.ncat.org/
new_pubs/attra-pub/organiccrop/origins.html.

At the 1992 Earth Summit in Rio de Janeiro (http://www.un.org/
geninfo/bp/enviro.html), attending nations passed Agenda 21, "a wide-
ranging blueprint for action to achieve sustainable development worldwide," the first worldwide recognition of sustainable development.

My understanding of certification issues and the politics that surround them
was augmented by interviews with Leif Pederson, project manager for biodiversity conservation in coffee, and his colleagues Luis D. Jimenez and
Robert Goodier, all at Rainforest Alliance in Costa Rica.

CHAPTER 4: GO SELL IT ON THE MOUNTAIN

See Conservation International at http://www.conservation.org. Scientific
Certification Systems (SCS) has a detailed website at http://www.scscerti-
fied.com, including information on Starbucks' C.A.F.E. Practices, which,
according to Starbucks, have "guidelines contain[ing] 28 specific indicators
that fall under five focus areas: product quality, economic accountability
[transparency], social responsibility, environmental leadership in coffee
growing and environmental leadership in coffee processing." The SCS
website also includes information about its own involvement in these
practices.

Bob Perillo of the U.S. Labor Education in the Americas Project helped me
understand the dynamics and dangers of Guatemala City and the impact of
U.S. immigration policy there.

The term *latte revolution* is widely credited to Luttinger and Dicum
(2006).

CHAPTER 5: MOVING UP ON EIGHTH STREET

On gentrification, see http://www.urbandictionary.com/define.php?term= gentrification; Michael Canning, "Starbucks Possibility Generates Local Buzz," *St. Petersburg Times*, May 28, 2004, available at http:// www.sptimes.com/2004/05/28/Citytimes/Starbucks_possibility.shtml; and Marianne Curphey, "Finding the Next Notting Hill," *Observer*, October 27, 2002, available at http://money.guardian.co.uk/homebuying/ movinghome/story/0,,820908,00.html.

The Blagojevich quotation is from Mickey Ciokajlo, "Homeowners Get Break; Government OKs a Dose of Tax Relief in 7% Cap on Property Assessment Hikes," *Chicago Tribune*, July 13, 2004, available at http://www.cook-countyassessor.com/ccao/press/NewsClips002.asp?ID=48.

See Gene Johnson, "Home Values Rise but Black Residents Are Priced Out; Influx of Whites Alters Central District," *Olympian*, November 6, 2001, available at http://news.theolympian.com/Census2000/133679.shtml.

On the Anacostia Starbucks, see Debbi Wilgoren, "$3 Cappuccinos Coming to Southeast," *Washington Post*, May 12, 2004, p. B01.

Starbucks maven Bryant Simon, director of American studies at Temple University, suggests that a Starbucks in a poorer neighborhood may be of greater benefit to the company's image than to the community. Check out his lecture on YouTube at http://www.youtube.com/watch?v= Fxpfx8W8C20.

See Klein (2000). When I did my first interviews at Starbucks, Klein's *No Logo* was prominently displayed on at least one vice president's bookshelf, but Klein is not a fan of the company. To delve into some of her objections, see chapter 6, "Brand Bombing," 129–41.

See Markman (February 16, 2005).

CHAPTER 6: THE CROSS-DRESSING OF COFFEE-COUNTER CULTURE

See Robert L. Badgett, "Frequently Asked Questions about Opening a Coffee Business," *Badgett's Coffee eJournal*, February 18, 2003, available at http://www.aboutcoffee.net/2003_02_16_bcearc.html.

Business survival rates are from the Small Business Administration's "Frequently Asked Questions," available at http://www.sba.gov/ advo/ stats/sbfaq.pdf.

The Interbrand quotation about the glories of branding can be found at "About Us—What We Believe" on the company's website (http://www.inter-brand.com).

Information about Leopold's Records and Tower Records are from the recollections of former Leopold's manager Michael Lauer and former Berkeley resident Alec Dubro.

On the culture jammers' attack, see Chuck Squatriglia, "Coffee Icon Hit in S.F.," *San Francisco Chronicle*, August 6, 2003, available at www.sfgate.com/cgi-bin/article.cgi?f=/chronicle/archive/2003/ 08/06/BA135034.DTL&NF=1.

For a provocative look at the interplay between culture and counterculture, see Joseph Heath and Andrew Potter, *Nation of Rebels: Why Counterculture Became Consumer Culture* (New York: HarperCollins, 2004), 9. The authors tip their hats, and I mine, to Thomas Frank's *The Conquest of Cool* (Chicago: University of Chicago Press, 1998). Rob Walker, who writes the "Consumed" column for the *New York Times Magazine*, provides ongoing, interesting thoughts on this theme.

On the chain coffee wars, see Julie Bosman, "This Joe's for You?" *New York Times*, June 8, 2006, p. C1; and Michael S. Rosenwald and Chris Kirkham, "Big Fight Brews for Average Joe," *Washington Post*, September 7, 2006, p. DO1.

For Schultz on Dunkin' Donuts, see David Gardner and Tom Gardner, "Starbucks' New Wavelength," *Motley Fool*, May 11, 2004, available at http://www.fool.com/Specials/2004/04051100sp.htm.

You can find the lyrics to Kristin Chenoweth's "Taylor, the Latte Boy" at http://artists.letssingit.com/kristin-chenoweth-taylor-the-latte-boy-m1d38rk.

The Japantown conflict was reported by Steven Tanamachi in two stories in the *Nichi Bei Times*: "Community Opposes Starbucks Bid for Japantown Location," May 23, 2005, available at http://news.ncmonline.com/news/view_article.html?article_id=0c96d39ce3a5a50beaf1660add395b7d ; and "The Buck(s) Won't Stop in San Francisco's Historic Japantown," June 6, 2005, available at http://news.pacificnews.org/news/view_article.html?article_id=eb1da1a5e4c32afc9d3626e2dee4ce3e.

The *Seattle Times* stories are all from October 22, 2006. The Lakeland ad appears on page E3. The Brett Zamore quotation on page E7 appears in a reprinted *Washington Post* article by Linda Hales, "Wanted: Fun, Modern and Affordable Architecture." The Margaret Carlson column is titled "Pennsylvania Stands Out in NE Liberal Corridor."

CHAPTER 7: WHEN WORKER MET PARTNER

The Starbucks cards mirror *The Green Apron Book*, a small and lovely booklet that lays out the five Starbucks "ways of being": welcoming, genuine, knowledgeable, considerate, involved. It is heavy on design, low on text. The green pages toward the end of the book offer checklists of behaviors that comprise the goals.

See Richard Sennett, *The Culture of the New Capitalism* (New Haven: Yale University Press, 2006), 63. This slim book of essays is thick with ideas about how we relate to our work and each other and what we are losing with the diminution of craft and trust.

On Wal-Mart, see Charles Fishman, *The Wal-Mart Effect* (New York: Penguin, 2006), 79. Other books on Wal-Mart include *The Bully of Bentonville* by Anthony Bianco (New York: Currency, 2006); and *Wal-Mart; the Face of Twenty-First-Century Capitalism*, edited by Nelson Lichtenstein (New York: New Press, 2006). There are also two union-sponsored websites: http://www.walmartwatch.com, organized and underwritten by the Service Employees International Union; and http://www.wakeupwalmart.com, sponsored by the United Food and Commercial Workers Union. To get the other side of the story, you can always go to the source: http://www.walmart.com.

Figures on employee turnover come from the Starbucks human resources department. The Alternet piece that precipitated the response was Liza Featherstone's "Workers of the World Unite against Starbucks," reprinted from the *Nation* and posted on May 21, 2007. The cited response can be found at http://www.alternet.org/workplace/52146/.

The Jef Keighley quotation from a 2003 interview with me.

Information on how Starbucks treats its workers comes from myriad interviews, including one with David Pace, the company's executive vice president for partner resources. The survey results are included in the fiscal 2006 CSR report.

Over the course of my research I spoke with individuals involved in all of the union campaigns I mention. None of the experiences were good.

See Liza Featherstone, "It's Business, Man! Unions and Socially Responsible Corporations," *Dissent*, March 2, 2000, available at http://www.labournet.net /ukunion/0002/hippycap.html.

On unions, see Schultz with Yang (1997, 108).

The Operating Engineers shared documentation regarding the fate of the union and its members at the roasting plant. A number of complaints to the National Labor Relations Board against Starbucks were settled for varying amounts and included clauses prohibiting the plaintiffs from talking about the cases. The case of Mark Tutalo, the veteran mentioned in the narrative, was settled in July 2007 for an undisclosed amount. My narrative was also informed by two tours of the roasting plant.

The text of Schultz's voicemail to the New York City baristas was released by the IWW. The voicemail was sent to the stores on May 19, 2004.

The IWW's website (http://www.iww.org) is a historical treasure trove. The preamble is in the culture section, under the list of official organizational documents.

On the IWW's two news scores, see Daniel Gross (not the union organizer), "Latte Laborers Take on a Latte-Liberal Business," *New York Times*, April 8, 2007, p. WK5; and David Segal, "Coffee Break: 'Top Employer' Starbucks Has a Crack in Its Image," *Washington Post*, April 12, 2007, p. C1.

See Katherine S. Newman, *Chutes and Ladders: Navigating the Low-Wage Labor Market* (New York: Russell Sage Foundation, 2006), 186–87. The book is a rare in-depth look at the fate over time of a group of low-wage workers.

On Andy Stern's personal history, see Andy Stern, *A Country That Works: Getting America Back on Track* (New York: Free Press, 2006); and Matt Bai, "The New Boss," *New York Times Magazine*, January 30, 2005, 38–45. Bai's is one of many stories published over the past three years that includes a good summary of Stern's career. My narrative was also informed by my membership in Stern's local during the 1970s and by my 2005 interview.

Stern announced SEIU's effective withdrawal from the AFL-CIO in Chicago as the AFL-CIO convention was beginning. See http://www.stronger-together.org /media/pressreleases.cfm?pr_id=1238.

On the nine principles, see Stern (2006, 105–6).

See Steve Early, "From Monsignor Sweeney to Reverend Andy: Labor's 'New' Agenda for America Hasn't Improved with Age," *Labor Notes*, available at http://www.labornotes.org/node/473.

See Richard B. Freeman and Joel Rogers, *What Workers Want* (Ithaca, N.Y.: Cornell University Press, 2006), 91, 33. The original version was published in 1999 in conjunction with the Russell Sage Foundation.

The Building Movement project, where I worked on several issues in 2005, has been studying generational change in nonprofit organizations, drawing on an extensive survey of the literature about leadership transition and the differences between generations. Many of the reports can be accessed online at http://www.buildingmovement.org.

See Barry Schwartz, Hazel Rose Markus, and Alana Conner Snibbe, "Is Freedom Just Another Word for Many Things to Buy?" *New York Times Magazine*, February 26, 2006, available at http://www.nytimes.com/2006/02/26/magazine/26wwln_essay.html.

On open source unions, see Freeman and Rogers (2006, 193–205).

I also drew on my personal experience with less conventional forms of unionism, having served as information director for the Screen Actors Guild from 1979 to 1985 and as executive director of the National Writers Union from 1986 to 1990. More recently, I worked on several writing projects at Working America.

Paul Garver was an organizer for the International Union of Food, Agricultural, Hotel, Restaurant, Catering, Tobacco, and Allied Workers' Associations (IUF), one of what are now fewer than a dozen Global Union Federations. From 1990 until 2006 he worked at IUF with member unions all over the world, including all those involved in bargaining with Nestlé and other transnational corporations. The quotation come from interviews with me in early 2007.

Schurman's comments are from an e-mail to me dated April 30, 2007.

CHAPTER 8: AT THE GLOBAL CROSSROADS

The story of the Ethiopian coffee trademarks began with various parties in the conflict telling contradictory stories. For months, I listened to all sides and interviewed many of the principals, trying to weave the different perspectives into a single narrative. Most of those involved took the struggle to heart; there was a great deal of tension. News coverage was incomplete and occasionally incomprehensible. The quoted interviewees are cited in the text, but I would not have been able to sort out as much as I did without the assistance of Shayna Harris and Seth Petchers at Oxfam; Dub Hay, Audrey Lincoff, Sandra Taylor, and Sue Mecklenburg at Starbucks; Ron Layton at Light Years IP; and Getachew Mengistie at the Ethiopian intellectual property office. In the end, the tale still had a few murky corners, but it also had a lot more light.

In Ethiopia, surnames are not generally used. Hence, I mention the surnames for Getachew and Tadesse only at first reference.

The Oromia Coffee Farmers Cooperative Union has a website (http://www.oromiacoffeeunion.org) that lists basic facts and figures about the cooperative.

The Tadesse quotation appears in a Starbucks interview transcript from the Africa Coffee Celebration, May 31–June 1, 2006.

The film *Black Gold*, produced and directed by Marc Francis and Nick Francis, was released in 2006 by Speak-It Films in association with Fulcrum Productions. The website is http://www.blackgoldmovie.com.

Tadesse's quotation comes from an Oxfam press release, "Starbucks Opposes Ethiopia's Plan to Trademark Specialty Coffee Names That Could Bring Farmers an Estimated $88 Million Annually," October 26, 2006, available at http://www.maketradefair.com/en/index.php?file=starbucks_10262006.htm.

The Benjamin Barber quotation is from the "Newsmakers" section of *Philanthropy News Digest*, March 20, 2003, available at http://foundationcenter.org/pnd/newsmakers/nwsmkr.jhtml;jsessionid=TH0IM30OZ5UWHTQRSI4CGXD5AAAACI2F?id=29100017.

Starbucks' goal of having five hundred European stores by the end of 2003 was reported in the unattributed article "Starbucks Springboard to Europe," *Tea & Coffee* (July 1999): 23–26.

See Thomas Friedman, *The Lexus and the Olive Tree* (New York: Anchor, 2000), 279.

The Rui Cheggang remarks are from a January 21, 2007, report in *Shanghaiist*, available at http://shanghaiist.com/2007/01/21/storm_in_a_coff.php.

The question of Schultz's supposed Zionism is a matter of many urban legends. Although he cares about Israel, he seems to be (as best I've been able to assess) in favor of a two-state solution. The Israel store-closing flare-up was debunked by the pro-Israel Anti-Defamation League (http://www.adl.org/rumors/starbucks_rumors.asp).

See the *Borowitz Report*, July 31, 2006, http://www.borowitzreport.com/archive_rpt.asp?rec=6553&srch.

Lara Wyss graciously shared some of the nuances of her work during a trip we took to the Kent roasting plant in early 2007.

Schultz's remarks about the Amman store were transcribed from remarks at the 2006 annual meeting.

I visited the Tokyo Starbucks in 2003.

My interviews and observations of Starbucks stores and other cafés in Paris and Berlin took place in 2004.

The Natsuno quotation is from Brad Spurgeon, "Organizing Your Life with a Mobile Phone," *International Herald Tribune*, October 25, 2004, p. 13.

See Sylvan Zaft, "Esperanto: A Language for the Global Village" (2002), available at *http://esperanto.ie/english/zaft/zaft.htm.*

See Kwame Anthony Appiah, "The Case for Contamination," *New York Times Magazine*, January 1, 2006, pp. 30–37. Appiah fleshes out and illuminates these ideas in his book *Cosmopolitanism* (New York: Norton, 2006).

Statistics on Ethiopia are from *http://hdr.undp.org/hdr2006/statistics/.* On per capita income and gross domestic product, see http://web.worldbank.org/WBSITE/EXTERNAL/DATASTATISTICS/0,,contentMDK:20535285~menuPK:1192694~pagePK:64133150~piPK:64133175~theSitePK:239419,00.html.

General information is courtesy of the CIA (https://www.cia.gov/library/publications/the-world-factbook/geos/et.html), the U.N. Office on Drugs and Crime (http://www.unodc.org/kenya/en/country_profile_ethi.html), and the British Foreign and Commonwealth Office (http://www.fco.gov.uk/servlet/Front?pagename=OpenMarket/Xcelerate/ShowPage&c=Page&cid=1007029394365&a=KCountryProfile&aid=1022070787685).

Specialty coffee information is from http://www.ethiopia-emb.or.jp/trade_e/index05.html—http://www.ico.org/prices/m1.htm. The dramatic difference in estimates of amount from the three regions is hard to reconcile: the lower figure is from coffee experts, the higher from my conversations with representatives of the Ethiopian government. One knowledgeable colleague suggests that the lower figure probably represents recent reality and the higher one future potential.

The U.S. Patent and Trademark Office has an extensive website; its trademark definition appears there at www.uspto.gov/web/offices/tac/tmfaq.

For information on TRIPs, see the WTO's "Overview: the TRIPS Agreement," available at http://www.wto.org/english/tratop_e/trips_e/intel2_e.htm.

On Big Pharma's efforts to prevent the development of generic alternatives, see Rohit Malpani and Mohga Kamal-Yanni, "Patents vs. Patients," Oxfam

Briefing Paper 95 (November 2006), available at http://www.oxfam.de/download/Patents_vs_Patients.pdf. For an introduction to Monsanto and seed privatization, see Matt Jenkins, "A History and Overview of Monsanto's Biotech Madness," *High Country News*, June 27, 2007, available at http://www.organicconsumers.org/articles/article_6024.cfm.

See Jake Batsell, "Starbucks' Attempts to Protect Trademark Could Grow Tougher," *Seattle Times*, March 14, 2003, available at http://archives.seattletimes.nwsource.com/cgi-bin/texis.cgi/web/vortex/display?slug=trademark14&date=20030314&query=sambucks. For a biased look at the HaidaBucks case, see http://www.lanebaldwin.com/hbc/about.htm.

For Starstrucks, see "Starbucks Steams at 'Starstrucks' Coffee Chain," *Reuters*, March 5, 2007, available at http://www.reuters.com/article/oddlyEnoughNews/idUSBOM20178420070305.

See Ron Layton, "Enhancing Intellectual Property Exports through Fair Trade," in *Poor People's Knowledge*, ed. J. Michael Finger (Washington, D.C.: World Bank and Oxford University Press, 2004), available at http://www.worldbank.org/research/Poor_Peoples_Knowledge.pdf.

On the symbolic, or brand, value of coffee, see Daviron and Ponte (2005, chap. 4).

See the undated press release from the Ethiopian Embassy, "Starbucks Aggressive over Trademarks, Says Former Ethiopian Ambassador to the U.S.," available as of June 2007 at http://www.ethiopianembassy.org/TradeMarkCampaign/Statement_by_the_Ethiopian_Ambassador_in_Berlin.

The Oxfam America website is http://www.oxfamamerica.org.

See Alison Maitland's "Starbucks Tastes Oxfam's brew" and "Starbucks and Oxfam Link to Fight Crisis," *Financial Times*, October 14, 2004, pp. 12, 27. The first is an excellent analysis of the relationship between companies and campaign organizations and is available at http://www.bidnetwork.org/article-12791-en.html.

Ted Lingle's comments, which he shared in a telephone interview, represent his personal views, not those of any organization with which he is affiliated.

Paul Katzeff's comments are from an e-mail to me on June 14, 2007.

Internal correspondence from Oxfam, expressing outrage with Starbucks and excitement over a possible confrontation, shows that the planning was underway by June 2006.

The comments of Nick Francis are from a telephone interview. At the time, there was also an extensive press packet available online. I viewed the film in mid-2006 at a screening in Washington, D.C.

For a review of *Black Gold*, see Ann Hornaday, "Brewing Black Gold," *Washington Post*, December 8, 2006, p. WE24.

Many Starbucks staff members feel great loyalty to the company, and others fear saying the wrong thing, so it's hard to ascertain the details of internal conflict. After piecing together all the narratives, though, I could see that there'd been dissension within the company, especially about how to respond to Oxfam. Although Dub Hay staunchly believed that trademarking was not a good idea, it's unclear who at the top actually insisted on a maintaining a hard line, even with growing bad publicity and internal disagreement.

Ambassador Ayele's comments are included in the previously cited Ethiopian Embassy release.

Petchers comments appear at http://www.oxfamamerica.org/newsand-publications/press_releases/press_release.2006-11-17.6908160357. Jo Lead-better of Oxfam's comments are from an interview the BBC Radio 4 program *Today*. Also see Joe Churcher and Tsegaye Tadesse, "Starbucks Accused of Unfair Trade over Coffee," *Scotsman*, October 27 2006, available at http://news.scotsman.com/international.cfm?id=1587982006. Linda Broom's quotation is from Derek Cheng, "Starbucks Costing Coffee Farmers Millions, Oxfam Claims," *New Zealand Herald*, October 26, 2006, available at http://www.nzherald.co.nz/section/2/story.cfm?c_id=2&objectid=10407752. For a pro-Ethiopia video, see http://www.youtube.com/watch?v=_Lfvp550PtU. A Dub Hay video appears at http://www.youtube.com/watch?v=WZGr2SBg-F8. Jim Donald's remarks are from Robin Pagnamenta, "Starbucks Seeks the Right Blend of Global Ambition and Ethical Trade," *Times of London*, December 11, 2006, available at http://business.timesonline.co.uk/tol/business/markets/africa/article667024.ece. Tilahun Garsamo's remarks appear in Janet Adamy and Roger Thurow, "Ethiopia Battles Starbucks over Rights to Coffee Names," *Wall Street Journal*, May 3, 2007, p. 1.

See Joyce Mulama, "Trade-Kenya: East Africans May Be Stripped of the Kikoi," *Inter Press Service News Agency*, March 30, 2007, available at http://www.ipsnews.net/interna.asp?idnews=37165.

Reverend Billy's extravagant quotations are from http://www.youtube.com/watch?v=cj6HfWfNrN8.

For a summary of the Kathie Lee Gifford/sweatshop story, see the CKUA Sound Archives Online Catalogue at http://66.244.199.219/CKUA_Archives/eng/archive/news_gifford.aspx.

For a profile of Charlie Kernaghan, see Charles Bowden, "Keeper of the Fire," *Mother Jones*, (July-August 2003), available at http://www.motherjones.com/news/feature/2003/07/ma_447_01.html.

On the fourth African Fine Coffee Conference, see Les Neuhaus, "Starbucks Says It Will Double Coffee Purchases from East Africa," *Associated Press*, February 15, 2007; and Elizabeth Gillespie, "Starbucks, Ethiopia Reach Licensing Deal, *Associated Press* June 20, 2007.

CHAPTER 9: THE VIEW FROM HEADQUARTERS

The Valentine's Day memo appears in full on *StarbucksGossip*, February 23, 2007, available at http://starbucksgossip.typepad.com/_/2007/02/starbucks_chair_2.html.

For Schultz's early concerns about growth, see Schultz with Yang (1997, 275–76).Chapter 20 is especially illuminating.

On the Starbucks way of business, see Joseph A. Michelli, *The Starbucks Experience: 5 Principles for Turning Ordinary into Extraordinary* (New York: McGraw-Hill, 2007), which was published with Starbucks' cooperation and imprimatur. The quirkiest book I've found is Leonard Sweet's *The Gospel According to Starbucks* (Colorado Springs: WaterBrook, 2007), which tells how you can find the essence of Christianity in Starbucks' principles.

There are many business school case studies on Starbucks of varying quality, and most cost plenty of money to see. Check Google Scholar for a listing.

American journalist Harold Coffin is usually credited with the "soulless corporation" statement, but it originated with Elizabethan jurist Sir Edward

Coke, writing in the Case of Sutton's Hospital, Report 32, cited in *Bartlett's Quotations*, ed. Emily Morison Beck, 15th ed. (Boston: Little, Brown, 1980), 172.

HMS owns many concessions along highways and in airports. I travel the Pennsylvania Turnpike regularly to visit my parents, so I often observe the work process at HMS concessions and have done a few interviews. Among rest-stop employees, working at Starbucks is considered a plum assignment with perks, but they are well aware that the benefits are better at the company-owned stores.

Foreign direct investment information is from the International Trade Centre and the United Nations Conference on Trade and Development; see http://www.investmentmap.org/invmap/en/glossary.aspx?prg=0.

Senator Larry Craig's voting record is available at http://www. ontheissues.org/senate/Larry_Craig.htm.

My thoughts on the Kent roasting plant are based on two visits and a number of interviews. Some interviewees did not wish to be identified, fearing company retaliation. Figures about the plant are courtesy of Gregg Clark, director of plant operations.

Concerning the protesters in cow suits demanding hormone-free milk, see http://dc.indymedia.org/newswire/display/136913/index.php. For an article linking caloric overdoses in Starbucks beverages to obesity, see, Martha Edwards, "How Many Calories . . . in a Starbucks Eggnog Latte?," November 11, 2006, available on http://www.thatsfit.com/2006/11/11/how-many-calories-in-a-starbucks-eggnog-latte/.

On the usual scalding coffee suits, see "Lawsuit: Starbucks Coffee Was Too Hot," *CBS Chicago*, July 19, 2006, available at http://cbs2chicago.com/local/local_story_200081846.html. On predatory real estate practices, see "Starbucks Sued for Trying to Sink Competition," CNNMoney.com, September 26 2006, available at http://money.cnn.com/2006/09/26/news/companies/starbucks/index.htm.

See the unattributed article "McDonald's Coffee Beats Starbucks, Says Consumer Reports," *Seattle Times*, February 2, 2007, available at http://seattletimes.nwsource.com/html/businesstechnology/2003553322_webcoffeetest02.

Reports of the March 2007 annual meeting are drawn from my own observations and my on-the-spot interviews. It was the first time I'd attended a Starbucks event at which members of the press were not shadowed by Starbucks staffers. Figures are from the 2006 annual report and speeches at the meeting. Again, most people associated with the company were reluctant to have their names connected to critical remarks.

CHAPTER 10: CAPITALISM IS LIKE FIRE . . .

This chapter would not have been possible without John Sage, who gave me not just the title but the provocation to grapple with my thinking.

Got a free evening? Spend it reading the entire text of NAFTA, available at http://www.international.gc.ca/nafta-alena/menu-en.asp.

See Duncan Foley, *Adam's Fallacy* (Cambridge: Belknap-Harvard, 2006), xiii–xiv. Foley's book came out while I was thinking about these issues, reflecting my concerns in a much more academic way.

The quotation from David Harvey comes from an interview about his book, *The New Imperialism* (Oxford University Press, 2005), conducted by Harry

Kreisler on March 2, 2004, at the Institute of International Studies at the University of California, Berkeley. It's available at http://globetrotter. berkeley.edu/people4/Harvey/harvey-con0.html.

The Paul Katzeff quotation is from an e-mail to me dated June 14, 2007.

I interviewed Vijay Prashad via phone. He writes on economic issues from a leftist perspective. His many books include *The Darker Nations: A People's History of the Third World* (New York: New Press, 2006); and with Teo Ballve, *Dispatches from Latin America: Experiments against Neoliberalism* (Boston: South End, 2006).

See Gregory Teverton, *CIA Intelligence and the Market State*, an undated, unclassified CIA study, which can be accessed at https://www.cia.gov/ library/center-for-the-study-of-intelligence/kent-csi/docs/v44i5a09p.htm.

See Leslie Sklair, *Globalization, Capitalism, and Its Alternatives* (Oxford University Press, 2002), 8.

The interview with William Robinson was conducted by the Greek newspaper *Eleftherotypia* on April 13, 2007, and was featured on *ZNet* at http:// www.zmag.org/content/showarticle.cfm?ItemID=12582.

See Edward Cody, "China and Marxism in an Era of Global Economics," *Washington Post*, December 5, 2005, A16.

See James McGregor, "How China Learned to Love Capitalism," *Guardian*, November 6, 2005, available at http://www.guardian.co.uk/china/story/ 0,7369,1635287,00.html.

See Joseph Stiglitz, "The Ethical Economist," *Foreign Affairs*, November-December 2005. It's a review of Benjamin M. Friedman's *The Moral Consequences of Economic Growth* (New York: Knopf, 2005) and is available at http://www.foreignaffairs.org/20051101fareviewessay84612/ joseph-e-stiglitz/the-ethical-economist.html.

In 2006 the Tomales Bay Institute reprinted its 2003 report on *The State of the Commons* and published a new one, *The Commons Rising*. The original report was written by Peter Barnes, Jonathan Rowe and David Bollier. Both can be downloaded at http://www.onthecommons.org. Peter Barnes's comments come from a D.C. presentation on his book, *Capitalism 3.0*, which can be downloaded at the same site under a Creative Commons Attribution-NonCommercial-ShareAlike license.

The insight on the personal and the political was provided by veteran organizer Heather Booth at a National Organizer Alliance gathering in Asheville, North Carolina, in 1999. Booth started out in the Student Nonviolent Coordinating Committee, became an early organizer of the women's movement, and continues to contribute her skills and inspiration to progressive campaigns for equity.

CHAPTER 11: GOODNESS AS BATTLEGROUND

The McElhaney quotation is from Michael Lewis, "The Irresponsible Investor," *New York Times Magazine*, June 6, 2004, available at http:// query.nytimes.com/gst/fullpage.html?res=9A01E1DA1431F935A35755C0 A9629C8B63.

The Bo Burlingham remarks are from a phone interview.

The Friedman-Mackey debate, which also included T. J. Rodgers of Cypress Semiconductor, appears in the unattributed article "Rethinking the Social Responsibility of Business," *Reason* (October 2005), available at http://www.reason.com/news/show/32239.html.

The Business for Social Responsibility website is http://www.bsr.org. I interviewed Aron Cramer by phone.

Information on the U.N.'s Global Compact was compiled from its website http://www.unglobalcompact.org and from discussions with practitioners in the field.

See Philip Mattera, "The Greenwashing of America," *Common Dreams*, June 7, 2007, available at http://www.commondreams.org/archive/2007/06/07/1709.

I conducted three interviews with Sandra Taylor over four years. The conversation reflected here took place early in 2007.

A phone interview with Kelle Louaillier from CAI provided useful context for this chapter as did my in-person discussion and e-mail correspondence with Kathryn Mulvey.

See Saul Alinsky, *Rules for Radicals* (New York: Vintage, 1972), 130.

Figures on Schultz's total compensation are extrapolated from the 2006 Starbucks annual report by Sarah Anderson at the Institute for Policy Studies.

See the Institute for Policy Studies report at http://www.faireconomy.org/reports/2006/ExecutiveExcess2006.pdf. Chuck Collins and Sam Pizzigati helped me clarify the data and reflect on its consequences.

Index

About the Author

Kim Fellner is a long-time organizer and communicator for unions and progressive community organizations. She and her husband, writer Alec Dubro, live in Washington, D.C., a short walk away from nine coffee joints. Visit her Web site at http://wrestlingwithstarbucks.com.